Communications
in Computer and Information Science   512

Commenced Publication in 2007
Founding and Former Series Editors:
Alfredo Cuzzocrea, Dominik Ślęzak, and Xiaokang Yang

More information about this series at http://www.springer.com/series/7899

Markus Helfert · Frédéric Desprez
Donald Ferguson · Frank Leymann
Víctor Méndez Muñoz (Eds.)

Cloud Computing and Services Sciences

International Conference in Cloud Computing
and Services Sciences, CLOSER 2014
Barcelona Spain, April 3–5, 2014
Revised Selected Papers

 Springer

Editors

Markus Helfert
School of Computing
Dublin City University
Dublin 9
Ireland

Frédéric Desprez
LIP/Inria
Ecole normale supérieure de Lyon
Lyon
France

Donald Ferguson
Dell
Round Rock
USA

Frank Leymann
University of Stuttgart
Stuttgart
Germany

Víctor Méndez Muñoz
Universitat Autònoma de Barcelona
Bellaterra
Spain

ISSN 1865-0929   ISSN 1865-0937 (electronic)
Communications in Computer and Information Science
ISBN 978-3-319-25413-5   ISBN 978-3-319-25414-2 (eBook)
DOI 10.1007/978-3-319-25414-2

Library of Congress Control Number: 2015952478

Springer Cham Heidelberg New York Dordrecht London
© Springer International Publishing Switzerland 2015

Printed on acid-free paper

Springer International Publishing AG Switzerland is part of Springer Science+Business Media
(www.springer.com)

Preface

This book includes extended and revised versions of a set of selected papers from CLOSER 2014 (the 4th International Conference on Cloud Computing and Services Science), held in Barcelona, Spain, in 2014, organized and sponsored by the Institute for Systems and Technologies of Information, Control and Communication (INSTICC). This conference was held in cooperation with the Association for Computing Machinery - Special Interest Group on Management Information Systems.

The purpose of the CLOSER series of conferences is to bring together researchers, engineers, and practitioners interested in the emerging area of cloud computing. The conference has five main tracks, namely, "Cloud Computing Fundamentals," "Services Science Foundation for Cloud Computing," "Cloud Computing Platforms and Applications," "Cloud Computing Enabling Technology," and "Mobile Cloud Computing and Services."

The three keynotes provided by Helge Meinhard (CERN, IT Department, Switzerland), Ignacio Martín Llorente (OpenNebula Director and CEO and Full Professor at UCM, Spain) and Paulo Gonçalves (Inria-DANTE, France) addressed cutting-edge questions in open discussion with the conference members.

CLOSER 2014 received 127 paper submissions from all continents. From these, 21 papers were published and presented as full papers, 40 were accepted as short papers, and another 27 for poster presentation. These numbers, leading to a full-paper acceptance ratio of 17 % and an oral paper acceptance ratio of 48 %, show the intention of preserving a high-quality forum for the next editions of this conference.

This book contains the revised papers selected among the best contributions taking also into account the quality of their presentation at the conference, assessed by the session chairs. Therefore, we hope that you find these papers interesting, and we trust they represent a helpful reference for all those who need to address any of the aforementioned research areas.

We wish to thank all those who supported and helped to organize the conference. On behalf of the conference Organizing Committee, we would like to thank the authors, whose work mostly contributed to a very successful conference, the keynote speakers, and the members of the Program Committee, whose expertise and diligence were instrumental for the quality of the final contributions. We also wish to thank all the members of the Organizing Committee, whose work and commitment was invaluable. Last but not least, we would like to thank Springer for their collaboration in getting this book to print.

April 2015

Markus Helfert
Frédéric Desprez
Donald Ferguson
Frank Leymann
Víctor Méndez Muñoz

Organization

Conference Chair

Markus Helfert   Dublin City University, Ireland

Program Co-chairs

Frédéric Desprez   LIP/Inria, France
Donald Ferguson   Dell, USA
Frank Leymann   University of Stuttgart, Germany
Víctor Méndez Muñoz   Universitat Autònoma de Barcelona, UAB, Spain

Organizing Committee

Marina Carvalho   INSTICC, Portugal
Helder Coelhas   INSTICC, Portugal
Ana Guerreiro   INSTICC, Portugal
André Lista   INSTICC, Portugal
Filipe Mariano   INSTICC, Portugal
Andreia Moita   INSTICC, Portugal
Carla Mota   INSTICC, Portugal
Raquel Pedrosa   INSTICC, Portugal
Vitor Pedrosa   INSTICC, Portugal
Cátia Pires   INSTICC, Portugal
Ana Ramalho   INSTICC, Portugal
Susana Ribeiro   INSTICC, Portugal
Rui Rodrigues   INSTICC, Portugal
André Santos   INSTICC, Portugal
Fábio Santos   INSTICC, Portugal
Mara Silva   INSTICC, Portugal
José Varela   INSTICC, Portugal
Pedro Varela   INSTICC, Portugal

Program Committee

Antonia Albani   University of St. Gallen, Switzerland
Vasilios Andrikopoulos   University of Stuttgart, Germany
Cosimo Anglano   Università del Piemonte Orientale A. Avogadro, Italy
Ashiq Anjum   University of Derby, UK
Claudio Ardagna   Università degli Studi di Milano, Italy
Danilo Ardagna   Politecnico di Milano, Italy

Alvaro Arenas	Instituto de Empresa Business School, Spain
José Enrique Armendáriz-Iñigo	Universidad Pública de Navarra, Spain
Matthew Arrott	University of California San Diego, USA
Benjamin Aziz	University of Portsmouth, UK
Zeina Azmeh	I3S Laboratory, University of Nice - Sophia Antipolis, France
Amelia Badica	University of Craiova, Romania
Henri E. Bal	Vrije Universiteit, The Netherlands
Janaka Balasooriya	Arizona State University, USA
Costas Bekas	IBM Zurich Research Lab, Switzerland
Karin Bernsmed	SINTEF ICT, Norway
Nik Bessis	University of Derby, UK
Luiz F. Bittencourt	IC/UNICAMP, Brazil
Stefano Bocconi	TU Delft, The Netherlands
Sergey Boldyrev	HERE Maps, Finland
Anne Boyer	Loria - Inria Lorraine, France
Francisco Brasileiro	Universidade Federal de Campina Grande, Brazil
Iris Braun	Dresden Technical University, Germany
Andrey Brito	Universidade Federal de Campina Grande, Brazil
Ralf Bruns	Hannover University of Applied Sciences and Arts, Germany
Anna Brunstrom	Karlstad University, Sweden
Rebecca Bulander	Pforzheim University of Applied Science, Germany
Tomas Bures	Charles University in Prague, Czech Republic
Massimo Cafaro	University of Salento, Italy
Manuel Isidoro Capel-Tuñón	University of Granada, Spain
Miriam Capretz	University of Western Ontario, Canada
Eddy Caron	École Normale Supérieure de Lyon, France
Noel Carroll	University of Limerick, Ireland
John Cartlidge	University of Bristol, UK
Humberto Castejon	Telenor, Norway
Rong N. Chang	IBM T.J. Watson Research Center, USA
Davide Cherubini	Alcatel-Lucent Ireland, Ireland
Augusto Ciuffoletti	Università di Pisa, Italy
Daniela Barreiro Claro	Universidade Federal da Bahia (UFBA), Brazil
Christine Collet	Grenoble Institute of Technology, France
Thierry Coupaye	Orange, France
António Miguel Rosado da Cruz	Instituto Politécnico de Viana do Castelo, Portugal
Tommaso Cucinotta	Alcatel-Lucent, Ireland
Eduardo Huedo Cuesta	Universidad Complutense de Madrid, Spain
Edward Curry	National University of Ireland, Galway, Ireland
Eliezer Dekel	IBM Research Haifa, Israel
Yuri Demchenko	University of Amsterdam, The Netherlands

Marco Winckler	University Paul Sabatier (Toulouse 3), France
Jan-Jan Wu	Academia Sinica, Taiwan
Hany F. El Yamany	Suez Canal University, Egypt
Bo Yang	University of Electronic Science and Technology of China, China
Ustun Yildiz	University of California, San Diego, USA
Michael Zapf	Georg Simon Ohm University of Applied Sciences, Germany
Wolfgang Ziegler	Fraunhofer Institute SCAI, Germany

Additional Reviewers

Laeeq Ahmed	PDC, Royal Institute of Technology, Sweden
Christophe Bobineau	Grenoble Institute of Technology, France
Damien Borgetto	Institut de Recherche en Informatique de Toulouse (IRIT), France
Philip Church	Deakin University, Australia
José Cordeiro	Polytechnic Institute of Setúbal/INSTICC, Portugal
Alevtina Dubovitskaya	HES-SO Valais Wallis, EPFL, Switzerland
Eugen Feller	Inria, France and Lawrence Berkeley National Lab, USA
Antonios Gouglidis	University of Macedonia, Greece
Katarina Grolinger	Western University, Canada
Christos Grompanopoulos	University of Macedonia, Greece
Leo Iaquinta	University of Milano-Bicocca, Italy
Sotiris Kotsiantis	Educational Software Development Laboratory, University of Patras, Greece
Wubin Li	Umeå University, Sweden
Giovanni Maccani	National University of Ireland Maynooth, Ireland
Ketan Maheshwari	Argonne National Laboratory, USA
Martin Meyer	Dublin City University, Ireland
Cataldo Musto	Università degli studi di Bari, Italy
P.-O. Östberg	Umeå University, Sweden
Nikos Parlavantzas	IRISA, France
Plamen Petkov	Dublin City University, Ireland
Eduardo Roloff	UFRGS, Brazil
Petter Svärd	Umeå University, Sweden
Luis Tomas	Umeå University, Sweden

Invited Speakers

Helge Meinhard, CERN, IT Department, Switzerland
Paulo Gonçalves, Inria-DANTE, France
Ignacio Martín Llorente, OpenNebula Director and CEO and Full Professor at UCM, Spain

Contents

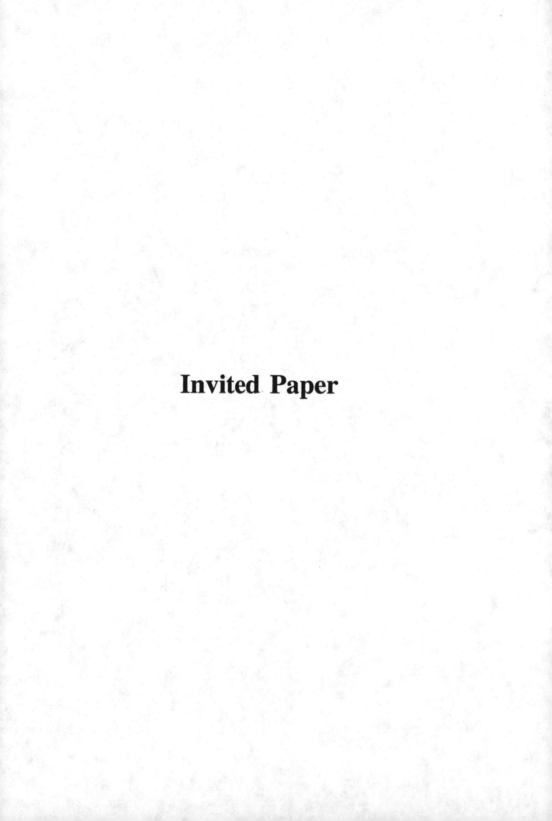

Invited Paper

A Cloud for Clouds: Weather Research and Forecasting on a Public Cloud Infrastructure

J.L. Vázquez-Poletti[1]([✉]), D. Santos-Muñoz[2], I.M. Llorente[1], and F. Valero[3]

[1] Departamento de Arquitectura de Computadores y Automática,
Facultad de Informática, Universidad Complutense de Madrid, 28040 Madrid, Spain
jlvazquez@fdi.ucm.es
[2] Agencia Estatal de Meteorología, 28071 Madrid, Spain
[3] Departamento de Física de la Tierra, Astronomía y Astrofísica II,
Facultad de Ciencias Físicas, Universidad Complutense de Madrid,
28040 Madrid, Spain

Abstract. The Weather Research & Forecasting (WRF) Model is a high performance computing application used by many worldwide meteorological agencies. Its execution may benefit from the cloud computing paradigm and from public cloud infrastructures in particular, but only if the parameters are chosen wisely. An optimal infrastructure by means of cost can be instantiated for a given deadline, and an optimal infrastructure by means of performance can be instantiated for a given budget.

1 Introduction

Cloud computing allows elastic, dynamic and on-demand provision of resources. Many applications, especially pertaining to the high performance computing area, have seen in the cloud a great ally for their optimal execution [1]. The appearance of public cloud providers, offering cloud services and charging only by usage, has created an interesting scenario where certain processes can be externalized, reducing the overall costs considerably [2].

However, the migration of scientific applications to public cloud infrastructures can be challenging. An example is the optimal selection of the provision parameters by means of cost and performance. An optimal computing performance setup will correspond to a specific budget and vice versa. With this in mind, we provide the optimal parameters for the execution of the Weather Research & Forecasting Model (WRF) on a public cloud infrastructure such as Amazon Web Services.

The present contribution starts with an overview of WRF in the next Section, followed by a short discussion on the use of public cloud infrastructures in Science (Sect. 3). Then, our approach for this particular problem is described in Sect. 4 and the paper ends with some conclusions.

This research was supported by the following projects: ServiceCloud (MINECO TIN2012-31518), MEIGA-METNET PRECURSOR (AYA201129967C0502) and Desarrollo y evaluacin de tcnicas de prediccin por conjuntos de eventos meteorolgicos extremos (MINECO CGL2011-25327).

M. Helfert et al. (Eds.): CLOSER 2014, CCIS 512, pp. 3–11, 2015.
DOI: 10.1007/978-3-319-25414-2_1

2   A Model to Forecast them All

The Weather Research & Forecasting (WRF) modelling system [3,4] is the result of an effort conducted by a collaborative partnership of different research agencies and universities to provide a next-generation data assimilation system and forecast model that advances both the understanding and prediction of mesoscale weather, accelerating the transfer of research advances into operation.

Two dynamical cores and data assimilation systems are continuously developed to create a state-of-the-art modelling system: the Advanced Research WRF (ARW) [3], supported by the NCAR Mesoscale and Microscale Meteorology Division, and the WRF-NMM (NMM)[1], supported by the Developmental Testbed Center (DTC).

WRF is designed to be a portable, flexible, and state-of-the-art code, especially efficient when executed in a massively parallel computing environment. It offers various physics options and can be used in a broad spectrum of applications across scales, ranging from meters to thousands of kilometers. It is currently used in many worldwide meteorological agencies and adopted by a huge community of users (over 20,000 in over 130 countries).

Several works have been conducted on WRF and other models from a meteorological point of view [4]. Also, the computational cost of high resolution simulations [5] and the ensemble prediction systems [6] have been studied. The execution of WRF is a typical high performance computing problem [7,8]. Moreover, different technologies ranging from multi-core computing clusters [9] to GPU [10] have been used.

However, the execution of WRF on cloud computing infrastructures has not been studied yet. As it will be explained in the next section, a specific type of these infrastructures offer an interesting environment. This is because cost, a metric that has gained much relevance nowadays, is managed in a different way.

3   Public Clouds for Science

Public cloud infrastructures are those where the bare metal resources are maintained by a different institution than that using their resources. A public cloud provider usually charges the usage of its services by unit of time, having to take care of the physical infrastructure on which their cloud is built.

This pay as you go model allows the user to scale the required services while sticking a given budget. However, public clouds do not offer control of the lower layers, so providers make the users choose between preconfigured sets of services.

Many scientific applications have benefited from the usage of public cloud infrastructures [11], specially those pertaining to the high performance computing area, where the required physical machines needed to palliate the computational peaks that break the budget [12]. Even, the usage of a physical infrastructure could be discouraged at all depending on the size and type of computational problem to be solved [13].

---

[1] http://www.dtcenter.org/wrf-nmm/users/docs/user_guide/V3/.

Executing scientific applications on a public cloud brings up some challenges that may discard this solution. The first one is about porting the application to the new environment. Although all architectures may be virtualized, other requirements could not be satisfied by a given provider. Moreover, a vendor lock-in may occur if there are no alternatives to the chosen infrastructure, or moving to another provider represents a great effort.

Application data security is a great challenge. The user has not total control of the physical machine where the instances are running and the data is transmitted over the Internet, where the connection can be eavesdropped.

Another challenge is data transfer by means of bandwidth and price. A great bottleneck in the execution of the application may appear if the data repository cannot be moved to the public cloud infrastructure.

The same applies to the components involved in the overall process. The level of parallelism could be increased and the resulting tasks could be distributed, but network latencies may decrease the application performance.

An optimal selection of provision parameters is needed once these challenges have been overcome. These parameters cannot pursue a unique solution by means of cost and performance, but a compromise between the two metrics.

In the present study we have worked at the lowest level of the cloud service model (Infrastructure as a Service) by using virtual machines provided by Amazon Web Services. Additionally relied on the next layer (Platform as a Service) for automatic node deployment.

4   Bringing the Clouds on the Cloud

The chosen version of WRF-ARW was 3.4.1, based on the forecast system physics suite run operationally at the National Centers for Environmental Prediction (NCEP). For our study we compiled it with the Distributed Memory and Message Passing Interface (MPI) option.

The next Section explains the differences between two data sets used to feed WRF and therefore provide different computational results. Section 4.2 describes the used infrastructure, and Sect. 4.3 shows and discusses the results.

4.1   A Tale of Two Models

Two different data sets pertaining to the most well-know and state-of-the-art global forecast systems have been used to run WRF: the Improved Forecast System from the European Centre for Medium-Range Weather Forecast (IFS-ECMWF) and the Global Forecast System from the National Center for Environmental Predictions (GFS-NCEP). Both models have different configurations and characteristics for producing realistic weather forecast.

The target area for this study has a resolution of 5×5 km (horizontal) and 28 levels (vertical), covering the Iberian Peninsula with a 301×250 grid points mesh. The simulations were carried out on a single run (starting at 00 UTC) with a 48-h forecast horizon.

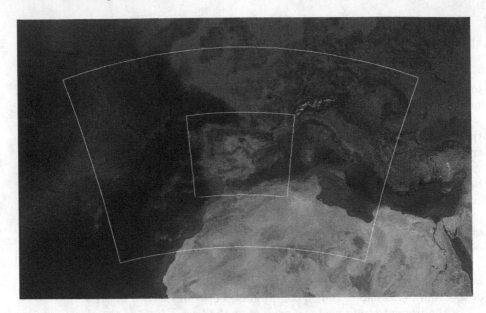

Fig. 1. Integration domains for GFS-NCEP global model data. The inner domain is the common one between WRF simulations initialized by both global models.

Table 1. Used Amazon EC2 instance characteristics. One EC2 Compute Unit (ECU) provides the equivalent CPU capacity of a 1.0–1.2 GHz 2007 Opteron or 2007 Xeon processor.

Type	Family	vCPU	ECU	Memory (GB)	Storage (GB)	Network perf
m1.small	General	1	1	1.7	1×160	Low
cc2.8xlarge	Compute	32	88	60.5	4×840	10 Gigabit
m2.4xlarge	Memory	8	26	68.4	2×840	High

Two different commercial policies are maintained by NCEP and ECMWF. Meanwhile the data for GFS-NCEP are allocated in a public server, the ECMWF has established a year cost for the use of the IFS-ECMWF data, which is $207,002.19 for this particular study.

The spatial extension of the IFS-ECMWF data has been selected to cover the outer domain in Fig. 1. Although it only feeds the inner domain in this study, the large spatial area coverage allows generating other integration domains over Europe and Northern Africa that could be interesting for other meteorological forecast areas.

4.2   Cloud Infrastructure

As stated before, we have chosen Amazon Web Services and, in particular, we relied on the Elastic Compute Cloud service, which focuses on the provision of virtual machines (instances).

Fig. 2. Examples of both cluster types deployed in Amazon EC2 and used during the experiments.

From the large list of offered instance types, we took into consideration those from Table 1. Hourly usage prices are \$0.06 for m1.small, \$2.40 for cc2.8xlarge and \$3.50 for m2.4xlarge.

In order to deploy computing clusters in Amazon, we used StarCluster[2], a PaaS solution that allows the automation and simplification of the building, configuration and management of Amazon EC2 instances. As shown at Fig. 2, two different clusters with variable number of nodes were deployed for running the experiments.

4.3   Computational Results

Figure 3 shows the execution times when using model data types on both cluster types with variable number of nodes. The cc2.8xlarge cluster scales worse as execution time is increased with more than 4 computing nodes. On the other hand, execution time with the m2.4xlarge cluster is decreased when adding nodes but seems to stabilize with the highest number used in the experiments.

Another interesting aspect is that the same number of m2.4xlarge instances team up less processor cores than using cc2.8xlarge ones (see Table 1), but execution times are the lowest while using the same data types.

This behavior is justified by the high I/O properties of the m2.4xlarge instances. Being memory oriented, they totally overcome the lack of processors compared with the cc2.8xlarge ones.

---

[2] http://star.mit.edu/cluster/.

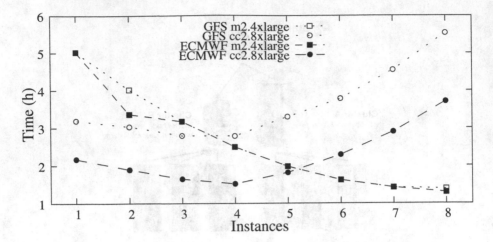

Fig. 3. Comparison of execution times for GFS and ECMWF with different number of Amazon EC2 instances.

On the other hand, execution times with different data models change dramatically from one instance type to the other. While in the m2.4xlarge cluster the differences are minor, using the free data set (GFS) produces higher execution times in the other cluster.

Figure 4 shows the execution costs for each proposed solution categorized by data set and instance type. These costs correspond to those charged by Amazon per hour and used instance, which were specified in the previous section.

The execution costs evolve almost in the same way as the execution times in Fig. 3. However, the inflection point is moved from 4 computing nodes to 5.

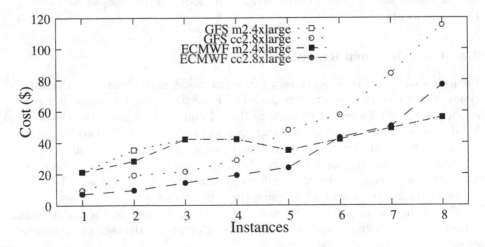

Fig. 4. Comparison of execution costs for GFS and ECMWF with different number of Amazon EC2 instances.

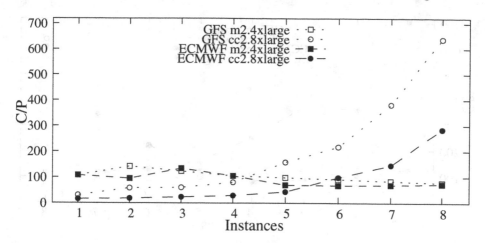

Fig. 5. Comparison of C/P values for GFS and ECMWF with different number of Amazon EC2 instances.

Before it, the highest costs correspond to the m2.4xlarge cluster, independently of the used data set. Then, they turn to produce the lowest costs. In average, the ECMWF data set is the one producing a fair cost over the time.

The values shown at Fig. 5 correspond to a metric introduced in [3.2] that associates cost and performance (C/P) and provides another point of view while deciding which is the optimal infrastructure for executing WRF. This metric is obtained by multiplying the infrastructure cost and the total execution time.

Being the best infrastructure that producing the lowest C/P value, the cc2.8xlarge cluster provides better results below 5 machines. The ECMWF data set is the optimal no matter which cluster is. However, the difference with GFS is reduced when moving to the m2.4xlarge cluster.

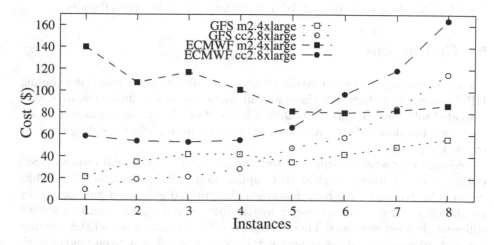

Fig. 6. Comparison of execution costs for GFS and ECMWF with different number of Amazon EC2 instances.

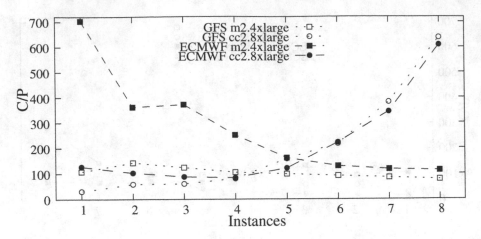

Fig. 7. Comparison of C/P values for GFS and ECMWF with different number of Amazon EC2 instances.

As explained before, using the ECMWF data set is not free. Its annual fee is $207, 002.19 when requested by a non-research purposes (VAT included).

In order to integrate the license cost in our study, we calculated the hourly fee of the data set, which is $23.61. This way, Fig. 6 shows the new comparison of execution costs.

As it can be seen, the license price has a dramatic effect in the compared to the previous comparison (Fig. 4). There is no single setup in which using the ECMWF data set is cheaper than GFS, with the exception of an 8 sized m2.4xlarge cluster.

On the other hand, Fig. 7 shows the new comparison of C/P values. This time, the GFS data set turns to be optimal when used in both a cc2.8xlarge cluster (1 to 4 nodes) and the m2.4xlarge cluster (5 to 8 nodes). The best setup when using the ECMWF data set is the m2.4xlarge cluster with no less than 6 nodes.

5   Conclusions

Cloud computing has been postulated as a great aid for applications demanding HPC power. Nowadays, the cloud and in particular public infrastructures have provided solutions to a great number of applications from a wide range of areas. However, the cloud offers a new level of indetermination when deciding the best execution parameters.

Along the present contribution we have provided experimental results of executing WRF, a meteorological HPC application, on the Amazon EC2 public cloud infrastructure. We have identified the optimal execution parameters by means of performance, cost and a metric that relates both, when considering different decision elements. These comprise different data sets and the instance types, throwing interesting experimental results that allow a given meteorological agency to understand better the elements to consider when externalizing the execution of WRF to a public cloud provider.

For future work we have two main directions. The first one is to provide a model that will allow to choose between the cloud and a physical infrastructure, like in [13], profiling the most used hardware setups done by meteorological agencies. The second direction is to provide an HTC cloud execution model for WRF, assuming a continuous execution with deadlines.

References

1. Deelman, E., Juve, G., Malawski, M., Nabrzyski, J.: Hosted science: managing computational workflows in the cloud. Parallel Process. Lett. **23**, 14 (2013)
2. Alford, T., Morton, G.: The economics of cloud computing (2009). http://www.boozallen.com/insights/insight-detail/42656904
3. Skamarock, W., Klemp, J.B., Dudhia, J., Gill, D.O., Barker, D., Duda, M.G., Huang, X., Wang, W.: A description of the Advanced Research WRF version 3. Technical report, National Center for Atmospheric Research (2008)
4. Kieran, A., Santos-Munoz, D., Valero, F.: Comparison of wind speed forecasts from MM5 and WRF ARW ensemble prediction systems over the Iberian Peninsula. In: Proceedings of 12th WRF Users' Workshop (2012)
5. Martin, M.L., Santos-Munoz, D., Morata, A., Luna, M.Y., Valero, F.: An objetively selected case heavy rain event in the Western Mediterranean Basin: a study through diagnosis and Numerical Simulations. Atmos. Res. **81**, 187–205 (2006)
6. Santos-Munoz, D., Martin, M.L., Valero, F., Morata, A., Pascual, A.: Verification of a short-range ensemble precipitation prediction system over Iberia. Adv. Geosci. **25**, 55–63 (2010)
7. Michalakes, J., Chen, S., Dudhia, J., Hart, L., Klemp, J., Middlecoff, J., Skamarock, W.: Development of a next generation regional weather research and forecast model. Developments in Teracomputing. In: Proceedings of 9th ECMWF Workshop on the Use of High Performance Computing in Meteorology (2001)
8. Michalakes, J., Dudhia, J., Gill, D., Henderson, T., Klemp, J., Skamarock, W., Wang, W.: The weather reseach and forecast model: software architecture and performance. In: Proceedings of 11th ECMWF Workshop on the Use of High Performance Computing in Meteorology (2004)
9. Shainer, G., Liu, T., Michalakes, J., Liberman, J., Layton, J., Celebioglu, O., Schultz, S.A., Mora, J., Cownie, D.: Weather Research and Forecast (WRF) model performance and profiling analysis on advanced multi-core HPC clusters. In: Proceedings of 11th LCI International Conference on High-Performance Clustered Computing (2008)
10. Michalakes, J., Vachharajani, M.: GPU acceleration of numerical weather prediction. Parallel Process. Lett. **18**, 531–548 (2008)
11. Sterling, T., Stark, D.: A high-performance computing forecast: partly cloudy. Comput. Sci. Eng. **11**, 42–49 (2009)
12. Vázquez-Poletti, J.L., Barderas, G., Llorente, I.M., Romero, P.: A model for efficient onboard actualization of an instrumental cyclogram for the mars metnet mission on a public cloud infrastructure. In: Jónasson, K. (ed.) PARA 2010, Part I. LNCS, vol. 7133, pp. 33–42. Springer, Heidelberg (2012)
13. Guerrero, G.D., Wallace, R.M., Vazquez-Poletti, J.L., Cecilia, J.M., Garcia, J.M., Mozos, D., Perez-Sanchez, H.: A performance/cost model for a CUDA drug discovery application on physical and public cloud infrastructures. concurrency Comput. Pract. Experience **26**, 1787–1798 (2013)

Papers

Semantic Generation of Clouds Privacy Policies

Hanene Boussi Rahmouni[1,3](✉), Kamran Munir[1],
Marco Casassa Mont[2], and Tony Solomonides[4]

[1] Centre for Complex Cooperative Systems, Department of Computer Science
and Creative Technologies, University of the West of England, Bristol, UK
{hanene2.rahmouni,kamran2.munir}@uwe.ac.uk
[2] Hewlett-Packard Labs, Cloud and Security Lab, Bristol, UK
marco_casassa-mont@hp.com
[3] Digital Security Research Unit, Sup'Com,
University of Carthage, Tunis, Tunisia
[4] Center for Biomedical Research Informatics (CBRI) Research Institute,
NorthShore University Health System, Evanston, USA
asolomonides@northshore.org

Abstract. The governance of privacy and personal information on cloud environments is challenging and complex. Usually many regulatory frameworks intervene to reflect diverse privacy wishes from several stakeholders. This includes data owners, data and services providers and also the end users. Focusing mainly on medical domains, this issue is particularly important due to the sensitivity of health related data in international data protection law. It is therefore essential to integrate heterogeneous privacy requirements in a semantic model and rules. Thereafter, overlaps, contradictions and similarities of privacy wishes could be detected and a final access control context would be captured before it is finally mapped to clouds operational policies. This paper describes an ontology-based semantic model of privacy requirements along with a logical formalism for mapping SWRL (Semantic Web Rule Language) privacy rules to a policy language that is implementable on clouds environments namely XACML. The underline implementation requirements for our formalism will be also explained.

Keywords: Privacy policies · OWL · SWRL · XACML · Cloud

1 Introduction

The protection of patients' privacy in a pan-European cloud infrastructure is challenging and requires combined solutions from legislation, organisational and social frameworks. In this regards, a European public cloud infrastructure is still a challenging goal to attend [1], but necessary for those nations wishing to collaborate for the advancement of medical research and public health. This challenge arises primarily due to the lack of harmonisation in legal frameworks governing privacy and data protection in Europe, not least the European Data Protection directive 95/46/EC [2, 3, 4]. For example, consent is not handled in the same way in Italy as in the UK. In Italy, consent

© Springer International Publishing Switzerland 2015
M. Helfert et al. (Eds.): CLOSER 2014, CCIS 512, pp. 15–30, 2015.
DOI: 10.1007/978-3-319-25414-2_2

could be provided for a broad purpose of data processing; whereas in the UK, obtaining a specific consent is a legal obligation [5, 6]. On top of this, there are significant conceptual and technical issues in-particular when expressing, interpreting and deriving operational consequences out of high-level policies. Finally, despite the attention that has been paid to security concerns for public and private clouds; such as infrastructure integrity and access control (typically authentication and authorization), this does not naturally extend to cover privacy concerns (often requiring context and purpose specification). Although they are newly emerging paradigms, clouds are very similar in many aspects to other distributed computing environments. Particularly, clouds are similar to large-scale systems that are based on virtualised technologies such as Grid systems [7]. These systems have high capabilities for sharing data and resources through the Internet. However they often fall short of providing measurable proof of compliance, which is required throughout the complete data sharing process. This is different than the case of traditional centralised systems, where the data security focus was directed only towards data access transactions. As such, it is an on-going challenge to search for ways to narrow the gaps between the various legal, technical, social and organizational aspects of the problem.

The approach presented in this paper is an attempt to show that the use of Semantic Web technologies [8] can allow both the specification and enforcement of privacy requirements that traditional access control languages and mechanisms cannot achieve. We start from the high-level regulations that govern privacy and data protection in Europe and we progress towards the integration of privacy constraints interpreted from them within access controls specifications. For this matter, policies' decisions cannot be deduced from data identifiers and access control conditions that are evaluated against their attributes' values. Instead, the evaluation of privacy policies requires more information about resources; and hence, we face the need to record metadata about the protected resources in a computational infrastructure. We believe, the existing access control solutions for the cloud need to evolve in order to allow for such integration and in order to enable enforcement of the full range of *privacy* constraints.

Although semantic based languages can adequately capture and conceptually specify the *contexts*, *facts* and *rules* necessary for reasoning about data manipulation obligations, it is rather not suitable for implementation in a cloud context. This is due to the necessity for answering two major clouds requirements namely *performance* and *standardisation*. In order to enable better interoperability, while exchanging data in the cloud, it is important to use standard data management languages and services. This includes both standard access control and security languages [7]. Moreover, the use of semantic access control languages requires customised enforcement architectures that are different from the ones adopted on the cloud infrastructure and that are designed to enforce policies specified in a standard format. A similar change might be very expensive from the point of view of clouds services and infrastructure providers. In order to be easily enforced at the cloud's system-level, we suggest that the presented policies should eventually be specified in a way that conforms to a widely adopted policy language or standard. In particular, a standard that has proven efficiency in the enforcement of privacy policies. Our choice is the eXtensible Access Control Mark-up Language (XACML) [9]. It is worth mentioning; and in order to eliminate confusion, that in the context of this work, we do not claim that XACML can handle privacy constraints in exactly the same way as it handles security constraints. The limitations of XACML, both as a policy language and as an enforcement mechanism, have been detailed in the literature [10, 11, 12]. Also additional limitations are presented in Sect. 3 of this paper. In this work, we seek to overcome some of these limitations. For a note to the readers, additional effort was also made in later version of XACML [30].

The remaining paper is organised as follows: Sect. 2 starts by clarifying the theory presented in this paper in comparison and continuation to the allied work that we have been doing previously in this domain. This Sect. 2 also clarifies the major contributions presented in this paper. Section 3 presents a synopsis of the main technologies on which we have based our privacy specification and enforcement approach, which are presented in later Sects. 4, 5 and 6. In particular, the Sect. 4 discusses the SWRL-based privacy policies specifications and Sect. 5 shows how they can be rewritten in a syntax conforming to the XACML standard. In Sect. 6, formalism for mapping SWRL privacy rules into XACML access controls is presented. This is followed by the requirements and recommendations for implementing the projected formalism in Sect. 7; and finally, the conclusions and relevant future orientations are presented in Sect. 8.

2 Semantic Modeling of Legal Privacy Requirements for Access Controls

In [13, 14], we have described how Semantic Web technologies have been used to classify the resources that we would like to protect. At that stage the resources were specified using the metadata captured within an ontology. We have also shown in this existing work, how different scenarios of data/resource sharing have been modelled within the same ontology. In this paper, we describe extensions to the previous model (with necessary metadata added) and extend the data sharing scenarios to include privacy policy contexts. We then show how this allows the specification and editing of privacy and access control policies in terms of existing concepts within the ontology. There is research reported in the literature (such as [15, 16, 17]) that has looked at the use of ontologies and Semantic Web technology in order to allow a better specification and enforcement of security and authorisation policies. Among these, only the "Consequence" project has looked at an approach that integrates requirements from high-level policies through the means of controlled natural language [17]. This approach translates high-level policies extracted from data sharing agreements into a natural language-like formalism in order to allow enforceability. This work did not stop at the *control of access to data*, but has rather focussed on ways of controlling any type of data usage even after the data were shared with a party belonging to an external domain. This functionality is worth further consideration and is discussed in the future work section of this paper. In comparison, the actual status of our approach allows the disclosure of data handling policies to external parties receiving personal data, but does not enforce these policies within the receiver's domain. However, the work in [17] included little effort to integrate within access control policies, privacy requirements that are interpreted from primary legislation (text law). It made rather a focus only on traditional security services such as authorisation and the trust aspect of it. Hence this approach couldn't fit in a solution aiming for the big picture of regulatory compliance.

This is because usually traditional security requirements covers only a very specific subset of jurisdictional requirements that are not general enough to cover any case of data sharing that might arise in the future.

3   An Overview of SWRL and XACML

In this section, an overview of the semantic web rule language (SWRL) and the extensible access control markup language XACML is presented. In this regard, an analysis of their expressiveness capabilities and utility for enforcing privacy policies in a cloud environment is also elaborated.

SWRL, the Semantic Web Rule Language (SWRL) [8] is based on a combination of the OWL-DL [17] and some sublanguages of the Rule Mark-up Language (RuleML) [18]. SWRL includes a high-level abstract syntax for Horn-like rules in both the OWL-DL and OWL-Lite sublanguages of OWL [19]. The proposal extends the set of OWL axioms to include Horn-like rules. It thus enables the rules to be combined with an OWL knowledge base. Some model-theoretic semantics are given to provide the formal meaning for OWL ontologies, including rules written in an abstract syntax. With the combination of an XML syntax based on RuleML, the OWL XML Presentation Syntax and an RDF [19] concrete syntax based on the OWL RDF/XML exchange syntax, SWRL presents an illustration of the extension of description logic into defeasible description logic [20]. This makes it a promising technology for the modelling of regulations.

The proposed rules are of the form of an implication between an *antecedent (body)* and a *consequent (head)*. The intended meaning can be read as: *whenever the conditions specified in the antecedent hold, then the conditions specified in the consequent must also hold.* Both the *antecedent (body)* and *consequent (head)* consist of *zero* or *more* atoms. An *empty antecedent* is treated as *trivially true* (i.e. satisfied by every interpretation), so the consequent must also be satisfied by every interpretation; an *empty consequent* is treated as *trivially false* (i.e., not satisfied by any interpretation), so the antecedent must also not be satisfied by any interpretation. Multiple *atoms* are treated as a *conjunction*. Note that rules with *conjunctive* consequents could easily be transformed into multiple rules, each with an *atomic consequent* [21]. Atoms in these rules can be of the form $C(x)$, $P(x,y)$, $sameAs(x,y)$ or $differentFrom(x,y)$, where C is an OWL description class, P is an OWL property, and x,y are either variables, OWL individuals or OWL data values. It is easy to see that OWL DL becomes undecidable when extended in this way as rules can be used to simulate role value maps [21].

XACML [9] is an XML specification and syntax for expressing policies controlling the access to information through the Internet. It provides the enterprises with a flexible and structured way of managing access to resources. The specification language is based on a subject-target-action-condition policy syntax specified in an XML document. As specified in the Fig. 1 [9] a *Policy* is composed of a *Target*, which identifies the set of capabilities that the requestor must expose along with a set of rules some Rules varying from one to many. Every Rule contains the specific facts needed for the access control decision-making. It also has an evaluation Effect, which can be either *Permit* or *Deny*. At policy evaluation time a policy combining algorithm is used to deal with *(permit/deny)* conflicts that might arise in the rule decisions. A *Target* is composed of four sub-elements: *Subjects*, *Actions*, *Resources*, and *Environments*. Beyond what is described in the Fig. 1, each target category is composed of a set of target elements, each of which contains an attribute identifier, a value and a matching function. Such information is used to check whether the policy is applicable to a given request. This could be specified in the condition section of a rule.

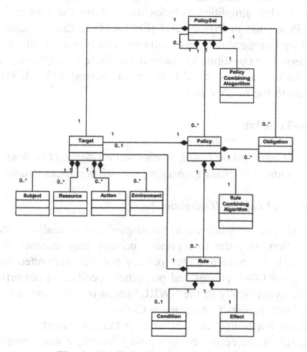

Fig. 1. XACMLv2's data flow model.

In most of the cases the language defines controls as a collection of attributes relevant to a principle. It includes both conditional authorisation policies and policies to specify *post* conditions such as notifications to data subject. Like other policies languages that are based on XML/XACML lacks the required semantics to allow for semantic heterogeneity and interoperability, especially when managing data access within environments that involve multiple organisations. The different data access requests coming from users in different organisations might refer to the same data item with different naming. Additional semantics are needed in order to allow semantic alignment to the different terms used to describe the same data item [15]. Moreover dealing with dynamic attributes such as the user's *age* or hierarchical attributes for example the user's *role* requires some additional semantics and integrated reasoning [22, 23, 24].

4 A SWRL-Based Privacy Policy Specification

We have examined the legal privacy rules and obligation dictated in many jurisdictional texts and we have noted that the rules are specified according to a specific vocabulary describing many conceptual entities. These entities are usually associated together in different combinations in order to build generic rules that could be modelled in the form of *if-then* rule template. Following this assumption and similarly to the work done in [31] that simplifies policies dictated by the Ontario's Freedom of Information and Protection of Privacy Act (FIPAA) [32, 33], we have expressed the policies specified by European data protection text law in a more simplified way using the different concepts that constitute its vocabulary. These concepts were captured in an OWL ontology that we have described in the previous work [13, 14, 31]. The policies were then matched to the rule template.

Privacy-Rule-Template:
If
[Context] and [Condition on User], [Condition on data], [Condition on Purpose],
[Condition on Other] (Including checking for privacy requirements)
Then
Allow [action] and Impose [Obligation]

The rule *privacy-rule-template* could be adapted and specialised, according to the context of application, in order to represent privacy requirements in a case based manner. On this basis, we have rewritten privacy policies interpreted from text law as SWRL rules using the OWL classes and properties specified in our privacy ontology. The rule conforms syntactically to the SWRL human readable syntax:

Antecedent Clause *implies* Consequence Clause

Or, in a different notation: `Antecedent` $\rightarrow$ `Consequent`

Adapting the rule to an access control policy format, it must conform to the following template:

`Rule: = Target` $\wedge$ `Conditions` $\rightarrow$ `Effect` $\wedge$ `Obligations`

Here we explain our SWRL privacy policies specification through a concrete rule example and a cloud data-sharing scenario:

Example: Purpose Compatibility Rule: In order to clearly explain our approach we start by specifying an example of high-level policy extracted from European privacy legislation. The policy is further taken trough series of transformations towards an operational status in the format of XACML syntax. In this example, we show how we model the privacy policy stating [4] that:

"A user may access a patient mammogram for a stated purpose provided that the patient has given informed consent for a specific processing purpose and the stated processing purpose is compatible with the purpose consented for".

We present below the application of the generic template of SWRL privacy rules to this rule example. For this we adopt a human readable SWRL syntax.

We denote by (R, T, Con, E and Ob) respectively the Rule elements (Rule, Target, Conditions, Effect and Obligations) described in the abstract syntax of privacy rules given above. The rule template is therefore rewritten as follows:
R: = T ∧ Con → E ∧ Ob

In order to implement our rule example, we need to apply it to a concrete data-sharing scenario. For this we present the example of data sharing in the cloud described in Fig. 2. The scenario we have chosen describes a case of data sharing in the *health* domain. We assume that two medical doctors belonging each to a different hospital in different European member states for example UK and Italy form the two data sharing parties. To be more precise, one of the medical doctors would like to get a second opinion on a patient's *Mammogram*.

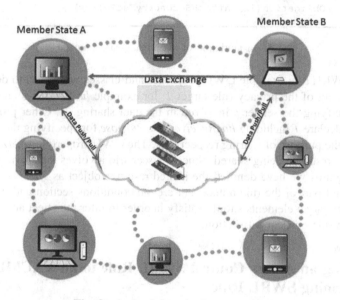

Fig. 2. A cloud data-sharing scenario.

The data will be exchanged on a cloud platform and it is required that the cloud security services could identify the right policy to apply in order to allow the sharing of the data, but in a lawful way. Since we are looking at a pan-European context, it wouldn't be always the case that the data processing law is interpreted and implemented in one member state in exactly the same way as in another. Stating as an example, when processing health data for the purpose of medical research, the patient consent must be a *specific consent* when referring to the law in the UK or France. However consent could be *broad* or *general consent* when referring to an Italian law.

For this more context information should be provided in the privacy rules specification for the cloud security processes in order to be able to make the right decision. It is therefore essential to indicate in the rule implementation the sender and receiver's locations and the member state from which the shared data comes. An instantiation of

R in the context of the rule example and the cloud data-sharing scenario is then interpreted in the Fig. 3.

```
T:
            hasSender(?x, ?s) ∧hasReceiver(?x, ?r) ∧ hasPurpose(?x, ?p)
Con:
        ∧  locatedIn(?s, UK)        ∧    locatedIn(?r, Italy)
        ∧  concerning(?x, ?m)       ∧    belongsTo(?m, UK)
        ∧  isForPatient(?m, ?pt)
        ∧  provided(?pt, InformedConsent)
        ∧  hasCollectionPurpose(?m, CollectionPurpose)
        ∧  compatibleWith(?p, CollectionPurpose)

E:          hasSharingDecision(?x, allow)
Ob:         hasObligation(?x, attachSecondaryUsePolicy)
```

Fig. 3. Instantiation of the privacy rule template.

In this SWRL rule example OWL properties and classes were used to describe the different element of the privacy rule target T, for example *hasSender* is an owl object property specifying the sender s involved in the data sharing $?x$. Other properties are also used to declare T including *hasReceiver*, *hasPurpose* for specifying the receiver of the data and the purpose of sharing respectively. The OWL property *concerning* is used to capture the resource being shared. Since the scenario involves the sharing of patient $?pt$ mammograms we have denoted the shared resource/object as $?m$.

The second part of the rule antecedent are the conditions section and it shows the constraints the target elements should satisfy in order to infer the effect and obligations shown in the rule consequent section.

5   Mapping an Access Control SWRL Rule to an XACML Conforming SWRL Rule

For easy mapping to an XACML rule, the SWRL rule has to be specified in terms of attributes of only the generic entities that constitute an XACML Rule Target (see above) and other elements that are used to specify the general policy that the rule in question belongs to, e.g. the purpose of processing. In this regard, the OWL property:

```
Provided (Patient, Informed Consent)
```

is a property of the patient whose data is to be shared and indicates that the patient has provided informed consent. The patient or the data subject is not one of the XACML "Rule Target" components; therefore, we express the same condition in terms of property of the class "O" (the resource or object. In our case it is the data the subject is requesting access to). The result is presented in Table 1. Note that we do not need to translate *provided(?pt, InformedConsent)* as we are not keeping constraints about patients in the XACML version of the rule. For example, in the XACML conforming SWRL Rule, the consent is an attribute of the object and not of the patient any more.

Table 1. Logical mapping from SWRL rule to XACML conforming SWRL rule.

Initial SWRL Privacy-Aware access control rule	XACML Conforming SWRL Privacy-Aware access control rule
`dataSharing(?x)`	`hasRuleContext(?r, ?rc)`
`∧ hasAction(?x, ?ac)`	`∧ hasContextAction(?rc, ?ac)`
`∧ hasSender(?x, ?s)`	`∧ hasContextSubject(?rc, ?s)`
`∧ hasReceiver(?x, ?r)`	`∧ hasReceiver(?ac, ?rec)`
`∧ concerning(?x, ?m)`	`∧ hasContextObject(?rc, ?o)`
`∧ hasPurpose(?x, ?p)`	`∧ hasContextPurpose(?rc, ?p)`
`∧ action(?ac, send)`	`∧ action(?ac, send)`
`∧ locatedIn(?s, UK)`	`∧ locatedIn(?s, UK)`
`∧ belongsTo(?m, UK)`	`∧ consent(?o, true)`
	`∧ hasConsentType(?o, InformedConsent)`
`∧ compatibleWith (?p,CollectionPurpose)`	`∧ compatibleWith(?p, ?cp)`
Rule Implication	
`hasSharingDecision(?x, allow)`	`hasRuleEffect(?r, allow)`
`∧ hasObligation(?x, attach-SecondaryUsePolicy)`	`∧ hasObligation(?r, attachSecond-aryUsePolicy)`

The rule described above is an extension or privacy aware version of traditional access control rules that pays no significant attention to privacy constraints and obligations. If specified in SWRL syntax, an example of this traditional access control rule would look as shown in the following instantiation of the privacy rule template (Fig. 4).

```
hasRuleContext(?r, ?rc)
∧        hasContextSubject(?rc, ?s)    ∧    hasContextObject(?rc, ?o)
∧        hasContextAction(?rc, send)    ∧    hasContextPurpose(?rc, ?p)
∧        hasRole(?s,doctor)             ∧    isForPatient(?o,?pt)
∧        isDoctorOf(?s,?pt)
→     hasRuleEffect(?r, allow)
```

Fig. 4. Instantiation of the privacy rule template.

The only constraints the rule above tests for before allowing the disclosure of the data is the role of the *subject* or *requestor*. In this case, the role of the subject must be a medical doctor of the patient whose data is to be disclosed.

XACML was designed to notate access control policies and to provide a reference framework for their enforcement. Its major focus is on security policies, although privacy is mentioned in the specification of version 2.0 [9]. It is verbose and complex and still lacks expressiveness. The XACML version 3.0 however, seems to provide a better privacy specification profile [30]. We have also noticed that some examples included in the XACML privacy profile, which were supposed to specify a policy compliant with the "specific and compatible purpose" privacy principle, in fact test for equality or matching of purposes rather than compatibility of purposes. We believe this is due to the language's lack of semantics and reasoning ability with regards to privacy constraints on protected data. If this lack is not addressed, a straightforward mapping from SWRL policies to XACML will not be possible. From the examples of the SWRL access control and privacy rules presented earlier in this paper, we conclude that privacy obligations should be specified for each rule as they are matched according to the data sharing context that we declare to be unique for each rule. This is different from the way obligations are specified in XACML. Obligations in XACML are related to a policy and not to the individual rules that a policy is made up of. We have resolved this problem by allowing each policy to include only one rule and its applicable obligations. Indeed, this decision was already implicit at the time we designed our SWRL privacy aware access control policies. For it, we decided to include one rule per policy. In fact, dealing with more then one privacy obligation at once might require a large amount of contextual information. Therefore, the equivalent SWRL rule would become too long and less readable.

6   Mapping of an XML Conforming SWRL Rule to an XACML Policy

In this section, we present an attempt to formalise a mapping of a SWRL rule to an XACML policy.

There is some existing work that has looked at formalisms of XACML with many purposes in mind such as in [25, 29, 27, 28, 29]. In particular, the work presented in [25, 26] has started from a BNF representation of an XACML rule and has produced a DL formalism that allows the mapping of an XACML rule to DL syntax. Our approach takes into consideration the syntactic difference between DL and SWRL. SWRL is an extension of OWL-DL that can be mapped to DL syntax. It has inherited *Horn-like* propositional logic syntax from RuleML and this characteristic would influence the deviation from a DL formalism provided in [25, 26]. The mapping process has already started from the previous section when we have transformed our SWRL access control rule into an XACML conforming representation. This was done by translating all the properties occurring in the antecedent and consequent to properties applied only on concepts that could be identified in the set of entities that occur in the XACML language model. After the transformation, we suggest that our SWRL access control rules can be generalised under the following formalism.

Formalism1:

Rule: = Target	∧	Conditions	→	Effect	∧	Obligations
R: = Tgt	∧	Con	→	Eft	∧	Ob

We denote by:

- **R:** an OWL concept representing an access control rule.
- **Tgt:** the target of a rule R that usually constitutes of the elements Subject, Object, Action and Purpose.

- **Con:** the constraints to be imposed on the different elements of a target and that should be satisfied in order for the decisions specified in the consequence clause to be satisfied.
- **Eft:** the effect of a rule R that could be a Permit or Deny
- **Ob:** the set of obligations that could be associated with the rule R

Formalism 1 may be mapped to Formalism 2 as described below:

Formalism 2:

$$\text{Rule}\,(R)\wedge[\textstyle\bigwedge_{i=0}^{3}\text{Pd}_i\,(R,\ \text{pd}_i\,(R))]\wedge[\textstyle\bigwedge_{i=3,k=n}\text{Pc}_k\,(C_i, pc_k\,(C_i))]\rightarrow \text{Eft}\,(R,e)\wedge[\textstyle\bigwedge_{j=0}^{m}\text{Ob}_j\,(R,ob_j\,(R))]$$

Where i, j and k are natural numbers ranging, respectively, over the number of rule target elements (0..3), the number of properties in our ontology (0..n), and the number of obligations that would be associated with the rule R (0..m), and where:

- $\wedge$ with limits is the symbol for multiple conjunctions;
- **Pd** denotes an OWL property used for declaration of the target elements of a rule R;
- **Pc** denotes an OWL property used for specifying constraints on the elements constituting a target of a rule;
- **C** represents a given class of our ontology with C0, C1, C2 and C3 representing respectively the entities constituting the elements of a target of a rule in the order: Subject, Object, Action and Purpose;
- **Eft** is an OWL property specifying the effect of a rule R, its value is a literal e where e belongs to {permit, deny}.

Table 2 provides a one to one mapping of the entities constituting an XACML rule and Formalism 2.

Table 2. Logical formalism of SWRL access control rules.

Entity	SWRL formalism
SWRL Rule: SR	$\text{Rule}(R)\wedge[\textstyle\bigwedge_{i=0}^{3}\text{Pd}_i\,(R,\ \text{pd}_i\,(R))]\wedge[\textstyle\bigwedge_{i=3,j=n}\text{Pc}_k\,(C_i, pc_k\,(C_i))]\rightarrow \text{Eft}(R,e)\wedge[\textstyle\bigwedge_{j=0}^{m}\text{Ob}_j\,(R,ob_j\,(R))]$
Effect	`Eft(R, e)` `e ::= Permit	Deny`
Target	`Subject(R,Sub)` $\wedge$ `Object(R,Obj)` $\wedge$ `Action(R,Act)` $\wedge$ `Purpose (R,Pur)` $::= \textstyle\bigwedge_{i=0}^{3}\text{Pd}_i(R,\ \text{pd}_i(R))$
Conditions	π`Conditions`π`(Sub)` $\wedge$ `Conditions`π`(Act)` $\wedge$ `Conditions`$\wedge\pi$`(Res)` $\wedge$ `Conditions`$\wedge\pi$`(Pur)` $::= \textstyle\bigwedge_{i=3,j=n}\text{Pc}_k\,(C_i, pc_k\,(C_i))$
Obliga-tions	$\pi\text{Ob}::= \textstyle\bigwedge_{j=0}^{n}\text{Ob}_j\,(R,ob_j\,(R))$

In order to be able to translate our SWRL rules to XACML rules we suggest allowing a one to one mapping between our SWRL Formalism 2 and the BNF formalism of an XACML rule provided in [25, 26]. To achieve this, we have extended the XACML BNF notation with the purpose element of a rule target and the rule obligations clause. The mapping is described in Table 3.

Table 3. SWRL to XACML mapping

Entity	SWRL formalism	XACML formalism
Rule	Formalism 2	R ::= (Rule Tgt Eft)
Effect	Eft(R, e) e ::= Permit | Deny	Eft ::= Permit | Deny
Target	Subject(R,Sub) ∧ Object(R,Obj) ∧ Action(R, Act) ∧ Purpose (R, Pur-pose) $::= \bigwedge_{i=0}^{j} Pd_i(R, pd_i(R))$	Tgt::= ((Sub) (Act) (Res) (Pur))
Condition Clause	ΠConditionsΠ Sub) ∧ ConditionsΠ(Act) ∧ Conditions∧Π(Res) ∧ Conditions∧Π(Pur) $::= \bigwedge_{i=0,j=\alpha} Pc_k(C_i, pc_k(C_i))$	Each Pc(C, Pc(C)) := Sub |Act | Res| Pur ::= Any | Fn Fn::= AV | Fn \ Fn | Fn [Fn | ¬ Fn AV::=(attr-id attr-val) attr-id attr-value
Obligations	$\pi Ob::= \bigwedge_{j=0}^{n} Ob_j(R, ob_j(R))$	Each Ob(R, ob(R))::= AV

Based on the above *one to one* mapping, we mapped the purpose compatibility SWRL rule produced earlier to the XACML Rule presented in Fig. 5. In this rule, we have chosen to name the *sender* and *receiver* specified previously in the cloud scenario (Sect. 4) as *Dr_House* and *Dr_Casa* respectively. Other context variable from the objet to be shared and the sharing purpose were also replaced with some values. We have chosen *M1* to indicate the mammogram being sent by *Dr_House* and the sending purpose were specified as *SecondOpinionOnTreatment*.

```
<Rule RuleId = "1" Effect="Permit">
<Target>
<Subjects>< Attribute AttributeId="Subject-Id" DataType= "String">
<AttributeValue> Dr_House </attributeValue>
< Attribute AttributeId = "Location" DataType= "String">
<AttributeValue> UK </attributeValue>
< Attribute AttributeId = "Receiver-Id" DataType= "String">
<AttributeValue> Dr_Casa</attributeValue>
< Attribute AttributeId = "Receiver-Location" DataType= "String">
<AttributeValue> Italy </attributeValue>
< Attribute AttributeId = "Role" DataType= "String">
<AttributeValue> Doctor </attributeValue>
</Subjects>
<Resources>< Attribute AttributeId = "ResourceId" DataType= "String">
<AttributeValue> M1</AttributeValue>
< Attribute AttributeId = "Consent" DataType= "Boolean">
<AttributeValue> true</AttributeValue>
</Resources>
<Action> >< Attribute AttributeId = "Action-Id" DataType= "String">
<AttributeValue>send</AttributeValue></Action>
<Purpose>
<Attribute AttributeId= "purpose-id" DataType="String">
<AttributeValue> SecondOpinionOnTreatment</AttributeValue>
</Attribute>
<Attribute AttributeId= "compatibleWith" DataType= "bag">
</Attribute>
</Purpose>
</Target>
<Condition
<Function FunctionId="urn:oasis:names:tc:xacml:1.0:function:string-equal"/>
<Apply FunctionId="urn:oasis:names:tc:xacml:1.0:function:string-is-in">
    -- Consent-Purpose is the purpose for which the data subject has consented or the purpose for
which the data (Resource) is legally stored on the grid database we have specified this purpose as
an attribute of the resource in question--
<ResourceAttributeDesignator attributeId= Consent Purpose DataType = "string"/> BreastCan-
cerDiagnosisAndTreatment
</ResourceAttributeDesignator>
</Apply>
<Apply>
<PurposeAttributeDesignator attributeId= "CompatibleWith"  DataType = "bag"/>
</Apply>
</Condition>
</Rule>
```

Fig. 5. Privacy aware XACML rule.

7 Mapping SWRL Rules to XACML Rules

In order to further automate the mapping of SWRL rules to XACML rules, we rely on
mapping templates where we can specify for each OWL property an equivalent
XACML attribute ID. Furthermore, we need a detailed *one to one* mapping between the
OWL axioms specifying conditions/constraints on the different elements of a rule target

and the standard XACML functions that could be used as alternatives to these axioms once applied on XACML attribute-ids.

In most of the cases, an XACML equality function/predicate would be the relevant function to allow the translation of an OWL property constraint. The two operands of the equality are first, the *attribute_id* that should hold the name of the OWL property and second the attribute value that should be the same as the OWL property value. XACML distinguishes between several equality checking functions depending on the *data types* of the *operands*. The equality functions in XACML include *string-equal*, *Boolean-equal*, *Integer-equal* and other types. Deciding on which one we need to select is based on a mapping between the OWL *data type* of the property *value* and XACML *data types*. If the property value is determined by an *object property* then an XACML attribute matching function of type *string* should be used. If the property value is determined by a *data type property*, then the XACML attribute matching function should have the same type as the *data type property value*. The work presented in [25, 26] provides a detailed mapping of XACML data types to OWL data types. A reverse mapping is needed in our case, since we are interested in mapping OWL axioms to XACML conditions instead.

8   Summary and Future Work

We have used OWL and SWRL to model high level policies interpreted from European and national data protection law as privacy aware access control policies. The high expressiveness power of semantic web languages allowed the integration of privacy requirements highlighted in text law such as requirements of consent and other safeguards of patient rights as policy constraints. Additionally we have used mapping templates to transform the Semantic Web access control policies into a de-facto and highly portable standard of access control notably XACML which is used in clouds security infrastructures. Among many investigated scenarios we have chosen the *"Medical Images Exchange"* example in order to validate the work. This permitted to conclude that the use of ontologies and semantic technologies could provide relatively easy interpretation of legislation at an operational level. Few challenges were faced when conducting this work that we have overcome by mapping the SWRL privacy policies to XACML policies. An interesting future work in this area for us is to produce an extended XACML enforcement architecture that is able to adequate the added semantic layer for the SWRL to XACML mapping task. This will require both an implementation of the mapping formalism and testing it on the extended enforcement architecture. A java implementation of the SWRL to XACML mapping tool is in progress.

References

1. Brandic, I., Dustdar, S., Anstett, T., Schumm, D., Leymann, F., Konrad, R.: Compliant cloud computing (C3): architecture and language support for user-driven compliance management in clouds. In: IEEE 3rd International Conference on Cloud Computing (2010)

2. EC.Directive 95/46/ECofthe European Parliament and of the Council (1995) (cited 2010). http://ec.europa.eu/justice/policies/privacy/law/index_en.htm#directive

3. McCullagh, K.: Study of data protection: harmonization or confusion? In: Proceeding of the 21st BILETA Conference: Globalisation and Harmonisation in Technology Law. Malta (2006)

4. Beyleveld, D., Townend, D., Rouillé-Mirza, S., Wright, J.: Implementation of the Data Protection Directive in Relation to Medical Research in Europe. Ashgate Publishing Limited, UK (2004). ISBN-10: 0754623696

5. Iversen, A., Liddell, K., Fear, N., Hotopf, M., Consent, W.S.: Confidentiality and the data protection act. Br. Med. J. (Clin. Res. Ed.) 332(7534), 165–169 (2006)

6. Italian Personal Data Protection Code (2003). http://www.privacy.it/privacycode-en.html. Legislative Decreeno. 196 of 30 June 2003 (cited 2012)

7. The Open Cloud Standards Incubator (OCSI): Architecture for Managing Clouds, White Paper from the Open Cloud Standards Incubator 1.0, DMTF DSP-ISO102 (2010). http://www.dmtf.org/standards/published_documents/DSP-IS0101_1.0.pdf

8. Horrocks, I., et al.: SWRL: a semantic web rule language combining OWL and RuleML (2004). http://www.w3.org/Submission/SWRL/. Accessed 2013

9. OASIS XACML: eXtensible Access Control Markup Language (XACML), version 2.0 (2005). http://docs.oasisopen.org/xacml/2.0/XACML-2.0-OSNORMATIVE.zip

10. Casassa Mont, M., Crosta, S., Kriegelstein, T., Sommer, D.: PRIME architecture V2. Deliverable D14.2.c. (2007). https://www.primeproject.eu/prime_products/reports/arch/pub_del_D14.2.c_ec_WP14.2_v1_Final.pdf. Accessed 2014

11. Sommer, D., Casassa Mont, M., Pearson, S.: PRIME architecture V3. Deliverable 14.2.d (2008). https://www.primeproject.eu/prime_products/reports/arch/pub_del_D14.2.d_ec_WP14.2_v3_Final.pdf. Accessed 2014

12. Casassa Mont, M., Shen, Y., Kounga, G., Pearson, S.: EnCoRe project deliverable D2.1. Technical Architecture for the First Realized Case Study [Online] (1.0) (2010). http://www.encoreproject.info. Accessed June 2014

13. Rahmouni, H.B., Solomonides, T., Casassa Mont, M., Shiu, S.: Privacy compliance and enforcement on European healthgrids: an approach through ontology. Philos. Trans. R. Soc. 368, 4057–4072 (2010)

14. Rahmouni, H.B., Solomonides, T., Casassa, M.M., Shiu, S., Rahmouni, M.A.: Modeldriven privacy compliance decision support for medical data sharing in europe. Methods Inf. Med. 50(4), 326–336 (2011)

15. Muppavarapu, V., Chung, S.M.: Semantic-based access control for grid data resources in open grid services architecture - data access and integration (OGSA-DAI). In: 20th IEEE International Conference on Tools with Artificia lIntelligence (ICTAI 2008), Dayton, Ohio, USA. IEEE Computer Society (2008)

16. Gowadia, V., Scalavino, E., Lupu, E., Aziz, B.: The consequence project, deliverable D3.1: models and framework for meta-data generation and policy infrastructure (2008). http://www.consequenceproject.eu/Deliverables_Y1/D3.1.pdf

17. Matteucci, I., Petrocchi, M., Sbodio, M.L.: CNL4DSA – a controlled natural language for data sharing agreements. In: Proceedings of the 2010 ACM Symposium on Applied Computing, Sierre, Switzerland. ACM (2010)

18. Boley, H., et al.: Schema specification of RuleML 1.0 (2010). http://ruleml.org/1.0/. Accessed 2012

19. Bechhofer, S., et al.: OWL web ontology language reference (2004). http://www.w3.org/TR/owl-ref/. Accessed 2013

20. Wang, K., Billington, D., Blee, J., Antoniou, G.: Combining description logic and defeasible logic for the semantic web. In: Antoniou, G., Boley, H. (eds.) Rules and Rule Markup Languages for the Semantic Web: Third International Workshop, RuleML. Lecture Notes in Computer Science, pp. 170–181. Springer, Heidelberg (2004)
21. Gruber, T.R.: Toward principles for the design of ontologies used for knowledge sharing. Int. J. Hum. Comput. Stud. **43**(4–5), 907–928 (1995)
22. Demchenko, Y., Koeroo, O., de Laat, C., Sagehaug, H.: Extending XACML authorisation model to support policy obligations handling in distributed applications. In: Proceedings of the 6th International Workshop on Middleware for Grid Computing. ACM (2008)
23. Priebe, T. et al.: Supporting attribute-based access control with ontologies. ARES, pp. 465–472 (2006). doi:10.1109/ARES.2006.127
24. Damiani, E., De Capitani di Vimercati, S., Fugazza, C., Samarati, P.: Extending policy languages to the semantic web. In: Fraternali, P., Koch, N., Wirsing, M. (eds.) ICWE 2004. LNCS, vol. 3140, pp. 330–343. Springer, Heidelberg (2004)
25. Kolovski, V.: Formalizing XACML using defeasible description logics. Technical report TR-233-11. University of Maryland - College Park (2006)
26. Kolosvki, V.: Logic-based framework for web access control policies. Ph.D. thesis, Digital Repository at the University of Maryland, College Park, Md (2008)
27. Kolovski, V., Hendler, J.: XACML policy analysis using descriptionlogics (2008). http://www.mindswap.org/~kolovski/KolovskiXACMLAnalysis-JCSSubmission.pd.   Accessed 2012
28. Masi, M., Pugliese, R., Tiezzi, F.: Formalisation and implementation of the XACML access control mechanism. In: Livshits, B., Scandariato, R., Barthe, G. (eds.) ESSoS 2012. LNCS, vol. 7159, pp. 60–74. Springer, Heidelberg (2012)
29. Bryans, J.W., Fitzgerald, J.S.: Formal engineering of XACML access control policies in VDM ++. In: Proceedings of the Formal Engineering Methods 9th International Conference on Formal Methods and Software Engineering, Boca Raton, FL, 14–15 November 2007
30. OASIS XACML: eXtensible Access Control Markup Language (XACML), version 3.0 (2013) http://docs.oasis-open.org/xacml/3.0/xacml-3.0-core-spec-os-en.pdf. Accessed 2013
31. Rahmouni, H.B., Solomonides, T., Casassa Mont, M., Shiu, S.: Ontology based privacy compliance for health data disclosure in Europe. Ph.D. thesis, University of the West of England, Bristol (2011)
32. Powers, C., Adler, S., Wishart, B.: EPAL translation of the freedom of information and protection of privacy act. In: White Paper, IBM Tivoli and Information and Privacy Commissioner, Ontario (2004)
33. Ontario: freedom of information and protection of privacy act (2008). http://www.elaws.gov.on.ca/html/statutes/english/elaws_statutes_90f31_e.htm. Accessed 2013

Dynamic Pricing in Cloud Markets: Evaluation of Procurement Auctions

Paolo Bonacquisto, Giuseppe Di Modica, Giuseppe Petralia,
and Orazio Tomarchio$^{(\boxtimes)}$

Department of Electrical, Electronic and Computer Engineering,
University of Catania, V.le A. Doria 6, 95125 Catania, Italy
{Paolo.Bonacquisto,Giuseppe.DiModica,Giuseppe.Petralia,
Orazio.Tomarchio}@dieei.unict.it

Abstract. One of the fundamental principles which cloud computing paradigm builds upon is that resources in the cloud may be accessed "on-demand", i.e., when they are required and for just the time they are required. This intrinsic technologic feature encouraged the cloud commercial providers to adopt the pay-per-use pricing mechanism as it turned to be the most convenient and the easiest to implement. Though pay-per-use ensures significant incomes to providers, still providers experience an underutilization of their computing capacity. It is a matter of fact that unemployed resources represent both a missed income and a cost to providers. In this paper a procurement auction market is proposed as an alternative sell mechanism to maximize the utilization rate of providers' datacenters. Benefits for the providers are achieved through the use of an adaptive strategy that can be easily tuned to cater for the provider's own business needs. Also, in the paper the resort to resource overbooking within the provider's strategy has been analyzed. The proposal's viability was finally proved through simulation tests conducted on the Cloudsim simulator.

Keywords: Cloud market · Procurement auction · Bidding strategy · Cloud simulations

1 Introduction

Cloud computing aims to provide computing resources to customers like public utilities such as water and electricity [3]. In an Infrastructure-as-a-Service (IaaS) cloud environment, physical resources are packaged into distinct types of virtual machines (VMs) and offered to customers. A cloud customer, on the other hand, will purchase VMs to run his applications, by looking for specific resource requirements in terms of CPU, memory and disk. Given the finite capacity for each type of resources in each data center, a fundamental problem faced by IaaS provider is how to select the price and allocate resources for each type of VM services in order to best match the interests of the customers while maximizing his revenue [9]. This issue is further complicated by the fact that, differently

© Springer International Publishing Switzerland 2015
M. Helfert et al. (Eds.): CLOSER 2014, CCIS 512, pp. 31–46, 2015.
DOI: 10.1007/978-3-319-25414-2_3

from traditional utility markets, cloud demand is strongly time varying and often burstly.

The resource allocation and trading mechanisms used by the current cloud computing systems are inefficient and inflexible due to the flat rate pricing model adopted. We argue that a fixed price-based resource allocation currently in use in cloud computing systems do not provide an efficient allocation of resources and do not maximize the revenue of the cloud providers. In a previous work [8], we already showed that a better alternative would be to use auction-based resource allocation mechanisms. In this paper we address issues related to the bidding strategies adopted by providers of computing resources in the context of procurement auctions. We try to analyze all the factors that mainly impact the strategic choices of providers in the acquisition of the goods allocated through auctions. The purpose of this work is not to devise an optimal bidding strategy, but rather, to prove that any strategy will have its objective guaranteed by the procurement mechanism. We also devised a tentative provider's strategy which adapts its aggressiveness to the earlier mentioned factors. In the addressed market scenario, we stress that our attention is devoted to the optimization of the utilization rate of providers' data centers and the utility of providers.

The remainder of the paper is structured as follows. Section 2 makes a review of the literature and gives some rationale of the work. Section 3 introduces the proposed idea and delves into technical details about procurement auctions, while Sect. 4 describes the proposed adative strategy. In Sect. 5 simulation results are presented and discussed. Finally, the work is concluded in Sect. 6.

2   Related Work

All main commercial IaaS providers impose a fixed price for the use of one hour of computing capacity[1]. So far, the only provider which successfully proposed an alternative approach to the fixed-price is Amazon with its *Spot Instance* model[2]. This model enables the customer to bid for what they call unused computing capacity. Virtual machines are charged the *Spot Price*, which is set by Amazon and fluctuates periodically depending on the supply/demand rate for computing capacity. The Spot Instance model represents the very first attempt to build up a virtual market of computing resources regulated by market prices, i.e., prices which dynamically fluctuate according to offer and demand. In spite of this, the model is still unclear (the formula of price fluctuation is not known) and is not proved to be resistant to potential malicious behaviors of customers [16]. Furthermore in [1] authors prove that the Amazon's Spot Price is not market driven, rather is typically generated as a random value near to the hidden reserve price within a tight price interval. The consideration stemming from this observation is that a provider, being an interested party, may not be a guarantee for the

---

[1] http://aws.amazon.com/ec2/, http://www.microsoft.com/windowsazure/, http://www.rackspace.com/.

[2] http://aws.amazon.com/ec2/spot-instances/.

correctness of the price determination. Instead, a third party broker should be in charge of calling out prices in auction-based contexts.

A quick review of the recent literature reveals that researchers are prone to apply auction mechanisms to the problem of the allocation (read "sale") of computing resources. In [14] authors propose a marketplace of computing resources where prices are determined using an exchange market. In [6] authors discuss several strategies that cloud providers should adopt in order to reach high performance and to overcome most of criticisms of auctions like high overheads and high latency using techniques like overbooking and Flexible Advanced Reservations. They propose several bidding functions but each one takes into account only one parameter among those monitored by a cloud provider.

For the majority of researchers, combinatorial auctions are the most appropriate sale mechanism for allocating virtual machines in the cloud. In combinatorial auctions the participants bid for bundles of items rather than individual items [7]. This mechanism seems to perfectly fit the Cloud context, as customers usually need to acquire not just one resource but a bunch of resources (e.g., one for hosting the database server, one for the application server and one for the web server). In [16] authors propose a suite of computationally efficient and truthful auction-style pricing mechanisms, which enable customers to fairly compete for resources and cloud providers to increase their overall revenue. [17] proposes a combinatorial auction-based protocol for resource allocation in grids. They considered a model where different grid providers can provide different types of computing resources. Buyya et al. [4] propose an infrastructure for auction-based resource allocation across multiple cloud systems. In [15] authors address the scenario of multiple resource procurement in the realm of cloud computing. In the observed context, they pre-process the user requests, analyze the auction and declare a set of vendors bidding for the auction as winners based on the Combinatorial Auction Branch on Bids (CABOB) model.

The discussed works mainly focus on solving the problem of the optimal sale of resources in combinatorial auctions, which is known to be NP-hard. The work we propose, instead of defining yet another sub-optimal allocation algorithm, takes a different direction. The profit of a provider strongly depends on its capability of keeping the hosts' average occupancy rate as high as possible. For their nature, computing resources can be regarded as perishable goods that need to be sold within a certain time frame otherwise they get wasted. Not selling a virtual machine in a given slot time means a profit loss for the provider, who anyway is spending money to keep the physical machines up and running. We then look at the trade of computing resources from a new perspective, in which providers, in the aim of maximizing their data center's occupancy rate, may be willing to attract customers by lowering the offer price. On their turn, customers may get what they need, at the time they need it, at a price which is lower than the standard price at which they usually buy. We advocate that the market model best fitting this perspective is the one which guarantees the sale of computing resources through **procurement auctions** [2]. Procurement auctions [10] (also called reverse auctions) reverse the roles of sellers and buyers, in the sense that the bidders are those who have interest in selling a good (the providers), and therefore the competition for acquiring the right-to-sell the good is run among providers.

3   A Procurement Auction Market

The purpose of this work is not to convince providers to abandon the direct-sell mechanism in favor of the procurement-based market. Providers have their regular customers, who issue requests which most of the times have a well known timing. For this kind of requests the most appropriate model is the *direct-sell/fixed-price*, in that it provides guarantees for both the provider and the customer. What we propose is the adoption of an alternative, dynamic pricing model for selling what is usually referred to as the *unused capacity*, i.e., the residual capacity that, on average, the provider is not able to sell through direct-sell.

Let us define the utilization rate $U(t)$ as the fraction of the overall unused capacity committed to serve customers' requests at the time t. The lower the U, the higher the profit loss for the provider. In the aim of maximizing the utilization rate (minimizing the residual capacity) providers need to adopt new selling strategies. The simplest strategy could just be lowering the price per computing unit. We argue that providers, in the aim of avoiding the "waste" of computing capacity, are willing to give up a portion of profit per computing unit (same as it happens for sale of perishable goods).

In this paper we propose the design of a market of computing capacity (see Fig. 1), to which any provider is admitted, and where computing resources can be sold through auction-based allocation schemes. The perspective is that of procurement auctions, where an initial price is called out and bidders iteratively have to call lower prices to win. The market mechanism is the following. Customers communicate their computing demand to the market. A *broker* will take care of requests. For each specific demand, the broker (auctioneer) will run a public auction to which any provider (bidder) can participate and compete for "acquiring" the demand. The winning provider (who offered the lowest price) will eventually have to serve the demand. Being the auctions open to the participation of multiple providers, the competition is granted. Providers will have to fight in order to gain the right-to-serve the demand. Bidding strategies enforced by providers can range from the most conservative to the most aggressive. The determination of the final price is driven only by the evaluation that each provider has on the goods to acquire (i.e., the customer's demand to be served). Customers will get their demand served at the lowest price. Further, they will have no more the burden to search for providers, as providers are gathered in the market.

We focus on three different types of procurement auctions. The common part of the three auction mechanisms is the auction preparation, which provides that upon the arrival of a demand, the broker issues a public "call for proposal" (CFP) to invite providers. The CFP shall specify a minimum set of auction parameters including the start-provision time, the stop-provision time, the initial price (from which discount bids are expected), the bidding rules (who can bid and when,

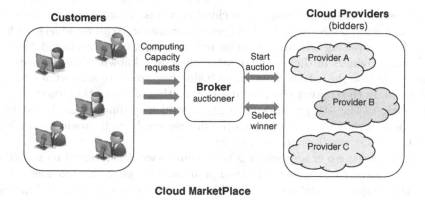

Fig. 1. The cloud marketplace scenario.

restrictions on bids) and the clearing policy (when to "terminate" the auction, who gets what, at what price). After collecting the willingness of providers to participate in the auction, the preparation phase ends up and the bargain starts according to what is specified in the bidding rules and the clearing policy. What characterizes one auction mechanism from another one is the information specified in the bidding rules and the clearing policy. For our purpose, in this paper the following auction types will be addressed: English Reverse (ER), First Price Sealed Bid (FPSB) and Second Price Sealed Bid (SPSB) [12].

4   A Provider's Adaptive Strategy

Main objective of this work is the study of an adaptive strategy for the providers that participate in procurement auctions. By strategy we mean a set of rules producing the decisions a provider should take to maximize their own business objective. Basically, a strategy shall drive the provider in choosing the right actions to be undertaken when competing for the acquisition of a good (e.g., whether to participate in a given auction, to bid in a given round, not to bid, which price to offer). In the strategy design, the first step was to outline the main factors that may impact such choices. Secondly, we tried to devise a dynamic strategy which accounts for the just mentioned factors and smoothly adapt their fluctuations. Finally, we set up and configured a test environment to analyze the results produced by the strategy.

According to the literature, the behavior of an auction's participant is mainly driven by the information the participant has on the value of the good being sold [10]. In respect to this information, two basic auction models are possible: (1) the *private-value* model, where each bidder has an estimate of the good for sale, and that estimate is private and unaffected by others' estimates, and (2) the *pure common-value* model, where the actual value of the object is the same for everyone, but bidders have different private information on how much that value actually is. Combined models can also be derived from the cited ones.

If we better analyze the context of cloud auctions, a computing resource can be seen as a good whose actual value (price) is common to all providers. In fact, though for computing resources we can not yet speak of conventional "market prices", all providers in their regular sales adopt well known, leveled prices. We can then conclude the actual values of such kind resources are somewhat common to providers. In the context of a procurement auction of computing resources, the estimate E_{pi} of the i-th provider for a given good may differ from the estimate E_{pj} of the j-th provider according to the diverse needs each provider may have in pursuing their own business objective.

Primary objective of a provider is to maximize what is referred to as *Utility*. Given a resource to be allocated through an auction sale, the provider's Utility for that request is defined as the difference between the winning bid price and the evaluation that the provider gives to the resource [16]. Of course, the provider aims at maximizing the average utility for the resources they compete for. Recalling the considerations made earlier, in the context of an auction sale of spare resources this objective can be pursued: (a) by keeping the data center's utilization as high as possible; (b) by bidding prices higher than the personal evaluation (which we will refer to as *lower bound*) and (c) by choosing the most profitable combination of customers' request to serve.

We identified a non-exhaustive list of factors which may strongly influence the strategy of a provider in a procurement auction.

- The duration of the customer task (demand) to be served (L). The longer the task, the higher the profitability for the provider, since the required capacity will be committed for a longer time. A provider, then, might prefer to participate in auctions where long tasks are traded.
- The type of VM instance required to serve the customer task (T). Of course, the profitability of a task is directly proportional to the task's requirements in terms of amount of computing capacity per hour, so providers may be motivated in pointing on auctions calling for a higher capacity/hour. But depending on the actual utilization level of both each single host and the whole data center, it might not be possible to serve further tasks requiring high capacity VMs.
- The gap between the potential revenue obtainable from serving the task the standard way (i.e., through the fixed-price market) and that obtainable by serving the task at the price called by the auctioneer (G_r). The revenue for serving a task is given by the L times the price (P) of the resource that will serve the task. This factor strongly depends on the provider's enforced revenue policy. A provider pointing on auctions to sell their unused capacity might accept a much lower revenue (bidding a lower price) in the case that expenses are already covered. Conversely, the provider might not be willing to excessively lower the price in the case that expenses are not yet covered.
- The utilization of the particular physical machine that is going to serve the customer's request. The marginal revenue, in fact, is affected by the utilization level of a host: if a host is already running and serving other tasks, adding more tasks to that host "costs" less than activating a new host.

Finally, some considerations need to be made about the *lower bound*. Each strategy must envision an "exit condition", which represents the condition that, when verified, forces the exit of the provider from the auction. When the provider decides to participate in an auction, they will have to set the lower bound price, which represents the maximum discount that the provider is willing to offer for the good being traded in that auction. Of course, this parameter only makes sense in multi-rounds auctions, as in single round auctions actually exit is imposed by the mechanism itself at the end of the first round. The lower bound parameter actually represents the evaluation of the provider for a given good (customer's request). It incorporates all provider's consideration regarding the costs for executing a VM, managing a VM's life cycle and supporting the customer.

The objective of a strategy is to suggest the provider the price to call for the next bid. In calling a price, a strategy may be more or less "aggressive", i.e., may propose higher or lower discounts. We discuss two different strategies. One is driven by randomness (aggressiveness is randomly chosen auction by auction, round by round). The other is adaptive, in the sense that is able to adapt the aggressiveness according to the above listed factors. For this kind of strategy, the aggressiveness can be tuned by adequately weighting the factors.

Recalling a formula presented in [11], the adaptive strategy will suggest the next bid as:

$$bid = \frac{n-1}{n-(1-\alpha)} * lastWinningBid \qquad (1)$$

where n is the number of bidders participating in the auction and *lastWinning Bid* is the price of the bid that won the last round. In case of single-round auctions and in the case of first rounds of multi-round auctions, *lastWinningBid* will be the auction's starting price. The parameter α is calculated as follows:

$$\alpha = w_1 * U(t) + w_2 * \frac{L}{L_{max}} + w_3 * \frac{P_a}{P_f} + w_4 * \frac{T_{vm}}{T_{max}} + w_5 * H(t) \qquad (2)$$

As we can see in the Eq. 2, α depends on:

- $U(t)$, the current utilization rate of the pool of spare resources; the less $U(t)$, the higher α, so the evaluated bid price will decrease (in a reverse auction, lowering the bid price means pointing to gain the good). As expected, the aggressiveness of a strategy increases with the reduction of the utilization rate.
- $\frac{L}{L_{max}}$, the ratio between the time period for which the computing resource is requested and the maximum time period for which a resource can be requested[3]. The ratio will increase for requests with longer execution time. The provider will be more aggressive in auctions where longer customer tasks are negotiated, as those ensure a higher utilization of the data center and, as a consequence, higher revenues.

---

[3] In real situations the time period for which a resource can be requested has no bound; in our simulation we will take into account tasks lasting no longer than 24 h.

- $\frac{P_a}{P_f}$ the ratio between the resource's starting price in the auction and the corresponding price in the standard fixed-price market. The provider's aggressiveness will be higher when the price at the start of a round is closer to the reference price (price at which resources are traded in regular markets, or, direct-sell price). The more the round price decreases, the lesser the provider's aggressiveness.
- $\frac{T_{vm}}{T_{max}}$ the ratio between the computing power of the resource being traded in the auction and the computing power of the highest resource. This factor increases the provider's aggressiveness in the case of customer tasks demanding high computing power. The higher the requested computing power, the higher the task's initial price. Further, a highly demanding task requires a bigger capacity on the data center, thus increasing the overall utilization rate.
- $H(t)$, the current utilization of the host on which the customer task to serve will be scheduled. This factor increases the α parameter and, therefore, increases the provider's aggressiveness. Recalling a previous consideration, the provider is more conservative in their strategy if for serving a task a new physical machine has to be activated.

Each parameter is weighted by a factor $(w_1, w_2, w_3, w_4, w_5)$, for which the following constraint applies:

$$\sum_{i=1}^{5} w_i = 1 \tag{3}$$

Different combinations of weights lead to different strategies. Finally, in the adaptive strategy the lower bound price will depend on α according to the following equation:

$$Lb = P_f * (1 - discount) \tag{4}$$

where $discount$ is

$$discount = (0.5 * \alpha) \pm rand * 0.03 \tag{5}$$

and P_f is the price of the resource advertised in the standard fixed-price market. The maximum $discount$ on the fixed price is evaluated as the 50 % of α; the higher alpha, the lower the bound. A variability of 3 % was also introduced to model a differentiation among providers, which reflects their respective personal evaluations.

4.1   Resource Overbooking

The auction mechanism causes a waste of computing resources at the provider's end. A provider may participate in many auctions (say m) at the same time. For each auction, no matter they win or lose, the provider will have to reserve a pool of resources to accommodate the customer's request for which they are competing. The number of auctions every provider will participate depends on the instant capacity of their free computing resources. In general, provider will win n auctions, being $n <= m$, thus, for the duration of all m auctions there may be a waste of resources proportional to the number of lost auctions $(m - n)$.

To overcome this limitation, the provider may decide to participate in more auctions and compete for customers'requests which they are not potentially able to meet. This mechanism, also known as resource *overbooking*, contributes to decrease the resource waste on the one hand, but on the other may bring to situations where the provider runs out of computing resources and may not honor one or more contracts signed at the time they won the auctions. In this cases, the *risk compensation* principle is applied [13], and the provider will incur penalties which are proportional to their actual bid.

In order to implement such mechanism in our market, we let the provider count on an amount of virtual computing capacity (namely, *overbooking capacity*) which is set to 20 % of their real capacity. The provider is then able to participate in $m + o$ auctions, where o is proportional to the overbooking capacity. This way the number of won auctions will increase, and the provider's utilization rate will get closer to 1. In the case the provider won more auctions than those they are actually able to serve, a penalty is due. When an auction appoints as winner a provider who is not eventually able to honor a request, the second best bidding provider is chosen. If, again, the latter is not able to serve the request, the third best is chosen, and so on. In this chain, all providers are subjected to penalties. The penalty is a monetary cost calculated as:

$$ penalty_{it} = \frac{P_i - bid_{it}}{P_i - winnerBid_i} * P_i * duration_i \tag{6} $$

where $penalty_{it}$ is the penalty for the i-th CFP due by provider t, P_i is the auction's starting price, bid_{it} is the bid called by provider t, $winnerBid_i$ is the winner's bid price and $duration_i$ is the time frame for which the computing resource is required by the customer. This law aims at penalizing the providers in a way that is proportional to their risk attitude. The auction winner who is eventually unable to meet the request will pay a penalty of $P_i * duration_i$. The following best bidders (2nd, 3rd, etc.) who on their turn are not able to serve the request will pay a lower penalty as their bid is higher than the winner's. If all participating providers happen to fail the provision due to the overbooking, the auction will be closed and a new auction will be called up.

5   Experimental Results

To prove the viability of our proposal a simulative approach was undertaken. A procurement market prototype was implemented on the well-known Cloudsim simulator [5]. We developed a new component (the **Auctioneer**) and modified the behavior of other existing components (**Datacenter**, **Broker** and **Cloudlet**). Cloudlet is the component of Cloudsim representing the task submitted by the customer, while Datacenter is representative of the provider that will compete for acquiring the task.

To test the adaptive strategy, we created a set of 11 Datacenters, ten of which adopt the proposed adaptive strategy, while one adopts a *Random strategy*: the latter makes its bids using the same equation of the adaptive strategy (Eq. 1),

Table 1. Weight setting for the datacenters' strategies.

Datacenter ID	Strategy	w_1	w_2	w_3	w_4	w_5
DC1	Adaptive	0.6	0.1	0.1	0.1	0.1
DC2	Adaptive	0.1	0.6	0.1	0.1	0.1
DC3	Adaptive	0.1	0.1	0.6	0.1	0.1
DC4	Adaptive	0.1	0.1	0.1	0.6	0.1
DC5	Adaptive	0.1	0.1	0.1	0.1	0.6
DC6	Adaptive	0.2	0.2	0.2	0.2	0.2
DC7	Adaptive	0.2	0.2	0.2	0.2	0.2
DC8	Adaptive	0.2	0.2	0.2	0.2	0.2
DC9	Adaptive	0.2	0.2	0.2	0.2	0.2
DC10	Adaptive	0.2	0.2	0.2	0.2	0.2
DC11	Random					

where the α parameter is assigned random values in the [0,1] range, without any specific objective to pursue. The weights characterizing the α parameter (Eq. 2) are shown in Table 1. As the reader may notice, strategies were expressly split in *unbalanced*, for which Datacenters point on just one factor, and *balanced*, for which all the weights are assigned the same value.

The objective of the simulation is to show that strategies actually guide Datacenters in the choice of tasks to compete for. Every Datacenter counts 70 hosts, each characterized by the following features:

- number of cores uniformly chosen in the range (64,128,256,512);
- RAM: 320 GB;
- Storage: 10 TB.

A core is modeled in CloudSim with a capacity of 2400 Mips.

Datacenters offer a restricted number of virtual machines (VM) configurations (instance types), which go from the very minimalist to the most powerful one. We will then assume that customers' demand will address the following VM instance types:

- **General Purpose**
  - M1.small - 32/64-bit architecture, 1 vCPU, 1 ECU, 1.7 GB RAM, 160 GB Storage, Low Bandwidth;
  - M1.medium - 32/64-bit architecture, 1 vCPU, 2 ECU, 3.75 GB RAM, 410 GB Storage, Moderate Bandwidth;
  - M1.large - 64-bit architecture, 2 vCPU, 4 ECU, 7.5 GB RAM, 820 GB Storage, Moderate Bandwidth;
  - M1.xlarge - 64-bit architecture, 4 vCPU, 8 ECU, 15 GB RAM, 1.6 TB Storage, High Bandwidth;
  - M3.xlarge - 64-bit architecture, 4 vCPU, 13 ECU, 15 GB RAM, 0 Storage, Moderate Bandwidth;

- **Compute Optimized**
  - C1.medium - 32/64-bit architecture, 2 vCPU, 5 ECU, 1.7 GB RAM, 350 GB Storage, Moderate Bandwidth;
  - C1.xlarge - 64-bit architecture, 8 vCPU, 20 ECU, 7 GB RAM, 1.6 TB Storage, High Bandwidth;
- **Memory Optimized**
  - M2.xlarge - 64-bit architecture, 2 vCPU, 6.5 ECU, 17.1 GB RAM, 420 GB Storage, Moderate Bandwidth.

Two experiments were conducted. The first was intended to assess the effectiveness of the proposed provider's strategy; in the second the impact of the overbooking mechanism was studied.

5.1 First Experiment

In the first battery of simulation we submitted 25000 cloudlets having a uniformly distributed length in the range $(1,24)$ h and requiring a uniformly distributed VM type in the set of the VMs listed above. The interarrival times of the cloudlets are distributed accordingly to a Poisson distribution, with $\lambda =$ 0.1 (10 s is the maximum time that lapses between the arrivals of two consecutive cloudlets). From early results, we noticed that the adaptive strategy of each Datacenter guarantees the achievement of the objective, regardless of the specific auction type.

The main parameter we measured is the utilization rate of the Datacenters, which is depicted in Fig. 2. We can observe that all the Datacenters (DC) pursuing one (or a combination) of these two objectives (1) to acquire VMs that require high capacity in terms of computing resources and (2) to obtain longer lasting tasks, actually reach an high level of utilization rate (in Table 1 DC2 and DC4 respectively).

DC11, that adopts the Random strategy, reaches an high level of utilization rate too, because it can easily win auctions for tasks that do not meet the objectives of other Datacenters (i.e. low performing VMs, short tasks). DC1's objective is to optimize the utilization rate; in the graph it can be noticed that after reaching an utilization rate between 60 % and 80 %, it is not able to further increase it, as its objective has almost been reached: the strategy's aggressiveness decreases so that no further auctions are won. The Datacenter obtaining the lowest utilization rate (around 20 %) is DC3; its strategy exhibits low aggressiveness as its objective is to acquire cloudlets with a price not too far from the standard on-demand fixed-price. However, as it can be seen in Fig. 3 where the revenue loss percentage of the Datacenters is shown, the objective of DC3 guarantees the lowest revenue loss. Datacenters with balanced strategy also avoid revenue losses while, at the same time, reaching a better utilization rate than DC3.

Finally, we report some graphs showing the cloudlet characteristics of auctions won by two specific Datacenters. Figure 4(a) shows the rate of auctions won by DC2, grouped by the length of the cloudlets expressed in hours. DC2 mainly won cloudlets with a length of more than eleven hours (the reader may check in

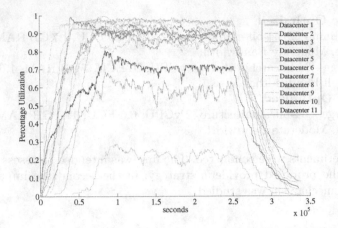

Fig. 2. Datacenters utilization: ER auction.

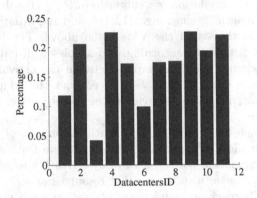

Fig. 3. Revenue loss percentage per datacenter.

Table 1 that the weight of parameter related to the length of the cloudlets is the highest). Figure 4(b) depicts the auctions won by DC4. It mainly wins auctions requiring high performing VMs, as its strategy is set to point on those VM types.

5.2   Second Experiment

We created a set of 8 Datacenters each enforcing an adaptive strategy with balanced weights ($w = 0.2$). First, the simulator was fed with 40.000 cloudlets having a length uniformly distributed in the range (1,12) h and poissonian arrivals with $\lambda = 0.01$. In Fig. 5(a) we may notice that all datacenters reach an utilization very close to 100 %. This is due to the fact that cloudlets are long-lived (in terms of time required by the task) and distant enough in time (100 s is the cloudlets' interarrival time). We then repeated the simulation with the same number of cloudlets but with a length uniformly distributed in (1,6) and poissonian arrivals with $\lambda = 0.06$ (17 s between consecutive cloudlets). In this case the average utilization decreases to 70–80%, as shown in Fig. 5(b).

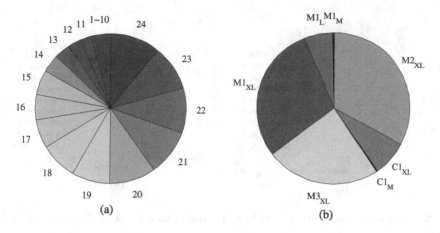

Fig. 4. Auctions won by DC2 and DC4, grouped by the Cloudlets' length (a) and the VM type (b).

The reason behind the poor performance obtained in the second case is easily explained. Being the interarrival time shorter, datacenters simultaneously engage in many auctions. Each datacenter happens to win a subset of these auctions, which are also short-lived (very short in time), thus it will not be able to commit all the capacity. In this specific case it may be of help to opt on the overbooking. To this purpose we ran a new simulation, where the cloudlet's parameters did not change, but four of the eight datacenters (DC1,DC2,DC3 and DC4 respectively) were configured to use a 20 % overbooking (i.e., those Datacenters could count on an extra virtual pool of computing resources whose size was 20 % the datacenter's nominal capacity).

Figure 6(a) shows that the overbooking datacenters (depicted in red) reach a very high utilization (close to 100 %). The side effect is of course that they incur penalties, which have been evaluated with the formula in 6. The revenue of datacenters enforcing the overbooking drops below the revenue of datacenters which do not use overbooking, as depicted in Fig. 6(b). The reader may notice that, despite the incurred penalties, datacenters enforcing the overbooking do have an acceptable revenue.

Last consideration is on single round auctions. As depicted in the Fig. 7 both the First and the Second Price Sealed Bid did not provide encouraging results in terms of utilization. This is because these types of auctions resolve in a very short time and the utilization of resources is not as dynamic as it actually is in multi-round auctions. We have then compared the performance of the First and the Second Price Sealed Bid auctions focusing on the average utility of the provider. As depicted in Fig. 8, the second price auction guarantees, on average, a better utility. This kind of auction, in fact, let the datacenter bid its real evaluation of the cloudlet preventing the utility from excessively decreasing.

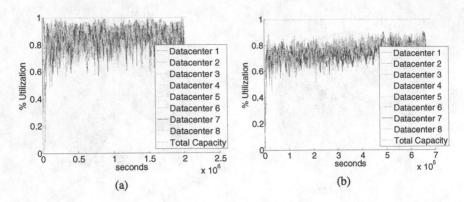

Fig. 5. Datacenters utilization WITHOUT overbooking for $\lambda = 0.01$ (a) and $\lambda = 0.06$ (b).

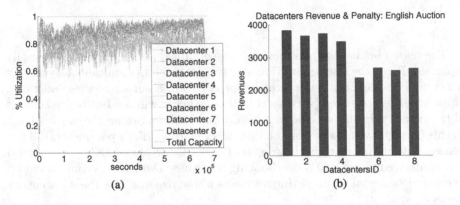

Fig. 6. Performance of overbooking datacenters: utilization rate (a) and incurred penalties (b) (Color figure online).

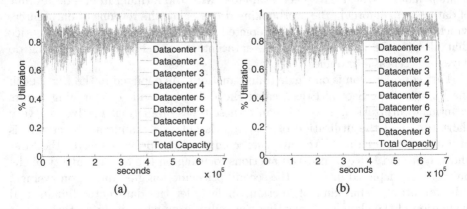

Fig. 7. Datacenters utilization WITH overbooking for auction types FPSB (a) and SPSB (b).

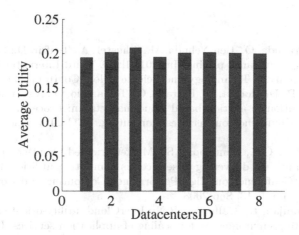

Fig. 8. Utility comparison between FPSB and SPSB.

6   Conclusions

Cloud computing has stimulated a great interest both in the academic community and in business contexts. More and more IT players look at this technology
as a great opportunity of increasing their profit. Though several studies report
the cloud services' market revenue is rocketing, economists say the business
potential of cloud computing is not yet fully exploited. There is not yet an open
market of cloud resources where providers and consumers can meet to satisfy
their needs. In this paper we propose a market of resources where demand and
offer of resources can be matched in auction-based sales. Specifically, we looked
at this market from the perspective of the provider, who needs a strategy to allocate at best their unused computing capacity. We proposed an adaptive strategy
that, suitably tailored to the provider's business objective, will help them to
maximize the revenue in the context of procurement auctions. Also, the resource
overbooking mechanism has been investigated as an optional strategy providers
may adopt in order to increase their revenue. Simulations run to test the proposed approach gave encouraging results, by showing that each provider is able
to reach their objectives by finely tuning the weights associated to their strategy. In the future, more factors will be taken into account in the definition of
the provider's strategy. Further, the business models of the broker of resources
(auctioneer) will also be investigated, in order to prove that a market model
based on procurement auctions can yield profit for all market actors.

References

1. Agmon Ben-Yehuda, O., Ben-Yehuda, M., Schuster, A., Tsafrir, D.: Deconstructing amazon ec2 spot instance pricing. In: 2011 IEEE Third International Conference on Cloud Computing Technology and Science (CloudCom), pp. 304–311 (2011)
2. Bonacquisto, P., Di Modica, G., Petralia, G., Tomarchio, O.: A strategy to optimize resource allocation in auction-based cloud markets. In: Proceedings - 2014 IEEE International Conference on Services Computing, SCC 2014, Anchorage, Alaska, USA, Jun 2014
3. Buyya, R., Yeo, C.S., Venugopal, S.: Market-oriented cloud computing: vision, hype, and reality for delivering it services as computing utilities. In: 10th IEEE International Conference on High Performance Computing and Communications (HPCC 2008), pp. 5–13, Sep 2008
4. Buyya, R., Ranjan, R., Calheiros, R.N.: InterCloud: utility-oriented federation of cloud computing environments for scaling of application services. In: Park, J.H., Yang, L.T., Yeo, S.-S., Hsu, C.-H. (eds.) ICA3PP 2010, Part I. LNCS, vol. 6081, pp. 13–31. Springer, Heidelberg (2010)
5. Calheiros, R., Ranjan, R., Beloglazov, A., De Rose, C.A., Buyya, R.: Cloudsim: a toolkit for modeling and simulation of cloud computing environments and evaluation of resource provisioning algorithms. Softw. Pract. Experience **41**, 23–50 (2011)
6. Chard, K., Bubendorfer, K.: High performance resource allocation strategies for computational economies. IEEE Trans. Parallel Distrib. Syst. **24**(1), 72–84 (2013)
7. Cramton, P., Shoham, Y., Steinberg, R.: Combinatorial Auctions. The MIT Press, Cambridge (2005)
8. Di Modica, G., Petralia, G., Tomarchio, O.: Procurement auctions to trade computing capacity in the Cloud. In: 8th International Conference on P2P, Parallel, Grid, Cloud and Internet Computing (3PGCIC 2013), Compiegne, France, Oct 2013
9. Di Modica, G., Tomarchio, O.: Matching the business perspectives of providers and customers in future cloud markets. Cluster Comput. **18**(1), 457–475 (2015)
10. Klemperer, P.: Auction theory: a guide to the literature. J. Econ. Surv. **13**(3), 227–286 (1999)
11. McAfee, R.P., McMillan, J.: Auctions and bidding. J. Econ. Lit. **15**, 699–738 (1987)
12. Parsons, S., Rodriguez-Aguilar, J.A., Klein, M.: Auctions and bidding: a guide for computer scientists. ACM Comput. Surv. **43**(2), 1–59 (2011)
13. Phillips, R.: Pricing and Revenue Optimization. Stanford University Press, CA (2005)
14. Risch, M., Altmann, J., Guo, L., Fleming, A., Courcoubetis, C.: The gridecon platform: a business scenario testbed for commercial cloud services. In: Altmann, J., Buyya, R., Rana, O.F. (eds.) GECON 2009. LNCS, vol. 5745, pp. 46–59. Springer, Heidelberg (2009)
15. Vinu Prasad, G., Rao, S., Prasad, A.: A combinatorial auction mechanism for multiple resource procurement in cloud computing. In: 2012 12th International Conference on Intelligent Systems Design and Applications (ISDA) (2012)
16. Wang, Q., Ren, K., Meng, X.: When cloud meets ebay: towards effective pricing for cloud computing. In: INFOCOM, 2012 Proceedings IEEE, pp. 936–944 (2012)
17. Zaman, S., Grosu, D.: Combinatorial auction-based allocation of virtual machine instances in clouds. J. Parallel Distrib. Comput. **73**(4), 495–508 (2013)

An Economic Model for Utilizing Cloud Computing Resources via Pricing Elasticity of Demand and Supply

Soheil Qanbari[1]([⊠]), Fei Li[1], Schahram Dustdar[1], and Tian-Shyr Dai[2]

[1] Distributed Systems Group, Technical University of Vienna, Vienna, Austria
{qanbari,Li,dustdar}@dsg.tuwien.ac.at
[2] Institute of Finance, National Chiao-Tung University, Hsinchu, Taiwan
d88006@csie.ntu.edu.tw
http://dsg.tuwien.ac.at, http://financelab.nctu.edu.tw

Abstract. In this study, we elaborate two economic variables which have direct impact on prospective aspects of trading like Cloud resource allocation over future demands. These variables are Pricing Elasticity of Demand (PEoD) and Pricing Elasticity of Provisioning (PEoP). To leverage the pricing elasticity of upcoming demand and supply, we employ financial option theory as a method to alleviate the risk in resource provisioning over future demands. Our approach finds the optimal option price of the federated resource in the Cloud to come to an equilibrium between PEoD and PEoP. The asset equilibrium price occurs when the supply resource pool matches the aggregate demand indicating an optimal resource utilization. This study proposes a novel Cloud Asset Pricing Tree (CAPT) model that finds the optimal premium price of the Cloud federation options efficiently. The CAPT enables cloud service providers to make proper decisions when to trade options in advance and when to exercise them to achieve more economies of scale. Our empirical evidences suggest that utilizing the CAPT model, exploits the Cloud federation market as an opportunity for more resource utilization and future capacity planning.

Keywords: Cloud price elasticity · Asset pricing · Financial options · Cloud federation · Cloud computing

1 Introduction

Cloud providers offer APIs associated with their pool of configurable computing resources (e.g., virtual machines) so that clients can access and utilize them by deploying their packages in runtime environments [7]. In a Cloud market, the right to benefit from these pools of Cloud resources with their utilization interfaces, can be delivered as *"On-Demand"* or *"Reserved"* instances. For clients, the reserved instances (RIs) are more reliable and economic assets. As a proof, the unit of a resource being studied here is an Amazon EC2 Standard Small

M. Helfert et al. (Eds.): CLOSER 2014, CCIS 512, pp. 47–62, 2015.
DOI: 10.1007/978-3-319-25414-2_4

Instance (US East) at a price[1] of $0.060/*hour* for an *on-demand* instance and for a *reserved* instance, costs $0.034/*hour* with an upfront payment of $61/*year*, which is almost half price. Therefore, financially, clients are more attracted to RIs. Faced with such dilemma, RIs pose the concern of less future utilization as far as it is not used by either the current or other on-demand clients. This motivates providers to take the opportunity to achieve more resource utilization by keeping all instances in use. Providers may reallocate unused RIs of current owner to other on-demand clients to keep all resources utilized. This approach makes the RIs unavailable for the current owner. Obviously, it is an obligation for providers to assure the availability of RIs associated with owners, otherwise, lack of resources leads to unmet demands and, while reflecting the SLA violations, leads to financial consequences and penalties. To assure asset availability when lacking resources, providers can seek for more affordable and cost-efficient Cloud open markets to outsource their clients demands. In addition to the fact that Cloud open marketplaces (e.g., Zimory, SpotCloud) and federation offerings (e.g., CloudKick, ScaleUp) offer more resource utilization mechanisms, they also enable further cost reduction due to the market competitive advantage among providers.

The decision to outsource the request to the federation parties is relatively dependent to the asset's price. In a similar model, the Amazon Web Services (AWS) also offer a spot instance pricing model, where the price fluctuates as the market supply and demand changes, and the spot instances will be provisioned to the bidders who won the competition. As soon as the asset's spot price goes above the winning bid, resources will be released. In open Cloud markets, the providers hardly can rely on such mechanism since there is no guarantee as they might lose the resources when the asset price crosses their bid. In order to encourage providers to benefit from the Cloud market, we need a dynamic economic model that keeps resource and financial elasticity sustainably balanced by controlling the asset price oscillation while demand and supply fluctuate. To this end, our contribution is twofold: (i) Analyzing the financial options and pricing elasticity concepts in Cloud federation market. (ii) The flexible pricing model that calculates the optimal premium price of the federation options efficiently and accurately.

The paper continues with a motivation scenario in support of an elastic economic model for pricing Cloud federation assets at Sect. 2. Section 3 presents the basic concepts and preliminaries where the conceptual basis and mathematical models are detailed. Based on this, CAPT pricing model is derived in Sect. 4. We simulate and evaluate our CAPT model and numerical results will be given in Sect. 5 to support the efficiency of our model. Subsequently, Sect. 6 surveys related works. Finally, Sect. 7 concludes the paper and presents an outlook on future research directions.

---

[1] http://aws.amazon.com/ec2/pricing/.

2   Motivation

Along with elastic resource provisioning, providers may face the limitations and insufficiency of their own resource pool supply. In effect, they can transfer the risk of lacking resources to the federation markets. Federation markets can be of interest for providers as well as for consumers. Clients may profit from lower costs and better performance, while providers may offer more sophisticated services [7]. However, hereinafter we focus on the provider perspective. Thus providers can benefit from the increasing capacity and diversity of federated resources. In our model, we employ financial option theory as an interface to elastically allocate an extra pool of federated resources. In finance, an option[2] is a contract which gives the buyer (the owner) the right, but not the obligation, to buy or sell an underlying asset or instrument at a specified strike price on or before a specified date.

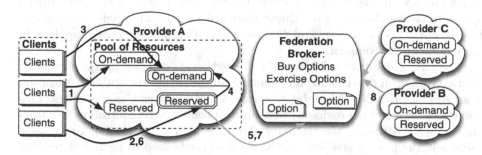

Fig. 1. Resource utilization in Cloud federation using options.

Pricing elasticity and resource trading among federation members lead to competitive contracting process, which aims at finding reasonable and fair price of the asset. The contracting process is to write an option that contains future aspects of trading. For instance, whenever the provider lacks the required resources, then can take advantage of exercising such options to allocate corresponding resources respectively. Using options, providers take the rights to provision seller's resources which match their demands among parties at a price equal or above to their expectation of the asset payoff. Now, the concern is, how to price an option to be reasonable for both parties? Obviously, option pricing is an elastic process [5], sensitive to the fluctuation of the asset price determined by supply and demand between federation parties in spot market. As a consequence, pricing elasticity that comes in two types of *Demand* and *Provisioning* may drive a wedge between the buying and selling price of an asset. Thus controlling the pricing elasticity of the demand and provisioning with respect to their effects on revenue stream by fair pricing of such options appears to be vital. This paper aims at addressing the pricing elasticity of the asset in federation market by fair pricing of the *option*. The option price is determined by a broker acting on behalf of the Cloud federation and therefore standardised across the federation.

---

[2] http://en.wikipedia.org/wiki/Option_(finance).

This option gives the right to obtain an instance at a given price, established at the agreement's stipulation time.

In this scenario, at stage 1 as shown in Fig. 1, the clients request for on-demand and RIs and keep using them. At stage 2 another client benefits from the existing RI. As soon as the RI is suspended, *Provider A* can utilize this instance by reallocating it to unmet on-demand request. Therefore, upon lacking resources, any incoming on-demand request at stage 3 will be responded by reallocation of the RI at 4 to a new client. At this moment, stage 5, *Provider A* buys an option from federation broker as a supporting mechanism for future resource capacity planning. The provider avoids buying resources at a price that is higher than the one charged to its own customers. As soon as the previous client claims for the RI at 6 which is now allocated to the request 3, the provider will take advantage of the option signed with *Provider B* by exercising it at 7 and the *Provider B* has an obligation to provision the promised resources at 8. Our focus lies on stages 5 and 7 where the provider is looking for a well priced option to be exercised later to achieve more utilization. In our federation model, *Provider A* is the demander and *Providers B & C* are the resource suppliers in the federated environment.

The fact that future valuation of federated assets depends on the correlated elasticity between provisioning and demand, suggests that the optimal utilization of an asset is primarily driven by its price volatility in open Cloud markets. This influences the trend of providers to be more concentrated on controlling this pricing elasticity. Although the elasticity of a demand is an initial impetus in asset valuation, the pricing elasticity of the demand might lead to inefficient revenue generation. For instance, the resource demand can be affected to a greater degree by minor changes in asset price. This leads to a question, how can volatility in price cause so much sensitivity in future demands? The reason is amplification. Blame is usually laid on asset price fluctuation and dynamic valuation. The price changes in federation market will be propagated across providers (such as domino effects), causing more sensitivity and concerns on provider's demand. The next question is, how can we control the pricing elasticity and decrease Cloud market sensitivity to future asset price changes? In this study we employ financial option theory which takes care of future valuation of the asset. Then by using the Binomial-Trinomial Tree (BTT) option pricing [3] methodology, we control the Cloud asset price changes and its propagation through the market. As the option price rises or falls, our CAPT model will adjust its structure to the price volatility to come up with an option price that is predictable and fair for both option holder and writer.

3   Terms and Preliminaries

In this section we present basic concepts, economic terms and numerical methods and their interpretations considered in the study.

3.1   Cloud Federation Contracts

In finance, an option is a contract but the major difference arise from the rights and obligations of an option's buyer and seller. A *Call* option gives the buyer the right, but not the obligation, to purchase the underlying asset at a specified price (the strike or exercise price) during the life of the option. The cost of obtaining this right is known as the option's *"premium"* which is the price that is offered in the exchange. We use the term *premium* for an *option premium* in this study. The option buyer's loss is limited to the premium paid. When you own a *Call*, what you do by exercising your right is to *Call for Resource Provisioning* from provider that offered the *Call* to you. The buyer's right becomes the seller's obligation when the option is exercised. An American option can be exercised at any time during the life of the contract while European option can only be exercised at maturity date. The CAPT is modeled with American call options.

American options are provided by a pool of providers and purchased by other providers as a hedge to cover potential excess demand. Using this method, providers are able to re-sell on-demand VMs that have previously been sold as RI. If the RI owner decides to use the instance then rather than violate an SLA, the excess demand can be covered by exercising previously purchased options to enable Cloud-bursting using the federated pool of resources. The option pricing model determines an option price that is inelastic (such that supply and demand are not highly sensitive to price), thereby reducing self-reinforcing oscillations in supply and demand. The paper demonstrates that the option pricing model converges to a more stable price over time and the simulated provider increases profit from outsourcing provisioning using options.

3.2   Cloud Asset Pricing Elasticity

In Cloud systems, elasticity is the ability to automatically increase or decrease resource allocation to asset instances as demand fluctuates. Cloud financial elasticity is a measure of how much resource buyers and sellers respond to changes in market conditions. It's a measure of the responsiveness of quantity demanded or provisioned to a change in one of its determinants like price or quality. In this paper we address the Cloud federation asset pricing elasticity. The law of demand states that a fall in the price of a resource raises the quantity demanded. To be more specific, the price elasticity of demand measures how willing providers are to buy less or more options as its price rises or falls. To sum up, the concept of *Price Elasticity of Demand* (PEoD) measures of how much the resource quantity demanded due to a price change. And the *Price Elasticity of Provisioning* (PEoP) measures how much the resource quantity provisioned due to a price change [8]. The PEoD and PEoP formulas are:

$$PEoD = \frac{(\%Change\ in\ Quantity\ Demanded)}{(\%Change\ in\ Price)} \tag{1}$$

$$PEoP = \frac{(\%Change\ in\ Quantity\ Provisioned)}{(\%Change\ in\ Price)}. \tag{2}$$

3.3   Pricing Elasticity Interpretation

Regarding interpretation, we analyze the Cloud asset price elasticity only with their absolute values. The PEoD variable values, denote how sensitive the demand for an asset is to a price change. In financial markets, the rule is if a provider's asset has a high elasticity of demand, the more the price goes up, the fewer consumers will buy and try to economise their needs. Correspondingly, in Cloud federation markets, a very high price elasticity suggests that when the price of a resource goes up, our provider will be more sensitive and demand for less assets or buy less call options. Conversely, when the price of that resource goes down, then the provider will demand for more assets or buy more call options. A very low price elasticity implies just the opposite, that changes in price have little influence on demand or exercising the call. To sum up, when demand is price inelastic, total revenue moves in the direction of a price change. When demand is price unit elastic, total revenue does not change in response to a price change. When demand is price elastic, total revenue moves in the direction of a quantity change. In order to see whether the price is elastic or inelastic we use the following rule of thumb:

$$\text{VM PEoD} = \begin{cases} > 1 & \text{Demand is price elastic.} \\ = 1 & \text{Demand is unit elastic.} \\ < 1 & \text{Demand is price inelastic.} \end{cases} \tag{3}$$

Next is price elasticity of provisioning in federation resource supply pool. The law of supply states that higher prices raise the quantity supplied. The price elasticity of supply measures how much the quantity supplied responds to changes in the price. Supply of a good is said to be elastic if the quantity supplied responds substantially to changes in the price. Supply is said to be inelastic if the quantity supplied responds only slightly to changes in the price. PEoP denotes how sensitive the provisioning of an asset is to a price change. In Cloud federation markets, a very high price elasticity of provisioning suggests that when the price of a resource goes up, Cloud federation members will be more sensitive to price changes and provision more assets or sell more call options to make more profit. Thus, the resource quantity supplied can respond substantially to price changes. Same as PEoD, in order to see whether the price is elastic or inelastic in PEoP, we use the following rule of thumb:

$$\text{VM PEoP} = \begin{cases} > 1 & \text{Provisioning is price elastic.} \\ = 1 & \text{Provisioning is unit elastic.} \\ < 1 & \text{Provisioning is price inelastic.} \end{cases} \tag{4}$$

Finding the right balance between these two polar approaches of PEoD and PEoP to come to a new equilibrium is a challenge as we address it using our CAPT model. In equilibrium, asset aggregate demand has to equal the asset supply. To be more specific, in our evaluation, we will show that our pricing model, calculates the fair price of the option that makes the demand, price inelastic and provisioning, price elastic. This leads to increasing demand, regardless of the asset price oscillation.

3.4   Assumptions

It is an indication that the following assumptions underlying our model has been considered for the proper positioning of this study. In a Cloud market, resources are virtualized to abstract concepts like virtual machines (VMs) and assumed as intangible assets. They are also seen as assets as long as associated with a contract that can be exercised by an option. Federation formation pose some concerns like contract management, data policies, SLA violations and etc. We believe these concerns should be addressed in the business models agreed among parties.

4   CAPT Model

The option pricing can be represented by numerical methods like trees. This section shows how to generate the CAPT tree for pricing options. The model benefits from the Binomial and Trinomial tree methods as detailed below. This section shows how to generate the CAPT tree for pricing options.

4.1   Binomial Tree

Binomial tree model is a numerical pricing method that approximates option price. Let a derivative on $S_{(t)}$ initiates at time 0 and matures at time T. A lattice partitions this time span into n equal-distanced time steps and specifies the value of $S_{(t)}$ at each time step which denotes the Cloud asset price. Let the length between two adjacent time steps be $\Delta t \equiv T/n$. The established Cox-Ross-Rubinstein (CRR) binomial tree [2] is shown in Fig. 2. As we move forward in time, each asset price S can either move upward to become S_u with probability P_u, or move downward to become S_d with probability $P_d \equiv 1 - P_u$. The CRR lattice adopts the following solution:

$$u = e^{\sigma\sqrt{\Delta t}}, d = e^{-\sigma\sqrt{\Delta t}}, P_u = \frac{e^{r\Delta t} - d}{u - d}, P_d = \frac{e^{r\Delta t} - u}{d - u} \tag{5}$$

where σ is price volatility, Δt is duration of a step and r denotes the interest rate.

4.2   Trinomial Tree

A trinomial tree can be built in a similar way to the binomial tree but has three possible paths (up, down, and stable) per node leading to more efficient pricing. The jump sizes (u, d) can be calculated in a similar way with doubled time spacing. The transition probabilities are given as:

$$P_u = \left(\frac{e^{\frac{r\Delta t}{2}} - e^{-\sigma\sqrt{\frac{\Delta t}{2}}}}{e^{\sigma\sqrt{\frac{\Delta t}{2}}} - e^{-\sigma\sqrt{\frac{\Delta t}{2}}}} \right)^2 P_d = \left(\frac{e^{\sigma\sqrt{\frac{\Delta t}{2}}} - e^{\frac{r\Delta t}{2}}}{e^{\sigma\sqrt{\frac{\Delta t}{2}}} - e^{-\sigma\sqrt{\frac{\Delta t}{2}}}} \right)^2 \tag{6}$$

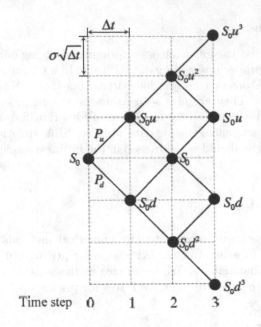

Fig. 2. CRR binomial pricing tree.

$$P_m = 1 - P_u - P_d \tag{7}$$

Now it is possible to find the value of the underlying asset, S for any sequence of price movements. It will generate a directed graph with nodes labeled as asset prices and edges connecting nodes separated by one time step and a single price up, down and middle jumps as N_u, N_d, N_m, where the price after i period at node j (or after i ups and j downs) is given by: $S_{(i,j)} = u^{N_u} d^{N_d} m^{N_m} S(t_0)$ where $N_u + N_d + N_m = i$. Finally, in both binomial and trinomial tree methods, the option value can be computed by standard backward induction method.

4.3   Growing the CAPT Tree

This section visualizes how the BTT tree is constructed for pricing the options briefly. In this model as illustrated in Fig. 3 the root of the tree is the node S which is formed by a trinomial tree and the rest of the tree is constructed using binomial method with the first two time steps truncated. The barriers (the black nodes) are H_0 and L_0 at time T_0 and H_1 and L_1 at time T_0+T_1. These barriers define the allowable range for the price fluctuation of the underlying asset serving to limit both, profits and losses, for federation parties. The tree adjusts and adapts its structure to the price volatility and the moving barriers to come up with an option price that is predictable and fair for both option holder and writer.

The combinatorial pricing algorithm [4] is used to evaluate the option values on the three CRR trees as shown in Fig. 3, with root nodes A, B, and C. The option price of the CAPT at node S is also evaluated by the backward induction method.

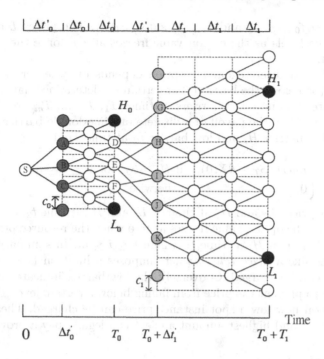

Fig. 3. Cloud option pricing using bino-trinomial tree.

4.4 The Role of Double Barriers

A barrier option is a cloud contract whose payoff depends on whether the Cloud underlying resource price path ever touches certain price levels called the barriers. A knock-in barrier option comes into existence if the resource price touches the barrier(s) before the maturity date, whereas a knock-out one ceases to exist if the resource price touches the barrier(s) before maturity.

The barrier(s) can also be moving due to the pricing elasticity of the resource which is a measure of relative quantity response to a change expressed in monetary parameters like *price*. A barrier event occurs when the Cloud resource price crosses the barrier level. For a continuous barrier option, the underlying stock price is monitored continuously from time 0 to time T. For instance, the payoff of a continuous double-barrier option on Amazon Cloud small on-demand instance[3] with a low barrier L and a high barrier H is:

$$
\begin{cases}
max(\theta S_T - \theta X, 0), & \text{if } S_{sup} < H \text{ and } S_{sup} < H, \\
0, & \text{otherwise,}
\end{cases}
\tag{8}
$$

---

[3] Amazon EC2 Small Instance: 1.7 GiB of memory, 1 EC2 Compute Unit, 160 GB of local instance storage, 32-bit or 64-bit platform.

where $S_{inf} = inf_{0 \leq t \leq T} S_t$ and $S_{sup} = sup_{0 \leq t \leq T} S_t$. The prices L and H are the critical price levels as the option value freezes at zero once the stock price reaches L or H.

The payoff of a discrete barrier option depends on whether the resource price is above (or below) the barrier(s) at certain predetermined dates called the monitoring dates. Assume the barriers at times T_1, T_2, ..., T_m are L_1, L_2, ..., L_m, respectively. Then the payoff of a discrete moving-double-barrier knock-out option with high barrier H_i and low barrier L_i at time T_i $(1 \leq i \leq m)$ is:

$$\begin{cases} max(\theta S_T - \theta X, 0), & \text{if } H_i > S_{T_i} \text{ for } 1 \leq i \leq m, \\ 0, & \text{otherwise,} \end{cases} \tag{9}$$

The barrier prices L_1 and H_1 at time t_1, L_2 and H_2 at time t_2, and so on are critical points as the option value freezes at zero when the resource price is lower than L_i or higher than H_i at time t_i, where $1 \leq i \leq m$. In summary, the high barrier behaves like a *price ceiling* where imposes a limit on how high a spot instance price can be charged. Conversely, the low barrier indicates *price floors* by attempting to prevent the price from falling below a certain level. Price floors exposes limits on how low a spot instance price can be charged. These barriers specify the lowest and highest amount a client can legally pay a provider.

5   Model Evaluation

Now, we present results from our simulation observation that show the efficiency of our model. We have implemented a Cloud federation environment using Cloud simulation platform, CloudSim [1]. The simulated Cloud federation uses our option pricing model for trading assets and VM provisioning. The unit of resource being observed is an Amazon EC2 Standard Small Instance (US East). At the date of simulation (Sept 2013), resources advertised at a price of $0.085/hour$ for an on-demand instance. For RIs, the same type instance for 12 months costs $0.034/hour$. For evaluation purposes, (i) the reserved capacity of the data center is considered as steady constant value during simulation. (ii) to economize the equations, we do not take into account the operational costs (i.e., hardware and software acquisition, staff salary, power consumption, cooling costs, physical space, etc.) of the data center. It imposes a constant value within the model.

5.1   Simulation Setup

The simulation environment is developed to capture the behavior of our CAPT model in Cloud federation where supply and demand fluctuate in daily patterns directly inspired by real-world market. For a provider, who benefits from this market, simulation was implemented with a resource pool capable of 400 simultaneous running VMs capacity including reserved and on-demand. We have implemented the following three components on top of *CloudSim* simulator. Further details of our option-based federation simulator entities and settings are as follows.

CAPT Request Generator (ReqG). The workload pattern generation was needed in order to mimic the real world IaaS Cloud requests. We implemented *CAPT-ReqG* agent to create jobs by using the *Cloudlet* class in *CloudSim*. In our model, each job has an arrival time as we scheduled the workload on a daily-basis pattern and a duration time which is the holding time of the instance by the job and metered to charge the consumer respectively. Given that our workload follows daily pattern based on normal Gaussian distribution for the 24 h of a day and considering standard business hours (from 9 to 17) as peak hours, we generate a randomly distributed arrival time for requests in each specific hour. The load decreased 60 % on weekends.

CAPT Resource Allocator (ResA). We have developed the *CAPT-ResA* agent to determine the association between jobs and federated resources. Our allocation policy finds a mapping between the batch of jobs outsourced to the federation and VMs associated to options. In the simulation, the VM provisioning policy is extended to best fit with respect to the option status. The providers are implemented using *DataCenter* class in CloudSim, as it behaves like an IaaS provider. The *CAPT-ResA* receives requests from *CAPT-ReqG*, allocates resources and binds the jobs to the VMs accordingly. For resource allocation, we have used shared pool strategy. In case of arriving a new on-demand job, the agent checks if the number of currently running on-demand jobs exceeds the capacity of on-demand pool and if so, it will allocate VMs from its reserved pool while buying an option from federated Cloud. As soon as it receives requests which can not be met in-house, the agent will exercise the options that were bought before and outsource the new jobs to federated pool.

CAPT Option Handler (OptH). Our *CAPT-OptH* agent implements the option pricing model as detailed in Sect. 4. It also routes the option exercising request to the *CAPT-ResA* agent to have the requested resource provisioned. The pricing policy is set to resource/hour consumed for each instance, for the duration an instance is launched till it is terminated. Each partial resource/hour consumed will be charged as a full hour. There are six metrics that affect the CAPT option pricing, (i) the current stock price, S_0 set to $0.034/$hour$ (ii) the exercise price (spot price), K is generated based on Amazon spot price observed pattern. (iii) the time to option expiration T set to 1 month (iv) the volatility σ which is the range and speed in which a price moves, set to 31.40 %per annum. It is observed by the *cloudexchange.org*[4] which is real-time monitoring of Amazon EC2 spot prices. (v) the interest rate, r is set to 19.56 % per annum since the Amazon EC2 SLA[5] interest rate is 1.5 % per month and (vi) the dividend expected during the life of the option is set to $5.17. Both *High* and *Low* barriers are set to $0.039 and $0.030. The simulation was run 50 times. The experiment duration is set to 6 months and the mean value of the results is evaluated to mimic the real-world environment.

---

[4] https://github.com/tlossen/cloudexchange.org.

[5] http://aws.amazon.com/agreement/.

5.2 Evaluation Measure

There are four empirical measures as we care to specify and observe their behavior during the simulation: (i) *Provider's profit* (P_{pr}), which our model claims to ensure the optimal utilization of the resources for providers. The profit measurement equation is:

$$P_{pr} = R_{on} + R_{res} + R_{(op,exe)} - C_{(op,pre)} - C_{(gen)} \qquad (10)$$

where R_{on} and R_{res} are the providers' total revenue received over their own on-demand and RIs. $R_{(op,exe)}$ is the revenue of exercising the options since the option exercise price is less than their own instance price sold to their clients before. $C_{(op,pre)}$ denotes the premium to be paid for the purchase of the option which our model calculates accurately. Finally, $C_{(gen)}$ covers general costs of provider as we assumed a constant value. (ii) Second measure is *QoS Violations* (QoS_v), that holds the number of rejected or unmet reserved and on-demand instances reflecting the SLA violations. Third and forth measures are (iii) *Price Elasticity of Demand* (ϵ_D) and (iv) *Price Elasticity of Provisioning* (ϵ_P) where their absolute values are highly correlated with the asset price changes. Their computation is done with these equations:

$$\epsilon_D(vm) = \frac{\%\Delta_{Qd}}{\%\Delta_{P_{vm}}} \ \ and \ \ \epsilon_P(vm) = \frac{\%\Delta_{Qp}}{\%\Delta_{P_{vm}}} \qquad (11)$$

The $\epsilon_D(vm)$ and $\epsilon_P(vm)$ denote the price elasticity of demand and provisioning of an asset, and measures the percentage change in the quantity of VM demanded and provisioned per 1 % change in the price of its option premium. Our economic model should make $\epsilon_D(vm)$ *"price inelastic"* and $\epsilon_P(vm)$ *"price elastic"* as interpreted in Sect. 3.2.

Table 1. Cloud federation market simulation summary (6 months).

Instance↓ Measures →	Workload	QoS violations		Profit		Price elasticity		Options	
		Reserved	On-demand	In-house	Option	PEoD	PEoP	Bought	Exercised
Amazon m1.small	98455	0	0	35293.63	3339.97	0.095	1.28	25676	14020

5.3 Results and Debate

The aggregate results imply utility and are reported as summary in Table 1. Results show that those providers are able to reach an utilization rate of 95 % and achieve gains both from the in-house instances and from those obtained by exercising the option's rights from other providers of the federation. Taking these results together, four points stand out in this simulation. First, is the profit made from exercising options. To interpret this, note that in our approach, providers buy the options that its exercise price are less than their own VM provisioning price. As observed, providers were able to meet 86 % of an incoming requests by inhouse provisioning and outsourced 14 % of their demands to the federation, in which are fully provisioned to celebrating 8.7 % more profit. Second, is the achievement over the QoS agreed with the client for resource delivery. For both reserved and on-demand, no QoS violation (no unmet request) is detected. Third, as our results indicate, the value of pricing elasticity of demand ($PEoD$) is kept less than 1 denoting that the demand became "*price inelastic*" serving to increasing demand, regardless of the asset price oscillation. From the federation perspective (resource suppliers side), the value of pricing elasticity of provisioning ($PEoP$) is more than 1 denoting that the provisioning became "*price elastic*" indicating the providers are flexible enough to adapt the amount of resources they provision. These values are consistent with the number of options purchased and exercised, leading to more economies of scale. Finally, is the utilization value, which is considerable. This indicates that optimal utilization of resources is achieved to exploit the efficiency and accuracy of our model.

To form a basis for comparison, our next two figures depict the dependencies between option pricing elasticity and its demand and provisioning. Figure 4, shows how CAPT controls the option pricing elasticity and converges to a more stable price smoothly. Our approach finds the optimal option price of the federated resource in the Cloud to come to an equilibrium between PEoD and PEoP. The asset equilibrium price occurs when the supply resource pool matches the aggregate demand indicating an optimal resource utilization. From the provisioning perspective, the $PEoP$ over 1 indicates an elastic supply. Since the asset pricing elasticity is controlled, we see a synchronous correlation between price and supply changes. As a result, the total revenue moves in the direction of price change.

6   Related Work

In relation to our approach, there are some alternatives that propose federation economic model more focused on the provider's perspective. A broker-based federation approach has been proposed by [9,10,14]. These studies decouple the brokerage strategies and federation economic valuation. Zhang proposes an economic model for the evaluation of the economic value of Cloud Computing Federation in providing one computing unit such as the power and human resources [15]. Just as Clouds enable users to cope with unexpected demand loads, a Federated Cloud will enable individual Clouds to cope with unforeseen variations of demand. Authors in [6] investigate the application of market-oriented mechanisms based on the General Equilibrium Theory of Microeconomics to coordinate the sharing of resources between the Clouds in the federated environment. In [16], authors present an online resource marketplace for open Clouds by adopting an eBay style transaction model based on auction theory. Here [11] establishes a novel economic sharing model to regulate capacity sharing in a federation of hybrid Cloud providers. The idea of financial options is used by [12] as a financial model for pricing Cloud compute commodities by using Moore's law on depreciation of asset values, to show the effect of depreciation of

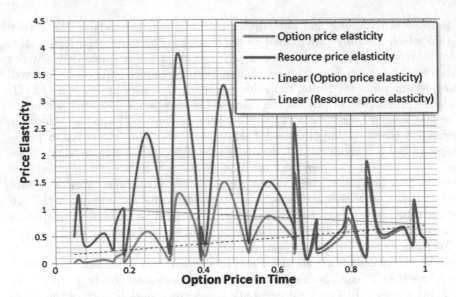

Fig. 4. Resource price elasticity controlled via options.

Cloud resource on QoS. In [13] authors incorporate financial options as a market model for federated Cloud environments. In contrast to existing approaches, we use financial option theory for asset trading and propose a dynamic and adaptive option pricing model which enhance profit by controlling the pricing elasticity of demand and provisioning in the Cloud federation.

7 Conclusions and Outlook

Providers consider federations as an alternative pool of resources to their expected consumption growth. Their demand to use the federated asset is dependent to the pricing elasticity of demand, as if the elasticity is high, then they will be more careful on buying options. In this paper, we proposed a financial option pricing model to address the pricing elasticity concerns in above situation. Our economical model is for implementing a future market of virtualized resources in a system where a federation of Cloud providers is used to reduce risks and costs associated with the capacity planning of Cloud providers. Providers will benefit by this model to make decisions when to buy options in advance and when to exercise them to achieve more economies of scale.

So far, we have proposed an economic model that considers future aspects of trading like capacity planning or resource allocation over upcoming demands. The CAPT model empowers vendors to get additional resources as and when required. This economic model aims for the leverage of demand and supply form the IaaS provider and third party providers point of view, finding suboptimal price policies between resources ownered by the provider and options to external providers using Cloud bursting when needed. This study covers two aspects of resource elasticity: *Resource Quantity* and *Price*. As an outlook, our future work includes further extension to the model that can also support the *Quality of Service (QoS)* aspect in federation environment.

Acknowledgements. The research leading to these results is sponsored by the Doctoral College of Adaptive Distributed Systems at the Vienna University of Technology as well as the Pacific Controls Cloud Computing Lab (PC3L) (http://pc3l.infosys. tuwien.ac.at/), a joint lab between Pacific Controls, Dubai, and the Distributed Systems Group at the Vienna University of Technology.

References

1. Calheiros, R.N., Ranjan, R., Beloglazov, A., De Rose, A.F., Buyya, R.: Cloudsim: a toolkit for modeling and simulation of cloud computing environments and evaluation of resource provisioning algorithms. Softw. Pract. Exper. **41**(1), 23–50 (2011). http://dx.doi.org/10.1002/spe.995
2. Cox, J.C., Ross, S.A., Rubinstein, M.: Option pricing: a simplified approach. J. Financ. Econ. **7**(3), 229–263 (1979)
3. Shyr Dai, T., dauh Lyuu, Y.: The bino-trinomial tree: a simple model for efficient and accurate option pricing. J. Deriv. **17**(4), 7–24 (2010)
4. Dai, T.-S., Lyuu, Y.-D.: An efficient, and fast convergent algorithm for barrier options. In: Kao, M.-Y., Li, X.-Y. (eds.) AAIM 2007. LNCS, vol. 4508, pp. 251–261. Springer, Heidelberg (2007)
5. Dustdar, S., Guo, Y., Satzger, B., Truong, H.L.: Principles of elastic processes. Internet Comput. IEEE **15**(5), 66–71 (2011)
6. Gomes, E.R., Vo, Q.B., Kowalczyk, R.: Pure exchange markets for resource sharing in federated clouds. Concurr. Comput. Pract. Exper. **24**(9), 977–991 (2012). http://dx.doi.org/10.1002/cpe.1659
7. Kurze, T., Klems, M., Bermbach, D., Lenk, A., Tai, S., Kunze, M.: Cloud federation. In: Computing (c), pp. 32–38 (2011)
8. Mankiw, N.G.: Elasticity and its applications. In: Principles of Microeconomics, 6th edn, pp. 89–109. Harvard University (2012)
9. Raj, G.: An efficient broker cloud management system. In: Proceedings of the International Conference on Advances in Computing and Artificial Intelligence, ACAI 2011, pp. 72–76. ACM, New York (2011). http://doi.acm.org/10.1145/2007052. 2007067
10. Rogers, O., Cliff, D.: A financial brokerage model for cloud computing. J. Cloud Comput. **1**(1), 1–12 (2012). http://dx.doi.org/10.1186/2192-113X-1-2
11. Samaan, N.: A novel economic sharing model in a federation of selfish cloud providers (2013)
12. Sharma, B., Thulasiram, R., Thulasiraman, P., Garg, S., Buyya, R.: Pricing cloud compute commodities: a novel financial economic model. In: 2012 12th IEEE/ACM International Symposium on Cluster, Cloud and Grid Computing (CCGrid), pp. 451–457 (2012)
13. Toosi, A., Thulasiram, R., Buyya, R.: Financial option market model for federated cloud environments. In: 2012 IEEE Fifth International Conference on Utility and Cloud Computing (UCC), pp. 3–12 (2012)

14. Villegas, D., Bobroff, N., Rodero, I., Delgado, J., Liu, Y., Devarakonda, A., Fong, L., Masoud Sadjadi, S., Parashar, M.: Cloud federation in a layered service model. J. Comput. Syst. Sci. **78**(5), 1330–1344 (2012). http://dx.doi.org/10.1016/j.jcss.2011.12.017
15. Zhang, Z., Zhang, X.: An economic model for the evaluation of the economic value of cloud computing federation. In: Zhang, Y. (ed.) Future Wireless Networks and Information Systems. LNEE, vol. 141, pp. 571–577. Springer, Heidelberg (2012)
16. Zhao, H., Yu, Z., Tiwari, S., Mao, X., Lee, K., Wolinsky, D., Li, X., Figueiredo, R.: Cloudbay: enabling an online resource market place for open clouds. In: 2012 IEEE Fifth International Conference on Utility and Cloud Computing (UCC), pp. 135–142 (2012)

Reducing Complexity in Service Development and Integration

Per-Olov Östberg[✉] and Niclas Lockner

Department of Computing Science, Umeå University, Umeå, Sweden
{p-o,lockner}@cs.umu.se

Abstract. The continuous growth and increasing complexity of distributed systems software has produced a need for software development tools and techniques that reduce the learning requirements and complexity of building distributed systems. In this work we address reduction of complexity in service-oriented software development and present an approach and a toolkit for multi-language service development based on three building blocks: a simplified service description language, an intuitive message serialization and transport protocol, and a set of code generation techniques that provide boilerplate environments for service implementations. The toolkit is intended for use in the eScience domain and is presented along with a performance evaluation that quantifies toolkit performance against that of selected alternative toolkits and technologies for service development. Toolkit performance is found to be comparable to or improve upon the performance of evaluated technologies.

Keywords: Creo · Service-Orientated Architecture · Service development

1 Introduction

In this paper[1] we discuss reduction of complexity in service-based software development; present a toolkit that demonstrates an approach to reduced complexity service description, development, and integration; and evaluate the communication efficiency of the presented toolkit against a set of alternative technologies and toolkits for service and distributed system component development.

Cloud computing has in recent years evolved to an established paradigm for provisioning of IT capacity. While this approach can offer several benefits compared to traditional static provisioning, e.g., facilitation of more flexible service types [4] and improvements in cost and energy efficiency of large-scale computing [5,25], it also places focus on a current and growing problem in distributed computing: the increasing complexity of development and management of systems in distributed computing environments [13].

---

[1] This paper is an invited extended version of the paper *Creo: Reduced Complexity Service Development* presented at CLOSER 2014.

© Springer International Publishing Switzerland 2015
M. Helfert et al. (Eds.): CLOSER 2014, CCIS 512, pp. 63–80, 2015.
DOI: 10.1007/978-3-319-25414-2_5

Service-Oriented Computing (SOC) is a popular approach to software development and integration in large-scale distributed systems. SOC is argued to be well suited for cloud environments as it places focus on representation of logic components as network-accessible services, and aims to facilitate development and integration of systems through coordination of service interactions. At architecture level, Service-Oriented Architectures (SOAs) define service interfaces as integration points and address system composition at interface or protocol level. While a number of SOA techniques have emerged, service development and integration are still complex issues and there exists a need for development tools that provide non-complex and low-learning-requirement environments for efficient development of service-based systems.

To illustrate these issues, we here take the perspective of eScience application development. In eScience[2], distributed computing techniques are used to create collaborative environments for large-scale scientific computing. In comparison to commercial software stacks, scientific computing tools are typically prototype-oriented, produced in projects with limited software development budgets, and often composed of heterogeneous components developed in multiple languages and environments. In addition, eScience applications also often use distributed or parallel programming techniques to exploit parallelism inherent to computational problems, further increasing the complexity of implementation and management of eScience software stacks. As many current eScience efforts are approaching construction of virtual infrastructures using cloud technology, they here serve as illustrative examples of the difficulties of developing multi-language software stacks in heterogeneous distributed computing environments.

In this work we address reduction of complexity in service-based software development, and present an easy-to-use toolkit for efficient cross-language integration of software services. The toolkit is based on three core components: a simplified syntax service description language, a transparent data serialization and transmission protocol, and a set of code generation tools designed to abstract complexity in service and service client development.

The remainder of the paper is structured as follows: Sect. 2 presents project background and a brief survey of related work, Sect. 3 outlines the proposed approach and toolkit, and Sect. 4 discusses use cases for the approach. In the second half of the paper, Sect. 5 contains a performance evaluation quantifying toolkit performance against selected alternative service development technologies, followed by conclusions and acknowledgements in Sect. 6.

2   Related Work

A number of tools for service development and middleware construction exist, ranging in complexity and abstraction levels from very simple fine-grained interprocess communication tools to advanced middleware construction toolkits featuring advanced data marshalling, call translation, and remote reference counting techniques. In general there exists trade-offs between complexity and efficiency

---

[2] Computationally intensive science in highly distributed network environments.

that make service technologies more or less suitable for certain situations, and many technologies have been developed for specific application scenarios.

For example, direct interprocess communication technologies such as traditional remote procedure calls (RPC) [6] and Java Object Serialization (JOS) [16] (over sockets) provide transparent development models but offer little in ways of complexity abstraction. Other approaches such as Java Remote Method Invocation (RMI) [26] and the Microsoft Windows Communication Framework (WCF) [14] offer development models tightly integrated into mature commercial software development environments, but lose some applicability in multi-platform application scenarios. There exists also standardized approaches to multi-language and multi-platform service development, e.g., the Common Object Request Broker Architecture (CORBA) [24], but while such standardized approaches typically are very expressive and capable of application in multiple programming styles, e.g., object-orientation and component-oriented development, this general applicability often comes at the price of very steep learning curves and high development complexity.

In service-oriented architectures, programming models such as SOAP and REST-style web services are widely used due to features such as platform independence, high abstraction levels, and interoperability. The SOAP approach to web services favors use of standardization of XML-based service description and message formats to facilitate automated generation of service interconnection code stubs, dynamic service discovery and invocation techniques, and service coordination and orchestration models. SOAP-style web services are however often criticized for having overly complex development models, inefficiencies in service communication, and low load tolerances in servers (although developments in pull-based parser models have alleviated some of the performance issues [11]).

The REpresentational State Transfer (REST) [8] web service model is often seen as a light-weight alternative to the complexity of SOAP-style web services. The REST approach discourages standardization (of message formats), promotes (re)use of existing wide-spread technology, and aims to give service developers more freedom in, e.g., choice of data representation formats and API structures. While this approach facilitates a development model well suited for smaller projects, it is sometimes argued to lead to more tightly coupled service models (that require service client developers to have knowledge of service-side data structures) and introduce technology heterogeneity in large systems.

Although service models are considered suitable for large-scale system integration, and some understanding of the applicability of web services has been gained [20], neither approach fully addresses the requirements of service-oriented software development and a number of technologies for hybrid service-RPC mechanisms have emerged. These include, e.g., interface definition language (IDL) based technologies such as Apache Thrift [22], an RPC framework for scalable cross-language service development, Apache Avro [2], a data serialization system featuring dynamic typing, and Google protocol buffers [10], a method for serializing structured data for interprocess communication. For high performance data serialization and transmission, there also exists a number of non-IDL based serialization formats and tools such as Jackson JSON [12], BSON [15], Kryo [7], and MessagePack [9].

In addition to trade-offs for technical performance and applicability, tools and development models often impose high learning requirements in dimensions orthogonal to the task of building distributed systems. For example, the Distributed Component Object Model (DCOM) requires developers to understand data marshalling and memory models, Java RMI distributed garbage collection, CORBA portable object adapters (type wrappers), and SOAP web services XML Schema (for type definition and validation). As distributed systems are by themselves complex to develop, debug, and efficiently analyze, there exists a need for software development tools that provide transparent and intuitive development models, and impose low learning requirements.

In this work we build on the service development model of the Service Development Abstraction Toolkit [17], and investigate an approach to construction of development tools focused on reducing complexity of service-based software development. The aim of this approach is to combine the high abstraction levels of SOAP-style web services (using a simplified service description syntax) with the communication efficiency of more direct RPC-style communication techniques, and produce tools with low learning requirements that efficiently facilitate service development. As the work is based on code generation, the approach can be seen akin to development of a domain-specific language [23] for service description, but the main focus of the work is to reduce overhead for exposing component logic as network-accessible services. The work is done in eScience settings, and presented results are primarily intended to be applied in scientific environments, e.g., in production of tools, applications, and middlewares for scientific simulation, experimentation, and analysis.

3 Creo

Service-oriented architectures typically expose components and systems as platform independent, network-accessible services. While this approach gracefully abstracts low-level integration issues and provides for high-level architecture design models, it can often lead to practical integration issues stemming from, e.g., complexity in service development models, steep learning curves of service development tools, and lack of distributed systems development experience in service client developers.

In this paper we build on earlier efforts presented in [17,19], and propose an approach to service development that places the responsibility of service client development on service developers. As this shift in responsibility introduces noticeable additional complexity in service development, e.g., in requirements for multi-language service client development, we note a need for tools to support the approach and present *Creo* - a service development toolkit based on simplified service description and automated code generation.

The Creo toolkit is aimed to reduce complexity in construction of network-accessible services by providing a development model that lowers learning requirements and increases automation in service development. While the toolkit is designed to be simple to use and targeted towards developers with limited distributed systems development experience, it also strives to provide service communication performance high enough to motivate use of the toolkit in mature service development scenarios.

To limit the scope of the work, we have initially designed the toolkit to support development of services in a single language (Java), and service client development in four languages common in eScience environments: C, C#, Java, and Python. The toolkit implementation patterns are however transparent and modularized, and all modules are designed to be extensible to code generation in additional languages. The intent of the toolkit is to provide robust service communication stubs in general purpose programming languages that can later be used to build integration bridges into special purpose environments such as R, Mathematica, and Matlab.

The choice of Java as service language is motivated by the language's rich development APIs, robustness in performance, platform independence, and widespread adoption in operating systems and server platforms. The design philosophy of the toolkit can be summarized as supporting advanced implementation of services while keeping generated code for clients as transparent, light-weight, and free of external dependencies as possible.

To combine the ease-of-use of high abstraction level tools with the communication performance of more fine-grained approaches, the toolkit development model is based on the service description approach of SOAP-style web services combined with a customized version of the RASP protocol presented in [19]. The toolkit service development process can be summarized in three steps:

1. Service Description. Service type sets and interfaces are defined in a custom service description (interface definition) language.
2. Communication Code Generation. Service and service client communication stubs are generated from service descriptions.
3. Service Integration. Logic components are exposed as services through implementation of generated service interfaces, and service clients are implemented based on the generated communication stubs for service interconnection.

In all steps of this process, the toolkit aims to reduce the complexity of service development by providing intuitive tools and formats for service description, data representation, and code generation.

3.1 Service Description

For data type and service interface definition, the toolkit employs a service description language comprised of three parts:

- Annotations. Define code generation parameters, e.g., service package names.
- Types. Specifies a primitive type set and basic type aggregation mechanisms.
- Interfaces. Define interfaces in terms of methods and method signatures.

Listing 1.1. Sample Creo service description.

```
// annotations
@PACKAGE("packagename")

// type definitions
struct MetaData
{
    String description;
    long timestamp;
}

struct Data
{
    MetaData metadata;
    double[] samples;
}

// interface definitions
interface DataService
{
    void storeData (Data[] data);
    Data retrieveData (String description);
}
```

To reduce the learning requirements for use of the toolkit, the toolkit's service description language format is based on the block syntax of the C/C++ family of languages. In the interest of simplicity, the primitive type set is restricted to a basic type set commonly occurring in most programming languages: `byte`, `short`, `int`, `long`, `float`, `double`, `char`, and `String`. The language supports direct aggregation of primitive types in structs and arrays as well as construction of compound types via aggregation of structs. This allows construction of hierarchical data types such as trees, but not direct definition of cyclic data types such as graphs. Listing 1.1 contains an example service description demonstrating the aggregation mechanisms of the Creo service description language. The example contains a basic type consisting of primitive types (`MetaData`), an aggregated type consisting of a struct and an array (`Data`), as well as a service interface (`DataService`) defining methods to store and retrieve `Data` instances.

While alternative representation formats with more advanced features exist, e.g., schema-based type set and data validation in XML and WSDL, the design philosophy of this work is to reduce complexity rather that offer advanced features. The goal of the description language is to provide a convenient format that has great expressive power, is as unambiguous as possible, and introduces as few learning requirements as possible. The primitive type set defined, as well as the concept of aggregation of fields in records and arrays, are prevalent in programming languages and should prove intuitive to developers regardless of background. To minimize the learning requirements of the tool, the type interpretations and syntax of the description language are based on a subset of the well-known Java programming language.

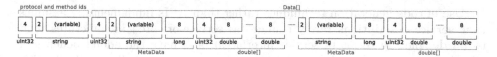

Fig. 1. Byte layout of the Creo protocol request message for the **sendData()** method of Listing 1.1. Data encoded in the order defined in service descriptions, arrays and strings prefixed with item counts. Byte block sizes and primitive types in black, protocol preamble (protocol and method ids) and aggregated (struct and array) types in red (Color figure online).

3.2 Data Representation

To promote transparency, the representation format specified in service description also directly outlines the data structures used in data serialization and transmission. For language and platform independence, all values are transformed to and from network byte order in transmission and support code is generated for programming languages not supporting description language features (e.g., byte order transformation, string classes, or array types). For aggregated types, types are serialized in the order declared (and stored in memory), with size counters prefixing data for array types and strings. As data are declared and stored in hierarchical structures (trees), data serialization is essentially a left-wise depth-first traversal of data trees, where individual node values are stored sequentially. In terms of invocation semantics, Creo defines call-by-value semantics for invocation of remote service methods. As data are serialized by value, the use of reference and pointer types inside data blocks passed to services is not supported. In particular, use of circular references (e.g., cyclic graphs) may lead to inefficient transmission performance or non-terminating loops.

For efficiency in transmission (i.e. minimization of system calls and alignment of network packet sizes to maximum transfer units), all data are serialized and deserialized via transmission buffers located in the generated code stubs. The protocol used for transmission of data between clients and services (illustrated in Fig. 1) is a customized version of the Resource Access and Serialization Protocol (RASP) of the StratUm framework [19]. The description language does not support encoding of explicit exception messages for propagating error information across process boundaries.

3.3 Code Generation

Service integration code is typically provided in one of two forms: APIs or service communication stubs. To reduce complexity in service client development, and increase the transparency of the service communication mechanisms, the Creo toolkit uses a code generation approach centered around immutable wrapper types and call-by-value interfaces. The aim of this design is to make use of generated client code as intuitive as possible, and to facilitate a client development model that doesn't require prior distributed systems development experience.

Use of code generation techniques rather than APIs fundamentally assumes that service descriptions rarely change (as service-oriented architectures tend to be designed in terms of service interfaces), and have the added benefits of allowing strongly typed languages to catch type errors earlier while keeping service client implementations loosely coupled to services.

Code Generator. From a high level, the Creo toolkit can be seen to be composed of three components: a service description parser, a framework generator, and a custom package generator. To promote flexibility and facilitate adaptation to new requirements, e.g., support for new programming languages or representation formats, the architecture of the toolkit is designed to be modular and extensible. The separation of code generation for frameworks and custom packages (i.e. code specific to data types and services defined in service descriptions) serves to facilitate third party implementation of code generator plug-ins. With this separation it is possible to contribute plug-in modules to support alternative implementations of, e.g., data serialization routines and client implementations, without having to deal with generation of framework code.

The service description parser is constructed using a combination of in-memory compilation of the service description types (after replacing selected keywords to make service descriptions Java compliant), use of the Java reflection API (to validate description structures), and a custom language parser (that extracts parameter information). To isolate code generators from document parsing, the parser provides a full internal API that completely describes the type sets and document structures of service descriptions.

Generated Code - Framework. To establish a uniform model for client-service communication, all service client code implements a framework model for connection establishment, data serialization, and transmission capabilities. This framework is structured around an identified core feature set that includes, e.g., primitive type representation and serialization (including network byte order transformations), array and string wrapper types (for languages not providing such types), and socket-level read and write transmission buffers.

The purpose of the framework is to separate service and client logic independent of the types and services defined in service descriptions, and reduce the complexity of generating code for service-dependent logic. Implementation of this framework pattern keeps all service client implementations lightweight and compatible with the service implementation, which facilitates development of client implementations in additional languages. On the service side, the framework code is connected to the service-dependent code through a provider-pattern implementation for service data type serializer factories.

Generated Code - Service Side. On the service side, the generated framework is extended with a lightweight service hosting environment containing basic server functionality such as thread and service management. The architecture of the service framework is based on the principle of abstracting as much as possible of the service boilerplate code required to expose components as services. It is the intent of the toolkit that service implementation should consist only of two steps - generation of the service framework from a service description file and implementation of a service (Java) interface.

The basic structure of the generated services is designed around the information flow in the system; a server hosts services, parses incoming requests, and passes request messages onto an incoming message queue for the requested service. The service implementation processes requests, generates and pushes response messages onto the outgoing message queue for the service. The server continuously monitors all service message queues and sends response messages when available. The core of the generated service framework is message-oriented and defined around the concept of asynchronous message queues, and does not restrict service implementations to use of only synchronous request-response communication patterns. However, while service implementations are free to define their own communication patterns in terms of the messages exchanged between clients and services, use of asynchronous communication patterns requires modifications of the generated service clients to fully support such exchanges. For reference, an asynchronous client (in Java) is provided with the generated service framework.

Generated Code - Client Side. The architecture of the generated service clients uses the same pattern in all implementing service client languages (C, C#, Java, and Python), and is designed to abstract fine-grained service communication tasks. A service API is generated exposing the methods defined in service descriptions, and all data are managed in immutable wrapper types based on the types defined in service descriptions. Service communication details, such as connection establishment and data marshalling, are abstracted by clients stubs.

The underlying philosophy of the toolkit is that it should be the responsibility of the service developer to provide integration code (service clients) and APIs for services, and the toolkit aims to abstract as much as possible of that process. To promote transparency, all client code generated is designed to follow the same design pattern and all generated service client code is designed to be as homogeneous as possible in architecture, code structure, and API functionality support. When applicable, all code is generated along with sample build environment data files (e.g., makefiles for C and ant build files for Java). In-memory compilation and generation of Java Archive (JAR) files are supported for Java.

4 Use Cases

To illustrate toolkit use, we here briefly discuss example application scenarios in the eScience domain. Intended use cases for the Creo toolkit include:

- Coordinated multi-language and multi-platform logging and configuration. Scientific applications in the eScience domain often consist of multiple components and systems developed in multiple programming languages. Coordinated logging of application state information can be very useful for visualization and management of application processes, which can be achieved by, e.g., developing a database accessor component in Java and exposing it as a service using the Creo toolkit. Client stubs generated by the toolkit can then be used to coordinate system logs from multiple sources without introducing external dependencies in systems. Similarly, multi-component systems can also use this technique to coordinate system configuration, allowing dynamic monitoring, reconfiguration, and scaling of systems (use cases from the StratUm [19] project).

– Multi-component system integration. Aequus [18] is a decentralized fairshare scheduling system designed for use in distributed computing environments such as high performance and grid computing infrastructures. While the core of the system is developed in Java, the system also contains specialized components and tools developed in other languages, e.g., scheduler integration plug-ins in C and visualization and statistics tools implemented in Python and Matlab. Use of the Creo toolkit allows smooth integration of different parts of the Aequus system without extensive distributed systems development effort.

– System evaluation experiments. Distributed computing infrastructure systems constructed as service-oriented architectures often require simulation experiments for testing and validation of functionality. The previously mentioned Aequus system is developed and evaluated using emulated system environments for system tests and scalability simulations. In these settings the Creo toolkit provides not only mechanisms for easy integration of multiple simulation components for surrounding systems (e.g., batch schedulers and accounting systems), but also the means for construction of large-scale emulation systems where system evaluation experiments can be run without modifications of the evaluated systems themselves.

– Application cloud migration. Many eScience applications are initially developed for use on single machines and later (for performance and scalability reasons) transformed into multi-component systems that use parallel and distributed computing techniques to exploit parallelism inherent to the computational problems modeled. As part of this process, staging of applications into cloud environments often requires some form of reformulation of computational algorithms to better adapt to scalability (e.g., data parallelism or horizontal cloud elasticity) models. The Creo toolkit can here be used to, e.g., build staging and monitoring tools or to facilitate remote communication with applications running in cloud data centers.

Use cases such as these illustrate not only the expressive power of tools for service development and component integration, but also the importance of keeping such tools simple and reducing the complexity of building distributed systems. Use of development tools with steep learning curves or advanced knowledge requirements for, e.g., serialization formats, marshalling techniques, and transmission formats, can greatly add to the complexity of building

Table 1. A brief overview of the feature sets of the evaluated service technologies.

	Creo	Thrift	PB	SOAP	REST	RMI
Interface type	IDL	IDL	IDL	IDL	protocol	stubs
Integration style	stubs	stubs	API	API/stubs	API/protocol	stubs
Data format	binary	text/binary	binary	text	text/binary	binary

distributed systems. For many purposes, and prototype development in particular, reduction of complexity and ease-of-use often outweigh the additional features of more advanced approaches.

5   Evaluation

Service-based software design is an area with many competing approaches to service development and integration, making objective evaluation of new tools non-trivial. In this work we identify three abstraction levels for development toolkits; low (fine-grained message level integration), intermediary (remote procedure call communication), and high (service-oriented component integration); and evaluate the proposed toolkit against selected tools from each abstraction level in the dimensions of serialization overhead, transmission overhead, and service response time. To facilitate future comparisons against third party tools, we select well-established and easily accessible tools for the evaluation.

For low level abstractions we compare the performance of the toolkit against that of Apache Thrift [3], a software framework for scalable cross-language service development, and Google Protocol Buffers (PB) [10], a message serialization framework developed for cross-platform integration. As the toolkit primarily targets service development in Java, we have for high and intermediary levels selected Java-based tools. For intermediary level we evaluate two related technologies: Java Remote Method Invocation (RMI) [26], an object-oriented remote procedure call mechanism that supports transfer of serialized Java objects and distributed garbage collection, and Java Object Serialization (JOS) [16], the object serialization technology used by Java RMI. For high level, we evaluate the toolkit against two popular web service technologies: REST web services (using the RESTlet framework version 2.0.15 [21]) and SOAP web services (using the Apache Axis 2 SOAP framework version 1.6.2 [1]). Table 1 provides a brief comparison of the feature sets of the evaluated service technologies.

5.1   Testbed and Experimental Setup

To evaluate the technical performance of the toolkit we measure three facets of service communication performance; serialization overhead, transmission overhead, and response time; and quantify these against corresponding measurements of selected alternative tools. *Serialization overhead* is here defined in terms of the computational capacity used for generation and parsing of service messages, and is included in tests as it can heavily impact the execution footprint of service-based tools. *Transmission overhead* is here defined to be the additional bandwidth requirements introduced by service data representation formats, and is measured by quantitative comparison of total message sizes and message payload (raw data) sizes. *Service response time* is here defined as the round-trip makespan of a service invocation, as seen from the service invoker perspective, and used to quantify the throughput performance of client-service combinations. To isolate the communication overhead components introduced by service tools in response time measurements, thin service implementations (that incur minimal service request processing times) are used.

Tests are performed using three types of request data; coarse-grained data (byte chunks), fine-grained number-resolved data (integer and double values), and fine-grained string-resolved data (text segments). For each test and request type, tests are performed with request sizes grown by orders of magnitude (blocks of 1 k, 10 k, 100 k, 1 M, 10 M and 100 M bytes). Coarse-grained requests consist of large chunks of bytes without structured format. For clients based on Creo, Thrift, PB, RMI, and JOS coarse-grained data are sent as raw byte arrays. For REST-based clients, requests are sent in HTTP POST requests as raw bytes with the MIME type "application/octet-stream". In SOAP-based clients, request data are encoded as Base64-encoded strings.

Data for fine-grained requests are created by aggregating 64 16-byte tuples (two 4-byte integers plus an 8-byte double for number-resolved data, two 4-character strings plus an 8-character string for string-resolved data) to form a 1024-byte data block. Larger data blocks are then formed by aggregating data blocks in groups of 10, for example, by aggregating ten 1 k data blocks to form a 10 k data block, ten 10 k data blocks to form a 100 k data block, etc.

For serialization overhead and service response time tests, all tests are done by measuring the client-side makespans of full operations, starting at the point of client invocation and ending when the client receives a uniform size 4-byte service response message. To isolate overhead components, all measurements are performed in closed loop system settings using sequential invocation patterns on dedicated machines with no competing load and isolated network segments. Experiments are repeated multiple (at least ten) times and average values are computed on the median measurements in experiments to minimize the impact of external factors on measurements. Parallel invocation tests are used to evaluate the load sensitivity and scalability of service tools. All services used in measurements are implemented in Java and service clients are implemented in C, C#, Java and Python. For tests of the service response time of REST and SOAP tools, message serializations are performed in JSON (using the reference library of http://json.org) and XML (using JAXB) respectively.

All tests are run on a dedicated symmetric cluster where nodes are equipped with dual 16 core 2.1 GHz AMD Opteron 6272 processors and 54 GB RAM. Nodes are interconnected with 1 Gbps links and networks are configured using MTU sizes of 1500 bytes. All nodes run Ubuntu Linux 14.04 kernel version 3.13,

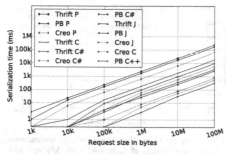

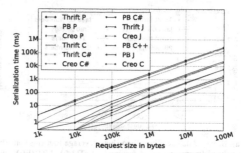

(a) Number-resolved data. Compared to Thrift, Creo shows average serialization time improvements of factors 34.99 (C), 1.66 (C#), 3.40 (Java), and 3.72 (Python). Compared to PB, Creo shows average serialization time improvements of factors 0.53 (C), 0.62 (C#), 1.00 (Java), and 2.69 (Python).

(b) String-resolved data. Compared to Thrift, Creo shows average serialization time improvements of factors 31.07 (C), 1.15 (C#), 2.86 (Java), and 1.94 (Python). Compared to PB, Creo shows average serialization time improvements of factors 2.16 (C), 0.35 (C#), 0.72 (Java), and 1.62 (Python).

Fig. 2. Creo, Thrift, and PB message serialization time. Axes logarithmic.

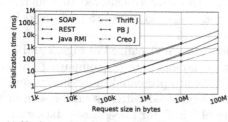

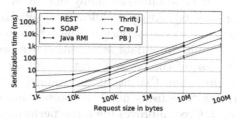

(a) Number-resolved data. On average Creo shows serialization time improvements of factors 34.54 (SOAP), 31.14 (REST), 6.10 (RMI), 3.40 (Thrift), and 1.00 (PB).

(b) String-resolved data. On average Creo shows serialization time improvements of factors 7.55 (SOAP), 13.24 (REST), 9.28 (RMI), 2.86 (Thrift), and 0.72 (PB).

Fig. 3. Message serialization time for Java-based tools. Axes logarithmic.

OpenJDK 1.7, Python 2.7.5, Mono 3.2.8, GLib 2.40, and GCC 4.8.2. All software are accessible from Ubuntu repositories.

5.2 Serialization Overhead

To isolate measurements of data serialization overhead it is necessary to make some modifications to the default behavior of the tools tested in serialization overhead tests. For example, to avoid impacting serialization overhead measurements with differences in data transmission behaviors (e.g., different types and sizes of transmission buffers), Creo, Thrift, and PB service clients (generated code and/or runtime libraries) are in tests modified to write directly to preallocated buffers instead of sending packets. Additionally, all tool's service clients are modified so that they do not read data from services after invocations.

To avoid modifications of Java RMI stacks, we here include measurements of the underlying serialization technology used (JOS) and assume measurements are representative of the serialization overhead of RMI. To quantify the serialization overhead of JOS, `ObjectOutputStream` instances are wrapped

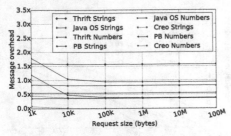 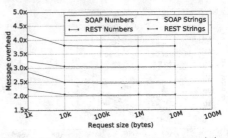

(a) Binary data encoding. Creo shows average transmission overhead improvements of factors 1.84 (Thrift), 1.24 (PB) and 1.40 (Java Object Serialization).

(b) Text data encoding. Creo shows average transmission overhead improvements of factors 4.76 (SOAP) and 4.03 (REST) for numbers, and 2.51 (SOAP) and 2.20 (REST) for strings.

Fig. 4. Message transmission (size) overhead. Horizontal axes logarithmic.

around non-buffered dummy output streams (no data transferred to underlying sockets). After modifications, serialization overhead tests are performed in the same way as service response time tests.

Results from data serialization overhead tests are visualized in Figs. 2 and 3. For ease of comparison, test results for multi-language tests (comparing Creo to Thrift and PB) using fine-grained data tests are presented individually, separating tests using number-resolved and string-resolved data. As can be seen in Fig. 2, Creo improves upon the performance of Thrift for fine-grained data with an average of factors 1.15 to 3.72 for C#, Java, and Python clients. Compared to the less mature Thrift C clients, Creo shows improvements of factors 31.07 to 34.99. When compared to Protocol Buffers, Creo shows performance improvements only for Python (ranging from factors 1.62 to 2.69) and string serialization in C (factor 2.16). When comparing the performance of Creo against that of other Java-based tools (illustrated in Fig. 3), Creo exhibits performance improvements of factors 6.10 to 34.54, which is attributed to use of more complex serialization techniques and text-resolved data representation formats in the other high-level tools. These tests illustrate the magnitude of serialization overhead incurred by complex serialization techniques, as well as the impact serialization overhead can have on service execution footprint and performance. For example, the JAXB serialization engine used in the SOAP tests is unable to process messages of sizes 100 MB in standalone settings, indicating a potential source for load issues when used inside service engines.

5.3 Transmission Overhead

To evaluate transmission overhead and response time for service communication a simple server component that counts and returns the number of bytes in requests is used. Service invocation makespan is measured on the client side and used to quantify transmission overhead for service invocations with known request payload sizes. Apache Thrift supports transmission of data using three protocols: text-resolved JSON and two binary protocols: TBinaryProtocol

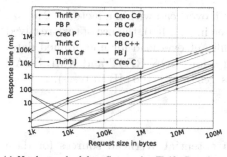 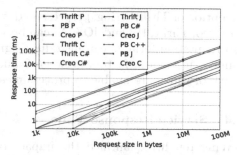

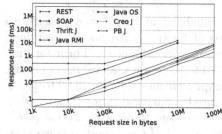 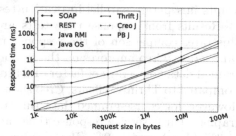

(a) Number-resolved data. Compared to Thrift, Creo shows average service response time improvements of factors 15.20 (C), 1.59 (C#), 2.15 (Java), and 2.51 (Python). Compared to PB, Creo shows average service response time improvements of factors 1.91 (C), 0.72 (C#), 0.59 (Java), and 1.69 (Python).

(b) String-resolved data. Compared to Thrift, Creo shows average service response time improvements of factors 9.93 (C), 1.24 (C#), 3.14 (Java), and 1.33 (Python). Compared to PB, Creo shows average service response time improvements of factors 1.29 (C), 0.46 (C#), 0.69 (Java), and 1.07 (Python).

Fig. 5. Creo, Thrift, and PB service response time. Axes logarithmic.

(a) Number-resolved data. On average Creo shows service response time improvements of factors 26.26 (SOAP), 41.78 (REST), 2.15 (Thrift), 1.53 (RMI), 1.21 (JOS), and 0.59 (PB).

(b) String-resolved data. On average Creo shows service response time improvements of factors 21.65 (SOAP), 19.52 (REST), 3.14 (Thrift), 5.34 (RMI), 3.38 (JOS), and 0.69 (PB).

Fig. 6. Service response time for Java-based tools. Axes logarithmic

and TCompactProtocol, where the former sends data as-is and the latter uses variable-length encoding of integers. The purpose of this encoding scheme; which for example encodes 16-bit integers as 1–3 bytes, 32-bit integers as 1–5 bytes, and 64-bit integer as 1–10 bytes; is to reduce the size of payload and commonly occurring metadata such as the length of strings, arrays, and collections. Protocol Buffers supports a similar scheme for variable-length encoding of integers, that in investigation incurs a minor performance overhead for a reduction in representation size. However, in tests we primarily use Thrift's TBinaryProtocol (and Protocol Buffer's corresponding non-compression encoding scheme) as it is supported in all languages, and evaluate the efficiency of variable-length encoding schemes in the languages supported (and quantify it against that of Creo and the binary protocol) in separate tests.

For ease of comparison, test results for compact binary representation formats (Creo, Thrift, PB, and JOS) and text-resolved formats (JSON REST and XML SOAP) are presented separately. As can be seen in Fig. 4(a), binary encoding schemes represent data efficiently and fine-grained data are (with the exception of Thrift strings) represented with overhead within a factor of 2 in size for Creo, Thrift, PB and JOS. As can be seen in Fig. 4(b), the use of text-resolved representation formats can introduce significant overhead for fine-grained data, ranging in tests in factors between 2 and 4 for JSON REST and XML SOAP (both of which are unable to process messages of size 100 MB in tests).

5.4   Service Response Time

Having roughly quantified the impact of potential overhead sources for data serialization and transmission, we analyze the communication performance of the evaluated tools in terms of service request response times. Using closed system loop settings (sequential invocations of services deployed in isolated systems), we measure invocation makespan from the client perspective and use it as a measurement of service response time. To verify the transfer of results from sequential tests to (more realistic) parallel invocation scenarios, we also validate results in separate parallel invocation tests.

Results from response time tests are visualized in Figs. 5 and 6. Figure 5 illustrates comparison of the response time of Creo, Thrift, and PB services. On average, Creo improves on the response time performance of Thrift for fine-grained data on average of factors 1.24 to 3.14 for C#, Java, and Python clients. Compared to Thrift C clients, Creo shows improvements of factors 9.93 to 15.20. However, for coarse-grained data (unstructured binary data, not illustrated in graphs), Thrift service response times are on average 16.6 % (C), 21.8 % (C#), 21.3 % (Java), and 15.9 % (Python) lower than that of Creo (performance averages calculated for request sizes of 1 MB, 10 MB, and 100 MB). Similarly, Protocol Buffer service response times are also on average 2.8 % (C), 9.7 % (C#), 11.0 % (Java), and -3.5 % (Python) lower than that of Creo. The higher response times of Creo for coarse-grained data are attributed to the use of asynchronous message queues and immutable data structures on the service side, which cause redundant data replications in message transmission.

When comparing the response time of Creo to that of other Java-based tools (illustrated in Fig. 6), we note performance improvements ranging from 1.53 to 5.34 (RMI), 19.52 to 41.78 (REST), and 21.65 to 26.26 (SOAP) for fine-grained data, and comparative performance for coarse-grained data. As expected from analysis of serialization and transmission overhead, REST and SOAP web services exhibit response time performance degradations from the use of text-based representation formats and associated message serializations.

6   Conclusions

In this work we investigate an approach to service-based software development and present a toolkit for reduction of complexity in service development and distributed component integration. The architecture of the toolkit is designed to be modular and extensible, and places focus on transparency and reduction of complexity. To reduce learning requirements, the toolkit employs a service description language based on the syntax and type interpretations of the well-known Java language. The service description language defines a set of primitive types and mechanisms for aggregation of types in arrays and structs.

The toolkit supports generation of code for construction of Java-based services as well as service clients in Java, C, C#, and Python. The toolkit uses the same code generation pattern for all languages, which defines immutable types that directly wrap the data types and aggregation patterns defined in service descriptions. For transparency, the service communication protocol serializes data in the order and types defined in the service description language.

A performance evaluation quantifying toolkit performance (in terms of message overhead and service response time) against Java Object Serialization, Java RMI, SOAP web services, REST web services, Apache Thrift, and Google Protocol Buffers is presented. Toolkit performance is found to be comparable to or improve upon the performance of the alternative techniques.

Acknowledgements. The authors acknowledge Mikael Öhman, Sebastian Gröhn, and Anders Häggström for work related to the project. This work is done in collaboration with the High Performance Computing Center North (HPC2N) and is funded by the Swedish Government's strategic research project eSSENCE and the Swedish Research Council (VR) under contract number C0590801 for the project Cloud Control.

References

1. Apache, Apache Web Services Project - Axis2, July 2014. http://ws.apache.org/axis2
2. Apache, Apache Avro, July 2014. http://avro.apache.org/
3. Apache, Apache Thrift, July 2014. http://thrift.apache.org/
4. Armbrust, M., Fox, A., Griffith, R., Joseph, A.D., Katz, R., Konwinski, A., Lee, G., Patterson, D., Rabkin, A., Stoica, I., et al.: A view of cloud computing. Commun. ACM **53**(4), 50–58 (2010)
5. Berl, A., Gelenbe, E., Di Girolamo, M., Giuliani, G., De Meer, H., Dang, M.Q., Pentikousis, K.: Energy-efficient cloud computing. Comput. J. **53**(7), 1045–1051 (2010)
6. Birrell, A.D., Nelson, B.J.: Implementing remote procedure calls. ACM Trans. Comput. Syst. (TOCS) **2**(1), 39–59 (1984)
7. Esoteric Software, Kryo, July 2014. https://github.com/EsotericSoftware/kryo
8. Fielding, R.T.: Architectural styles and the design of network-based software architectures. Ph.D thesis, University of California (2000)
9. Furuhashi, S.: MessagePack, July 2014. https://github.com/msgpack/msgpack/
10. Google, Protocol Buffers, July 2014. https://developers.google.com/protocol-buffers/
11. Govindaraju, M., Slominski, A., Chiu, K., Liu, P., Van Engelen, R., Lewis, M.J.: Toward characterizing the performance of SOAP toolkits. In: Proceedings of the Fifth IEEE/ACM International Workshop on Grid Computing, pp. 365–372. IEEE (2004)
12. Jackson, July 2014. https://github.com/FasterXML/jackson

13. Kephart, J.O., Chess, D.M.: The vision of autonomic computing. Computer **36**, 41–50 (2003)
14. Mackey, A.: Windows communication foundation. In: Introducing. NET 4.0, pp. 159–173. Springer (2010)
15. MongoDB Inc., BSON, July 2014. http://bsonspec.org
16. Oracle, Java Object Serialization, July 2014. http://docs.oracle.com/javase/7/docs/platform/serialization/spec/serialTOC.html
17. Östberg, P.-O., Elmroth, E.: Increasing flexibility and abstracting complexity in service-based grid and cloud software. In: Ivanov, I., Leymann, F., van Sinderen, M., Shishkov, B. (eds.) Proceedings of CLOSER 2011 - International Conference on Cloud Computing and Services Science, pp. 240–249. SciTePress, Noordwijkerhout (2011)
18. Östberg, P.-O., Espling, D., Elmroth, E.: Decentralized scalable fairshare scheduling. Future Gener. Comput. Syst. - Int. J. Grid Comput. eScience **29**, 130–143 (2013)
19. Östberg, P.-O., Hellander, A., Drawert, B., Elmroth, E., Holmgren, S., Petzold, L.: Reducing complexity in management of escience computations. In: Proceedings of CCGrid 2012 - The 12th IEEE/ACM International Symposium on Cluster, Cloud and Grid Computing, pp. 845–852 (2012)
20. Pautasso, C., Zimmermann, O., Leymann, F.: Restful web services vs. big web services: making the right architectural decision. In: Proceedings of the 17th International Conference on World Wide Web, pp. 805–814. ACM (2008)
21. Restlet, Restlet Framework, July 2014. http://restlet.org
22. Slee, M., Agarwal, A., Kwiatkowski, M.: Thrift: scalable cross-language services implementation. Facebook White Pap. **5**, 8 (2007)
23. Van Deursen, A., Klint, P., Visser, J.: Domain-specific languages: an annotated bibliography. sigplan Not. **35**(6), 26–36 (2000)
24. Vinoski, S.: Distributed object computing with CORBA. C++ Rep. **5**(6), 32–38 (1993)
25. Walker, E.: The real cost of a CPU hour. Computer **42**(4), 35–41 (2009)
26. Wollrath, A., Riggs, R., Waldo, J.: A distributed object model for the Java system. Comput. Syst. **9**, 265–290 (1996)

Generating Secure Service Compositions

Luca Pino[1]([✉]), George Spanoudakis[1], Andreas Fuchs[2],
and Sigrid Gürgens[2]

[1] Department of Computer Science,
City University London, London, UK
{luca.pino.1,g.e.spanoudakis}@city.ac.uk
[2] Fraunhofer Institute for Secure Information Technology,
Darmstadt, Germany
{andreas.fuchs,sigrid.guergens}@sit.fraunhofer.de

Abstract. Ensuring that the compositions of services that constitute service-based systems satisfy given security properties is a key prerequisite for the adoption of the service oriented computing paradigm. In this paper, we address this issue using a novel approach that guarantees service composition security by virtue of the generation of compositions. Our approach generates service compositions that are guaranteed to satisfy security properties based on *secure service orchestration (SESO) patterns*. These patterns express primitive (e.g., sequential, parallel) service orchestrations, which are proven to have certain global security properties if the individual services participating in them have themselves other security properties. The paper shows how SESO patterns can be constructed and gives examples of proofs for such patterns. It also presents the process of using SESO patterns to generate secure service compositions and presents the results of an initial experimental evaluation of the approach.

Keywords: Software services · Secure service compositions · Security certificates

1 Introduction

The security of service based systems (SBS), i.e., systems that are composed of distributed software services, has been a critical concern for both the users and providers of such systems [3, 17, 24]. This is because the security of an SBS depends on the security of the individual services that it deploys, in complex ways that depend not only on the particular security properties of concern but also on the exact way in which these services are composed to form the SBS. Consider, for example, the case where the property required of an SBS is that the integrity of any data D, which are passed to it by an external client, will not be compromised by any of its constituent services that receive D. The assessment of this property requires knowledge of the exact services that constitute the SBS, the exact form of the composition of these services and the data flows between them, and a guarantee that each of the constituent services of SBS that receives D will preserve its integrity. Such assessments of security are required both during the design of an SBS and at

© Springer International Publishing Switzerland 2015
M. Helfert et al. (Eds.): CLOSER 2014, CCIS 512, pp. 81–99, 2015.
DOI: 10.1007/978-3-319-25414-2_6

runtime in cases where one of its constituent services S needs to be replaced and, due to the absence of any individual service matching it, a composition of services must be built to replace S. Whilst the construction of service compositions that satisfy functional and quality properties has been investigated in the literature (e.g., [1, 2, 27]), the construction of secure service compositions is not adequately supported by existing research.

In this paper, we present an approach for generating compositions of services, which are guaranteed to satisfy certain security properties. Our approach is based on the application of *SEcure Service Orchestration patterns* (SESO patterns). SESO patterns specify primitive service orchestrations, which are proven to have particular global (i.e., composition level) security properties, if their constituent services satisfy other service-level security properties. A SESO pattern specifies the order of the execution (e.g., sequential, parallel) of its constituent services and the data flows between them. It also specifies rules dictating the security properties that the constituent services of the pattern must have for the orchestration to satisfy a global security property. These rules express security property relations of the form *IF P THEN* $\wedge_{i=1,...,n} P_i$ where P is a global security property required of the service orchestration and P_i are security properties, which must be satisfied by the services of the pattern for P to hold. These security property relations are formally proven. The constituent services of a SESO pattern are abstract "placeholder" services that need to be instantiated by concrete services when the pattern is instantiated.

When a constituent service S of an SBS needs to be replaced at runtime and no single alternative service S' satisfying exactly the same security properties as S can be found, SESO patterns can be applied to generate compositions of other services that have exactly the same security properties as S and could replace it within SBS. SESO patterns determine the criteria (security, interface and functional) that should be satisfied by the services that could instantiate them. These criteria are used to drive a discovery process through which the pattern can be instantiated. If this process is successful, i.e., different combinations of services that satisfy the required criteria and fit with the orchestration structure of the pattern are discovered, any combination (composition) of services that is built according to the pattern is guaranteed to have the required global security property by construction.

An earlier account of our approach has been given in [20, 22]. In this paper, we extend [22] by presenting the method that underpins the proof of security properties in SESO patterns, showing additional examples of concrete proofs of security properties for specific SESO patterns, and presenting the composition algorithm that generates secure service compositions that functionally relevant to the needed service.

The rest of this paper is organized as follows. Section 2 presents an overview of our approach. Section 3 discusses the validation of SESO patterns and provides examples of proofs of security properties for some patterns. Section 4 discusses the encoding of SESO patterns. Section 5 presents the SESO pattern driven service composition algorithm. Section 6 provides the results of an initial experimental evaluation of our approach. Section 7 overviews related work. Finally, Sect. 8 provides conclusions and directions for future work.

2   Overview

The service composition approach that we present in this paper extends a general framework developed at City University to support runtime service discovery [28]. This framework supports service discovery driven by queries expressed in an XML based query language, called *SerDiQueL*, which supports the specification of interface, behavioural and quality discovery criteria. The execution of queries can be reactive or proactive. In reactive execution, the SBS submits a query to the framework and gets back any services matching the query that are discovered by the framework. In proactive execution, the SBS submits to the framework queries that are executed in parallel, to find potential replacement services that could be used if needed, without the need to initiate and wait for the results of the discovery process at this point [28].

To take into account service security requirements as part of the service discovery process, we have extended the above framework in two ways. Firstly, we have extended *SerDiQueL* to enable the specification of the security properties that are required of individual services as querying conditions (the new language is called *A-SerDiQueL*). Secondly, we have developed a module supporting the generation of possible compositions of services that could replace a given service in an SBS in cases where a discovery query cannot find any single matching service. The generation of service compositions is based on the approach presented in this paper. In particular, this paper focuses on the process of searching for and constructing secure service compositions and the SESO patterns used in this process.

The key problems during the composition process are to ensure that the constructed composition of services: (a) provides the functionality of the service that it should replace, and (b) satisfies the security properties required of this service. To address (a), our approach uses abstract service workflows. These workflows express service coordination processes that realize known business processes through the use of software services with fixed interfaces. Such workflows are available for specific application domains such as telecom services (IBM BPM Industry Packs [13]), logistics (RosettaNet [25]), and are often available as part of SOA architecting and realization platforms (e.g., IBM WebSphere). Service workflows are encoded in an XML based language that represents the interfaces, and the control and data flows between the workflow activities.

To address (b), we are using SESO patterns. These patterns are based on primitive service orchestrations that have been proposed in the literature (e.g., sequential and parallel service execution) but augment them by specifying concrete security properties $P_1,\ldots, P_n$ that must be provided by the individual services that instantiate the pattern for the overall orchestration to satisfy a required security property P_0. The derivation of these security properties is based on rules that encode formally proven relations between the security properties of the individual placeholder services of the pattern and the security property required of the entire service orchestration represented by the pattern. Once derived through the application of rules, the security properties required of the individual partner services of the orchestration are expressed as queries in *A-SerDiQueL*. These queries are then executed to identify concrete services with the required security properties, which could instantiate the placeholder services of the pattern. If such services are found the pattern is instantiated. The pattern instantiation process is gradual and, if it is completed successfully, a new concrete and executable service composition that satisfies the overall security property guaranteed by the pattern is generated.

A key element of our approach is the formal validation of the relations between the security properties of the individual placeholder services of a SESO pattern and the security property of the entire composition expressed by the pattern. The validation of such relations is discussed in the next section.

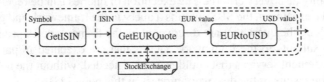

Fig. 1. Composition to replace *GetStockQuote*.

To illustrate our approach assume that a *Stock Broker* SBS that uses an operation *GetStockQuote* from a service *StockQuote* to obtain price quotations for a given stock. *GetStockQuote* takes as input a string *Symbol* identifying a stock and returns the current value of that stock in USD. If *StockQuote* becomes unavailable at runtime, then it becomes necessary to replace it with another service or a service composition (if no single replacement service can be discovered). A composition that may replace *Stock-Quote* is shown in Fig. 1. This composition contains three activities connected by two sequential patterns (indicated as dashed areas in workflow). The first placeholder of the outer sequence contains the activity *GetISIN*, which converts the *Symbol* identifying the Stock into the *ISIN* (another unique stock identifier). The second placeholder corresponds to the inner sequence. Within this inner sequence, the first placeholder is the activity *GetEURQuote* that involves *StockExchange* and returns the current stock value in EUR given the Stock *ISIN*. The second placeholder is the activity *EURtoUSD*, which converts a given amount from EUR to USD.

3   Validating Secure Service Compositions

In this section we introduce our approach for formally proving security properties of service compositions. This is based on generic models of service systems that take into account the different types of agents and actions that can be part of such systems. We then transform SESO patterns into different compositions of generic system models and show that such compositions satisfy specific security properties given that the individual system models satisfy some other security properties. In particular, we show that a sequential composition of two generic service models provides specific data integrity properties. Instantiating these service models with the concrete services of our example results in assurance that their sequential composition satisfies the respective concrete data integrity properties.

The task of formally validating the security of a service composition requires a three-step approach. It starts with a formal model of the service to be replaced and the formal models of the services to be composed. Firstly, the service composition is represented in terms of a formal model derived from the models of the individual services by applying a set of formal construction rules. These rules project the respective security properties of each of the composed services as well as the targeted property of the service to be replaced into the composed system. Secondly, additional properties are added to the composed system regarding the behaviour of the orchestrator, i.e., the primitive service orchestration pattern. Finally, the desired property is verified using the properties of the composed services and the orchestrator.

For the formal system representation and validation of security properties we utilize the Security Modeling Framework SeMF developed by Fraunhofer SIT [9–11]. In SeMF, a system specification is composed of a set $\mathbb{P}$ of agents and a set Σ of actions, $\Sigma_{/P}$ denoting the actions of agent P, and other system specifics that are not needed in this paper and are thus omitted. The behaviour B of a discrete system *Sys* can then be formally described by the set of its possible sequences of actions. Security properties are defined in terms of such a system specification. Relations between different formal models of systems are partially ordered with respect to different levels of abstraction. Formally, abstractions are described by so called alphabetic language homomorphisms that map action sequences of a finer abstraction level to action sequences of a more abstract level while respecting concatenation of actions. Language homomorphisms satisfying specific conditions are proven to preserve specific security properties, the conditions depending on the respective security property. Further information about SeMF can be found in [9–11].

Based on the representations of each of the service systems in the composition, we present a general construction rule using homomorphisms that map the service composition onto the individual services by preserving the individual services' security properties. This allows us to deduce the respective security properties to be satisfied by the composition. The different SESO patterns are translated into behaviour of the orchestrator regarding the invocation of the respective services. This includes functional and security related property statements. Based on this information it is possible to deduce the overall security properties of the composition system and validate whether they meet the expected results. In the next three sections, we illustrate our approach by exemplarily proving a specific data integrity property. The formal representation of services, composition and security properties is given in terms of generic agents and actions that are later instantiated by the SESO patterns towards concrete services and security properties. While our example focus on a single property on a specific set of orchestrations, our approach can handle various different orchestrations patterns, proving different instantiations of various security properties regarding integrity and confidentiality [21].

3.1 Formal Representation of Generic Service Composition

The formalization of a generic composition structure for service based systems is based on the following types of agents:

- *Clients C.* These are agents that use the service. They are thus specific to the service, and their actions are derived from the service's WSDL.

- *Service S.* This is the agent representing the service's communication interface (corresponding to its WSDL).
- *Backend Agents S-*.* These are service specific agents representing the implementation specifics, i.e. the internal functionality of a certain service (e.g. a backend storage used by the service).
- *Global agents G-*←*representing third parties that are known to be identical for all services (e.g., some service providing external information).
- *R (the "rest of the word").* This is a default global external agent that is used to represent any agent other than those identified in *C, S-** and *G-*.*

In the following, we denote (i) the system model of the service S^0 to be replaced by a composition by Sys^0, (ii) the system models of the services S^1 and S^2 to be composed by Sys^1 and Sys^2, respectively, and (iii) the composition system by Sys^c. The sets of agents and actions are denoted analogously (i.e. by $\mathbb{P}^i$, Σ^i, for $i = 0, 1, 2$). We mark service specific agents with the corresponding superscripts. We also mark global agents, even though being global, with superscripts in order to indicate the context of invocation (i.e. a global agent G-A being invoked by S^i is denoted by G^i-A. A generic system Sys^0 with service S^0, client C^0, a backend agent S^0-A and a global agent G^0-A can for example be instantiated by a service *StockbrokerService* using a backend storage service *StockbrokerService-Storage* for logging of client data and a global service *StockExchange* for actually retrieving the stock data.

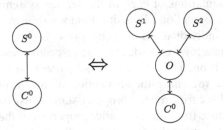

Fig. 2. Service Composition.

The principal idea of substituting a service by a composition is depicted in Fig. 2. More specifically, we assume two services S^1 and S^2 to act independently of (i.e., not to invoke) each other and utilize an orchestration engine O for their composition that takes the roles of both the clients C^1 and C^2 of Sys^1 and Sys^2 respectively, as well as the role of the service S^0 in Sys^0 to be replaced. Any global agent of Sys^0 will be part of the composition system and will be invoked by either S^1 or S^2. Furthermore, backend agents of Sys^0 will be removed, their functionality will be provided by the services S^1 or S^2 or their backend agents which will be part of the composition as well. This gives rise to the following set of agents of the composition:

$$\mathbb{P}^c = \left(\mathbb{P}^0\backslash\{S^0, S^0- *, G^0- *\right) \cup \left(\mathbb{P}^1\backslash\{C^1\}\right) \cup \left(\mathbb{P}^2\backslash\{C^2\}\right) \cup \{O\}$$

We then view the systems Sys^0, Sys^1 and Sys^2 as homomorphic images of the composed system Sys^c.

In order to determine the action set Σ^c of the composition we use a generic renaming function $r_{P \to Q}:\Sigma \to \Sigma_{r_{P \to Q}}$ that replaces all occurrences of agent P in an action by Q. Based on this function, we define functions $r^i:\Sigma^i \to \Sigma^c$ ($i = 0, 1, 2$, $j = 1, 2$) that formalizes the orchestrator taking the roles of S^0, C^1 and C^2 as follows:

$$r^0(a) = r_{S^0 \to O}(a)$$
$$r^j(a) = r_{C^j \to O}(a)$$

The resulting set Σ^c of actions of the composed system is then as follows:

$$\Sigma^c = r^0\left(\Sigma^0_{/C^0} \cup \Sigma^0_{/S^0}\right) \cup r^1\left(\Sigma^1\right) \cup r^2\left(\Sigma^2\right) \cup \Sigma^c_{/O}$$

$\Sigma^c_{/O}$ represents additional actions taken by the orchestration engine beyond the communication with client and services. These actions depend on the specific orchestration pattern used and will be discussed in the next section.

Now we need to assure that for all actions in Sys^0 exists an equivalent provided by either S^1 or S^2, i.e. the above set Σ^c of actions must satisfy the following:

$$\forall a \in \Sigma^0, \exists i \in \{1,2\}, \exists a' \in \Sigma^c: \quad r_{G^0-*\to G^i-*}(a) = a' \vee$$
$$r_{S^0-*\to S^i-*}(a) = a'$$

Since the functions r^i are injective we can now use their inverse image in order to define the homomorphisms that map the composition system onto the abstract systems: each homomorphism h^i abstracts Σ^c to Σ^i. Regarding the actions corresponding to those in Σ^i, h^i is simply the inverse of r^i, and all other actions are mapped onto the empty word. Hence for $i = 0, 1, 2$ and $j = 1, 2$ we define $h^i:\Sigma^c \to \Sigma^i$ as follows:

$$h^0(a) = \begin{cases} a' & \text{if } \exists a' \in \Sigma^0: r^0(a') = a \\ a'' & \text{if } \exists a'' \in \Sigma^0, \exists i \in \{1,2\}: r_{G^0-*\to G^i-*}(a'') = a \\ a''' & \text{if } \exists a''' \in \Sigma^0, \exists i \in \{1,2\}: r_{S^0-*\to S^i-*}(a''') = a \\ \varepsilon & \text{else} \end{cases}$$

$$h^j(a) = \begin{cases} a' & \text{if } \exists a' \in \Sigma^j: r^j(a') = a \\ \varepsilon & \text{otherwise} \end{cases}$$

These homomorphisms serve as a means to relate not only the models of the individual systems to the composition model but also to relate - under certain conditions - their security properties. A homomorphism that fulfills certain conditions "transports" a security property from an abstract system to the concrete one, i.e. if the conditions are satisfied and the property holds in the abstract system, the corresponding property will also hold in the concrete system. Thus, the homomorphism *preserves* the property. The conditions that must be satisfied depend on the property in question; see [9, 10] for example. We use this approach to prove specific security properties for a composition of services based on the security properties of these services.

3.2 Formally Representing Sequential Composition

Our methodology for service composition has been applied to various different patterns, proving different instantiations of various security properties (see [21] for more details). In the following, we will focus on a specific case for a sequential service composition that corresponds to the example introduced in Sect. 2.1 in order to illustrate our approach. We assume the original service S^0 to invoke a global agent G–A (denoted by G^0–A). For its substitution, the pattern for sequential composition of services realizes the subsequent invocation of two services S^1 and S^2, where the output of S^1 serves as input for S^2. The global agent G–A will be invoked by either S^1 or S^2 (denoted by G^1–A and G^2–A, respectively).

The actions of the systems are constructed from the generic service operations op_0, op_1, and op_2 (that represent the operations of concrete services' WSDL) as prefix, followed by one of the suffixes *IS, IR, OS, OR* to represent *InputSend, InputReceive, OutputSend, OutputReceive*, respectively. This naming scheme corresponds to our method of transforming a service's WSDL into sets of agents and actions introduced in [12]. The actions of the global agents, not being part of the service's WSDL, do not follow this notation. This leads to the following specification of systems Sys^i:

$$\mathbb{P}^i \supseteq \{C^i, S^i\} \quad \Sigma^i \supseteq \left\{ \begin{array}{l} op_i\text{–}IS\left(C^i, S^i, data_i\right), \\ op_i\text{–}IR\left(S^i, C^i, data_i\right), \\ op_i\text{–}OS\left(S^i, C^i, f_i(data_i)\right), \\ op_i\text{–}OR\left(C^i, S^i, f_i(data_i)\right) \end{array} \right\}$$

$$\mathbb{P}^j \supseteq \{G^j\text{–}A\} \quad \Sigma^j \supseteq \{\text{act}(G^j\text{–}A, in_{G^j\text{–}A}, out_{G^j\text{–}A})\}$$

with $i = 0,1,2$, and $j = 0,1$ for Sys^1, and $j = 0,2$ for S^2.

In the system Sys^0, when S^0 receives some data $data_0$ from the client, before forwarding it to the global agent it applies a function f_I^1. In our stockbroker example introduced in Sect. 2.1, this function could for instance remove the client's name or account). The global agent (*StockExchangeService* in the example) acts on receiving the input $in_{G^0\text{–}A}$ and produces the output $out_{G^0\text{–}A}$ (say, the stock value in Euros and the bill for the service provided). The global agent's input and output may or may not be functionally related. Such a relation is necessary in case an integrity property shall be expressed that involves the complete sequence of actions, starting with the client providing the input data and ending with the client receiving the final output. The case we investigate below considers only half of this sequence, starting with the global agent's output, thus a relation between global agent's input and output is not needed. Accordingly, G^0–A returns $out_{G^0\text{–}A}$ to S^0. The service then applies a function f_O^0 and sends the result to the client. The stockbroker service in our example could for instance remove the bill and just keep the stock value, and convert it to US dollar.

In the sequential composition pattern, the orchestrator forwards $data_0$ received from C^0 to S^1. In case it is S^1 that invokes the global agent, before doing so the service computes $f_I^1(data_0)$ (removes the client's name and account) and sends this to G^1-A. As in Sys^0, the global agent produces out_{G^1-A} and returns this to S^1. Note that input as well as output of the global agent are the same as in Sys^0 (otherwise the global agent would not be global). Now S^1 applies f_O^1 (removes the global agent's bill) and sends $f_O^1(out_{G^1-A})$ to the orchestrator. These data are then forwarded by the orchestrator to S^2 who applies f^2 (converts euro to dollar) and returns $f^2(f_O^1(out_{G^1-A}))$ which the orchestrator finally returns to the client. A similar sequence of actions occurs if the global agent is invoked by S^2. In a more complex scenario the orchestrator can for example alter (e.g., split) the client data and combine the output of S^1 with some data resulting from the client's input and send this to S^2. A proof for this more complex construction is achievable analogously to the one presented below.

The agent and action sets of the composition are constructed as specified in the previous section, using the functions r^0, r^1 and r^2. Function r^0 for example maps action op_0-$IS(C^0, S^0, data_0)$ onto op_0-$IS(C^0, O, data_0)$, hence $h^0(op_0$-$IS(C^0, O, data_0)) = op_0$-$IS(C^0, S^0, data_0)$, while $h^0(op_2$-$OR(O, S^2, f_2(data_2))) = h^0(r^2(op_2$-$OR(C^2, S^2, f_2(data_2)))) = \varepsilon$., with $data_1 := data_0$ and $data_2 = f_O^1(out_{G^1-A})$.

3.3 Validation of Integrity Preserving Compositions

Our approach of proving security properties of service compositions is generic and has already been applied to various integrity and confidentiality properties (see [21] for more details). As an example of such proofs, we will now present the proof regarding a specific data integrity property of S^0 being provided by the orchestration specified above. The definition of (data) integrity that we assume in our example is taken from RFC4949, i.e. "The property that data has not been changed, destroyed, or lost in an unauthorized or accidental manner." [26]. In SeMF, this property of data integrity is expressed by the concept of *precedence*: *pre(a, b)* holds if all sequences of actions $\omega \in B$ that contain action b also contain action a. Obviously, precedence is transitive (we omit the trivial proof). Further, precedence is preserved by any homomorphism if $h(B) \subseteq B'$ (see [11] for a proof). With $B^c = h^{1^{-1}}(B^1) \cap h^{2^{-1}}(B^2) \cap \{\omega \in \Sigma^c | \forall\ Prop \in prop_0 : prop\}$ all precedence properties are preserved in the following, with $Prop^0$ denoting the orchestrator assumptions (see P4 and P5 below).

Out of the many properties related to integrity and sequential composition we now investigate one that is related to transmission of data between a global agent and a client which results into four different properties. On the one hand, we can investigate the integrity of data transmitted from the client to a global agent vs. the one transmitted from a global agent to the client. On the other hand, we can differentiate between the global agent being invoked by either S^1 or S^2. Exemplarily we use the case where S^1 invokes the global agent and assume S^0 to provide the following integrity property: Each time client C^0 receives data from service S^0, this data originates from the global agent that was properly manipulated by S^0. Formally:

P0: $\forall data: op_0\text{-}OR\left(C^0, S^0, data\right) \in alph\left(\omega\right) \rightarrow data = f_O^0\left(out_{G^0\text{-}A}\right) \wedge$
$\quad pre\left(act\left(G - A, in_{G^0\text{-}A}, out_{G^0\text{-}A}\right), op_0\text{-}OR\left(C^0, S^0, f_O^0\left(out_{G^0\text{-}A}\right)\right)\right)$

As explained above, precedence shall be preserved by h^0 (as constructed in Sect. 3.1). Since the global agent's action in the composition is identical to the one in Sys^0, it must receive the same input in order for the composition to achieve the same functionality, hence $f_I^0 = f_I^1$. Also, what C^0 receives in the composition must be identical to what it receives in Sys^0. This implies $f_2 \circ f_O^1 = f_O^0$ which results in the following property of the composition (corresponding to P1') that we want to prove:

P1: $\forall data: op_0\text{-}OR\left(C^0, O, data\right) \in alph\left(\omega\right) \rightarrow data = f^2\left(f_O^1\left(out_{G^1\text{-}A}\right)\right) \wedge$
$\quad pre\left(act\left(G\text{-}A, in_{G^1\text{-}A}, out_{G^1\text{-}A}\right), op_0\text{-}OR\left(C^0, O, f^2\left(f_O^1\left(out_{G^1\text{-}A}\right)\right)\right)\right)$

For our proof, we assume that the services Sys^1 and Sys^2 provide the properties:

P2': $\forall data: op_1\text{-}OR\left(C^1, S^1, data\right) \in alph\left(\omega\right) \rightarrow data = f_O^1\left(out_{G^1\text{-}A}\right) \wedge$
$\quad pre\left(act\left(G^1\text{-}A, in_{G^1\text{-}A}, out_{G^1\text{-}A}\right), op_1\text{-}OR\left(C^1, S^1, f_O^1\left(out_{G^1\text{-}A}\right)\right)\right)$

P3': $\forall data: op_2\text{-}OR\left(C^2, S^2, data\right) \in alph\left(\omega\right) \rightarrow data = f^2(data_2) \wedge$
$\quad pre\left(op_2\text{-}IS\left(C^2, S^2, data_2\right), op_1\text{-}OR\left(C^1, S^2, f^2(data_2)\right)\right)$

The homomorphisms h^1 and h^2 as constructed in Sect. 3.1 preserve these precedence properties. Accordingly, the corresponding properties in Sys^c are:

P2: $\forall data: op_1\text{-}OR\left(O, S^1, data\right) \in alph\left(\omega\right) \rightarrow data = f_O^1\left(out_{G^1\text{-}A}\right) \wedge$
$\quad pre\left(act\left(G^1\text{-}A, in_{G^1\text{-}A}, out_{G^1\text{-}A}\right), op_1\text{-}OR\left(O, S^1, f_O^1\left(out_{G^1\text{-}A}\right)\right)\right)$

P3: $\forall data: op_2\text{-}OR\left(O, S^2, data\right) \in alph\left(\omega\right) \rightarrow data = f^2(data_2) \wedge$
$\quad pre\left(op_2\text{-}IS\left(O, S^2, data_2\right), op_1\text{-}OR\left(O, S^2, f^2(data_2)\right)\right)$

In addition, the orchestrator must act according to the pattern (as specified in Sect. 3.2), i.e., satisfy the following properties:

P4: $pre\left(op_1\text{-}OR\left(O, S^1, data\right), op_2\text{-}IS\left(O, S^2, data\right)\right)$
P5: $pre\left(op_2\text{-}OR\left(O, S^2, data\right), op_0\text{-}OR\left(C^0, O, data\right)\right)$

Proof. Assume there is $\omega \in B$ with $op_0\text{-}OR\left(C^0, O, data\right) \in alph(\omega)$. Property P5 implies that $op_2 - OR\left(O, S^2, data\right) \in alph(\omega)$. By P3, $data = f^2\left(data_2\right)$ and further $op_2\text{-}IS\left(O, S^2, f^2\left(data_2\right)\right) \in alph(\omega)$. In the next step, Property P4 implies that $op_1 - OR\left(O, S^1, f^2\left(data_2\right)\right) \in alph(\omega)$. By P2, we can deduce $data_2 = f_O^1(out_{G^1\text{-}A})$, i.e. $data = f^2\left(f_O^1\left(out_{G^1\text{-}A}\right)\right)$, and $act\left(G^1 - A, in_{G\text{-}A}, out_{G^1\text{-}A}\right) \in alph(\omega)$ which implies that property P1 holds.

Due to the simplicity of the precede property, the above proof is simple. In [21] we have proven other integrity properties (e.g. the global agent being invoked by S^2). We have also proven several confidentiality properties. All proofs use the approach presented in this paper: (i) deriving the formal model of the service composition from the formal models of the individual services, (ii) relating these models by using property preserving homomorphisms and thus representing the individual services' security properties in terms of the composition model, and (iii) using appropriate security properties to be satisfied by the orchestrator. Whilst we assume the orchestrator to behave correctly and hence to satisfy these additional properties, the security properties we assume for the individual services of the composition are translated into inference rules, which are then used in order to construct a concrete service compositions. The proofs of security properties for specific SESO patterns need to be constructed offline and encoded in the patterns as rules. At runtime, the rules encoding the patterns are used to deduce the security properties that must be satisfied by the candidate services that may instantiate the pattern.

4 Secure Service Orchestration Patterns

Proofs of security properties, like the one that we discussed in Sect. 3, form the basis of SESO patterns in our approach. More specifically, an SESO pattern encodes: (a) a primitive orchestration describing the order of the execution and the data flow between placeholder services, and (b) the implications between the security properties of these services and the security property of the whole orchestration. The placeholder services within a primitive orchestration can be atomic activities (i.e., abstract partner services) or other patterns. The implications in (b) are of the form:

"IF P is a primitive orchestration with placeholders S_1, ..., S_n and ρ^P is a security property required for P THEN ρ^P is guaranteed if each S_i in P satisfies the security properties ρ_j (j =1, ..., m_i)".

These implications reflect proofs of security properties, developed based on the approach discussed in Sect. 3. They are encoded as inference rules and used during the composition process to infer the security properties that would be required of the placeholders of a pattern P for it to satisfy ρ^P. The benefit of encoding proven implications as inference rules is that there is no need to reason from first-principles when attempting to construct compositions of services, based on SESO patterns.

To be more specific, SESO patterns and implications of the above form are encoded as Drools production rules [8]. Drools is a rule-based reasoning system supporting reasoning driven by production rules. Production rules in Drools are used to derive information from data facts stored in a Knowledge Base (KB). A production rule in Drools has the general form: *when* <*conditions*> *then* <*actions*>. When a rule is applied, the rule engine of Drools checks, through pattern matching, whether the conditions of the rule match with the facts in the KB and, if they do, it executes the actions of the rule. This execution can update the contents of the KB. Table 1 shows the encoding of integrity in the sequential orchestration pattern that was presented in Sect. 3.3 as a Drools rule. This rule uses the following definitions of integrity:

Table 1. Integrity Rule for Sequential SESO Pattern.

```
 1:  rule "Integrity on Sequential. Case GA at S1 to C"
 2:  when
 3:     $outGA : Parameter()
 4:     $f1-outGA : Parameter(functionOf == $outGA)
 5:     $f2-f1-outGA : Parameter(functionOf == $f1-outGA)
 6:     $GA1 : GlobalAgent(parameter == $outGA)
 7:     $S1 : Activity(globalAgents contains $GA1,
                         outputs contains $f1-outGA)
 8:     $S2 : Activity(inputs contains $f1-outGA,
                         outputs contains $f2-f1-outGA)
 9:     $P : Sequential(activity1 == $S1, activity2 == $S2)
10:     $ rhoP : IntegrityGA2C(subject == $P, GA == $GA1,
                         data == $f2-f1-outGA)
11:  then
12:     insert(new IntegrityGA2C($S1, $GA1, $f1-outGA));
13:     insert(new IntegrityE2E($S2, $f1-outGA, $f2-f1-outGA));
14:     retract($rhoP);
15:  end
```

Definition 1. The integrity of data X generated by a global agent GA and sent to the client by S^1: $IntegrityGA2C(S^i, GA, f^i(X)) = pre(act(GA, \_, X), op_i\text{-}OR(C^i, S^i, f^i(X)))$

Definition 2. The end-to-end integrity of the data, from input to output (i.e. the property investigated in a former version of this work [22]): $IntegrityE2E(S^i, X, Y) = pre(op_i\text{-}IS(C^i, S^i, X), op_i\text{-}OR(C^i, S^i, Y))$.

Using such more abstract security properties in the rules avoids the need to encode in the rule the formalism that the proof is based on. This makes it also possible to use SESO patterns proven through different formalisms in our approach.

Returning to the rule in Table 1, lines 3–9 describe the primitive orchestration that the security property refers to. More specifically, the rule can be applied when a sequential pattern ($P) with two placeholders, i.e., activity $S1 followed by activity $S2, is encountered. Activity $S1 interacts with a global agent $GA1 that generates output $outGA. The rule defines the parameters of these activities: $S1 has an output parameter $f1-outGA, that is a function of $outGA, and $S2 uses the input parameter $f1-outGA in order to generate the output parameter $f1-f2-outGA, as shown in Table 1. Line 10 describes the original security requirement requested on the composition pattern $rhoP, i.e. integrity on the pattern $P of the data $f2-f1-outGA originally generated by $GA1. This requirement is equivalent to the property P1 presented in Sect. 3.3. Lines 12–14 (i.e., the then part of the rule) specify the security properties that are required of the activities of the pattern in order to guarantee $rhoP, namely: (i) integrity on the output ($f1-outGA) of $S1 generated by $GA1, as stated by the precedence property P2, and (ii) end-to-end integrity on the input ($f1-outGA) and output ($f2-f1-outGA) of $S2, as required from P3. Additionally, we assume the framework executing the orchestration to satisfy properties P4–P5, hence these need not be mentioned in the rule.

Finally, according to the rule, once the original requirement $rhoP is guaranteed by the new ones, it can be removed from the KB.

Similar encodings of other SESO patterns have been expressed using this approach. SESO pattern encoding rules, like the one presented above, are used during the composition process to infer the security properties that are required of the concrete services that may instantiate the placeholder services in a workflow. This process is discussed next.

5 SESO Pattern Driven Service Composition

The service composition process is carried out according to the algorithm shown in Table 2. This algorithm is invoked when an SBS service needs to be replaced but the service discovery query specified for it cannot identify any single service matching it.

In such cases, the structural part of the query, which defines the operations that a service should have and the data types of the parameters of these operations, is used to retrieve from the repository of the discovery framework abstract workflows that can provide the required service functionality. An abstract workflow represents a coarse grained orchestration of activities, which collectively offer a specific functionality, and is exposed as a composite service. Such workflows are fairly common (e.g., [5, 19]) and result from reference process models in specific domains [13, 25]. The activities of an abstract workflow are orchestrated through a process consisting of the primitive orchestrations that underpin the security patterns, as discussed in Sect. 4. If such workflows are found the generation of a service composition is attempted by trying to instantiate each abstract workflow.

As shown in Table 2, initially, the algorithm identifies the abstract workflows that could be potentially used to generate a composition that can provide the operations of the required service (see STRUCTURALMATCH function in line 3). This is based on the execution of the query associated with the service to be replaced (Q_S). If such workflows are found, the algorithm continues by starting a process of instantiating the activities of each of the found workflows with services. The activities of the workflows are instantiated progressively, by investigating each workflow W in a depth-first manner. More specifically, the algorithm takes the first unassigned activity A in W (in the control flow order) and builds a query Q_A based on the workflow specification and the discovery query Q_S. In particular, the structural part of Q_A is taken from the description of A in the abstract workflow. The security conditions in Q_A are generated through the procedure SECURITYCONDITIONS(Q_S, W).

This procedure infers the security conditions for A based on the Drools rules that encode the SESO patterns detected within the current workflow. More specifically, all the information about the workflow, its patterns, activities, security properties and requirements are put into the KB. Then the rules that represent the detected SESO patterns are fired (i.e. applied), propagating the requirements through the workflow. The generated requirements for the unassigned activity are then retrieved and converted to query conditions. The propagation of security requirements is possible as each workflow can be seen as a recursive application of primitive orchestrations.

Table 2. Service Composition Algorithm.

```
Require: Qₛ - query for the required service
Ensure: ResultSet - set of instantiated workflows
 1:   procedure SERVICECOMPOSITION(Qₛ)
 2:      for all abstract workflows AW in the repository do
 3:         if STRUCTURALMATCH(Qₛ, AW) == true then
 4:            Put a copy of AW in WStack
 5:         end if
 6:      end for
 7:      while there are more workflows in WStack do
 8:         Get the first workflow W in the WStack
 9:         Pop the first unassigned activity A from W
10:         Extract the structural query Qₐ for A from W
11:         SecCond := SECURITYCONDITIONS(Qₛ, W)
12:         Add to Qₐ the security conditions SecCond
13:         Res := SERVICEDISCOVERY(Qₐ)
14:         for all services S* in Res do
15:            W_{S*} := W[A/S*]            //i.e. substitute S* for A in W
16:            if exists an unassigned activity in W_{S*} then
17:               Push W_{S*} in WStack
18:            else
19:               Add W_{S*} to ResultSet
20:            end if
21:         end for
22:      end while
23:      return ResultSet
24: end procedure
```

Figure 3 shows the order of propagation through the use of the rules, on a workflow shown in (c). A security requirement ρ^S is initially given for a service S (Fig. 3(a)). The first rule that will be fired by Drools is the one for the outermost pattern of the workflow: a choice pattern (i.e., the *if-then-else* primitive orchestration in Fig. 3(b)). The security requirement is then propagated by the relevant rule (if such a rule exists) to the place-holders A and B returning the requirements ρ^{A1}, ..., ρ^{An} and ρ^{B1}, ..., ρ^{Bm} (with $n, m \geq 0$ and $n + m \geq 1$). For each security requirement ρ^{Ai} (with $i = 1, ..., n$), a rule is fired to propagate the requirement to the sequential pattern that instantiates A (Fig. 3(c)). This process generates the security requirements for placeholders C and D.

If a security requirement cannot be propagated to the atomic activity level (e.g., no rules are defined for the given pattern or security property) then Drools returns an error state to point out that a security requirement cannot be guaranteed by the existing set of rules. This ensures that no security requirements are ignored.

After constructing Q_A, the query is executed by the runtime discovery framework in [28] to identify a list of candidate services for Q_A. The candidate services (if any) are then used to instantiate the activity A in W. Note that the composition algorithm implements a depth-first search in the composition generation process in order to explore fully the instantiation of a particular activity within a pattern before considering other activities. This spots dead-ends sooner than a breadth-first search.

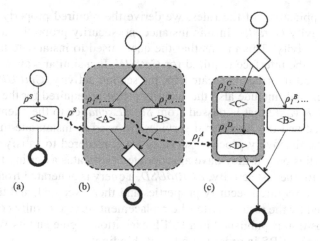

Fig. 3. Recursive applications of secure service orchestration patterns.

As an example of applying the algorithm in Table 2, consider the Stock Broker example introduced in Sect. 2.1. Suppose that the Stock Broker SBS has a security requirement regarding integrity of the output data of its *StockQuote* service, and would consider replacement services that can offer the same operation only if they satisfy this particular security requirement. To deal with potential problems with *StockQuote* at runtime (e.g., unavailability), *Stock Broker* can subscribe a service discovery query Q_{SQ} for replacing *StockQuote* to the discovery framework and request its execution in proactive mode. Q_{SQ} should specify the functional and security properties that the potential replacement services of *StockQuote* must have. If the execution of Q_{SQ} results in discovering no single service matching it (i.e., when single service discovery fails), the service composition process is carried out. At this stage, according to the algorithm of Table 2, the framework will query the abstract workflow repository to locate workflows matching Q_{SQ}.

Suppose that this identifies the abstract workflow W_{SQ} shown in Fig. 1 that matches the query. This workflow contains a sequence of three activities: *GetISIN*, *GetEURQuote* and *EURtoUSD*. The framework then infers the security properties required for each of the services that could instantiate the activities of W_{SQ} and uses them to query for such services. Initially, a rule for integrity of data D on a sequential pattern with the global agent generating D in the second activity is fired on the external sequential pattern. This rule and the related proof are given in [21] (Sect. 3.3.3, case 2). The rule is applied because the property required for the external sequential pattern is that the output of the workflow (i.e., *USD value*) must have been computed from the value returned by *Stock-Exchange*. From the required security property, the rule derives only one property about the integrity of *USD value* (again, from the value coming from *StockExchange*) for the inner sequential pattern. This newly generated property fires the rule shown in Table 1 resulting in two security properties: (1) integrity from the global agent *StockExchange* to the client for *GetEURQuote* output *EUR value*, and (2) end-to-end integrity on inputs and outputs of *EURtoUSD*.

After the application of the rules, we derive the required property for the first unassigned activity *GetISIN*. In this instance, no security properties are requested from the first activity. This means that the query used to instantiate the workflow consists only of the interface required for *GetISIN*. In a similar way, a query specifying the required interface is created for the second activity, *GetEURQuote*. This query, however, will include also the security property required for the activity i.e., integrity of *EUR value* that is passed from *StockExchange* to the client. The query is then executed and the discovered services are used to instantiate the workflow. Note that in the discovery process, services are considered to satisfy the required security properties only if they have appropriate certificates asserting these properties. Similarly for the last activity, *EURtoUSD*, a query is generated from the service interface and the required security properties and then executed, and the workflow gets instantiated by the results. After the replacement service is fully composed, the service composition is published in a BPEL execution engine and its WSDL is sent to the *Stock Broker* SBS in order to update its bindings.

6 Tool Support and Experiments

To implement and test our approach, we have developed a prototype realizing the composition process and integrated it with the runtime service discovery tool described in Sect. 2. The prototype gives the possibility to select a service discovery query and execute it to find potential candidate services and service compositions. If alternative service compositions can be built, the alternatives are presented to the user who can select and explore the services in each of them.

Early performance tests of our approach have been carried out using service registries of different sizes. Table 3 shows average execution times for single service and service composition discovery obtained from using our tool on an Intel Core i3 CPU (3.06 GHz) with 4 GB RAM. The reported times are average times taken over 30 executions of each discovery query. In the experiments, we used service registries of four sizes (150, 300, 600 and 1200), 25 abstract workflows and 3 patterns.

As shown in the table, the time required for building service compositions is considerably higher than the time required for single service discovery. The main part of this cost comes from the process of discovering the individual services to instantiate the partner links of the composition. Although the overall composition time is high, its impact is not as significant, since as we discussed in Sect. 2 our framework can apply discovery and service composition in a proactive manner, i.e., discover possible service compositions in parallel with the operation of an SBS and use them when a service needs to be replaced. Furthermore, the cost of compositions can be reduced or kept under a given threshold by controlling the number of alternative compositions that the algorithm in Table 2 builds. In [28], the authors have shown the benefits of a proactive execution of the service discovery process used in our approach. Hence, we believe that the proactive generation of compositions could also reduce execution time but this would need to be confirmed experimentally.

Table 3. Execution times (in msecs).

Registry size	150	300	600	1200
Single service discovery time	194	275	355	642
Composition discovery time	777	2214	4943	12660
No. of generated compositions	4	12	24	40

7 Related Work

Existing work in service composition has focused on creating compositions that have certain functional and quality of service properties (e.g., [1, 2, 14, 17, 23, 24, 27]) and provides only basic support for addressing security properties in service composition, which is the main focus of our approach.

The creation of service compositions that satisfy given security properties has been a focus of work on model based service composition (e.g., [4, 6, 7]). In this area, service compositions are modeled using formal languages and their required properties are expressed as properties on the model. Our approach to composition is also model based. However, it uses model based property proofs to identify how overall security properties of compositions can be guaranteed through the security properties of the individual components (services) of the composition. Existing work on model based service composition could provide proofs of additional security properties, which could be used to extend the patterns used in our approach, even if they use different formalisms. The compositionality results for information flows discussed in [18], for example, can be easily converted into SESO patterns.

Other work on service composition focuses on discovering services that have given security properties (e.g., [3, 5, 15, 16, 19]). Some of these approaches focus on specific types of security properties (e.g., [16, 19]) whilst other focus on how to express and check security properties but only for single partner services of a composition (e.g., [3, 5, 15]). In contrast, our approach can support arbitrary security properties and properties of entire service compositions.

Two ontology-based frameworks for automatic composition are described in [15] and [19]. The first framework defines a set of metrics for selecting amongst different compositions but provides limited support for security. The second framework introduces hierarchies of security properties but does not support the construction of secure service compositions. In [16] planning techniques have been used to build sequential compositions guarantying access control models, and [5] introduces an approach to security aware service composition that matches security requirements with external service properties. The focus of [3] is on generating test-based virtual security certificates for service compositions, derived from the test-based security certificates of the external services that form the composition.

8   Conclusion

In this paper, we have presented an approach supporting the discovery of secure service compositions. Our approach is based on secure service orchestration (SESO) patterns. These patterns comprise specifications of primitive orchestrations describing the order of the execution and the data flow between placeholder services, and rules reflecting formally proven relations between the security properties of the individual placeholders and the security property of the whole orchestration. The formal proofs (and patterns) developed so far cover different integrity and confidentiality properties for different forms of primitive orchestrations. During the composition process, the proven relations between security properties are used to deduce the actual properties that should be required of the individual services that may instantiate an orchestration for the orchestration to satisfy specific security properties as a whole. In order to facilitate reasoning, SESO patterns are encoded as Drools rules. This enables the use of the Drools rule based system for inferring the required service security properties when trying to generate a service composition.

Our approach has been implemented and integrated with a generic framework supporting runtime service discovery that is described in [28]. We are currently investigating the validity of our approach through a series of focus group evaluations. We are also investigating further SESO patterns (e.g., for availability), and conducting further performance and scalability analysis of our prototype. We are also exploring the use of heuristic controls over the number of compositions generated by the algorithm to speed up the processing.

Acknowledgements. The work reported in this paper has been partially funded by the EU F7 project ASSERT4SOA (grant no.257351).

References

1. Aggarwal, R., et al.,: Constraint driven web service composition in METEOR-S. In: Proceedings of the IEEE International Conference on Services Computing (SCC 2004), pp. 23–30 (2004)
2. Alrifai, M., Risse, T., Nejdl, W.: A hybrid approach for efficient Web service composition with end-to-end QoS constraints. ACM Trans. Web **6**(2), 7:1–7:31 (2012)
3. Anisetti, M., Ardagna, C., Damiani, E.: Security certification of composite services: a test-based approach. In: Proceedings of the IEEE 20th International Conference on Web Services, pp. 475–482 (2013)
4. Bartoletti, M., Degano, P., Ferrari, G.L.: Enforcing secure service composition. In: Proceedings of the 18th Computer Security Foundations Workshop (CSFW), pp. 211–223. IEEE Computer Society (2005)
5. Carminati, B., Ferrari, E., Hung, P.C.K.:. Security conscious web service composition. In: Proceedings of the International Conference on Web Services (ICWS), pp. 489–496. IEEE Computer Society (2006)
6. Deubler, M., et al.: Sound development of secure service-based systems. In: Proceedings of 2nd International Conference on Service Oriented Computing, pp. 115–124 (2004)
7. Dong, J., Peng, T., Zhao, Y.: Automated verification of security pattern compositions. Inf. Softw. Technol. **52**(3), 274–295 (2010)

8. Drools. http://www.jboss.org/drools/
9. Gürgens, S., Rudolph, C., Ochsenschläger, P.: Authenticity and provability - a formal framework. In: Rees, O., Frankel, Y., Davida, G.I. (eds.) InfraSec 2002. LNCS, vol. 2437, pp. 227–245. Springer, Heidelberg (2002)
10. Gürgens, S., Ochsenschläger, P., Rudolph, C.: Abstractions preserving parameter confidentiality. In: di Vimercati, S., Gollmann, D., Syverson, P.F. (eds.) ESORICS 2005. LNCS, vol. 3679, pp. 418–437. Springer, Heidelberg (2005)
11. Gürgens, S., et al.: D05.1 Formal Models and Model Composition. ASSERT4SOA Project, Technical report (2011). http://assert4soa.eu/public-deliverables/
12. Gürgens, S., et al.: D05.3 Model Based Certification Artefacts. ASSERT4SOA Project, Technical report (2013). http://assert4soa.eu/public-deliverables/
13. IBM BPM industry packs. http://www.ibm.com/software/products/us/en/business-process-manager-industry-packs/
14. Jaeger, M.C., Rojec-Goldmann, G., Muhl, G.: QoS aggregation for web service composition using workflow patterns. In: Proceedings of the 8th IEEE International Enterprise Distributed Object Computing Conference, pp. 149–159 (2004)
15. Khan, K.M., Erradi, A., Alhazbi, S., Han, J.: Security oriented service composition: A framework. In: Proceedings of International Conference on Innovations in Information Technology (IIT), pp. 48–53 (2012)
16. Riabov, A.V., Liu, Z., Lelarge, M.: Automatic composition of secure workflows. In: Ungerer, T., Yang, L.T., Jin, H., Ma, J. (eds.) ATC 2006. LNCS, vol. 4158, pp. 322–331. Springer, Heidelberg (2006)
17. Majithia, S., Walker, D.W., Gray, W.A.: A framework for automated service composition in service-oriented architectures. In: Bussler, C.J., Davies, J., Fensel, D., Studer, R. (eds.) ESWS 2004. LNCS, vol. 3053, pp. 269–283. Springer, Heidelberg (2004)
18. Mantel, H.: On the composition of secure systems. In: Proceedings of the 2002 IEEE Symposium on Security and Privacy (SP2002). IEEE Computer Society (2002)
19. Medjahed, B., Bouguettaya, A., Elmagarmid, A.K.: Composing web services on the semantic web. VLDB J. 12(4), 333–351 (2003)
20. Pino, L., Spanoudakis, G.: Constructing secure service compositions with patterns. In: Proceedings of 2012 IEEE 8th World Congress on Services, pp. 184–191 (2012)
21. Pino, L., et al.: D02.2 ASSERT aware service orchestration patterns. ASSERT4SOA Project, Technical report (2012). http://assert4soa.eu/public-deliverables/
22. Pino, L., Spanoudakis, G., Gürgens, S., Fuchs, A.: Discovering secure service compositions. In: Proceedings of the International Conference on Cloud Computing and Services Science (2014)
23. Ponnekanti, S.R., Fox, A.: Sword: a developer toolkit for web service composition. In: Proceedings of the 11th World Wide Web Conference, pp. 7–11 (2002)
24. Raman, B., et al.: The SAHARA model for service composition across multiple providers. In: Mattern, F., Naghshineh, M. (eds.) PERVASIVE 2002. LNCS, vol. 2414, pp. 1–14. Springer, Heidelberg (2002)
25. RosettaNet. Available: http://www.rosettanet.org/
26. Shirey, R.: Internet Security Glossary, Version 2. RFC 4949 (Informational), IETF (2007). Available: http://www.ietf.org/rfc/rfc4949.txt
27. Tan, W., Fan, Y., Zhou, M.: A petri net-based method for compatibility analysis and composition of web services in business process execution language. IEEE Trans. Autom. Sci. Eng. 6(1), 94–106 (2009)
28. Zisman, A., Spanoudakis, G., Dooley, J., Siveroni, I.: Proactive and reactive runtime service discovery: A framework and its evaluation. IEEE Trans. Softw. Eng. 39(7), 954–974 (2013)

A Scalable Monitor for Large Systems

Mauro Andreolini[1]([✉]), Marcello Pietri[2], Stefania Tosi[2],
and Riccardo Lancellotti[2]

[1] Department of Physics, Computer Science and Mathematics,
University of Modena and Reggio Emilia, Via Campi 213/a, 41125 Modena, Italy
mauro.andreolini@unimore.it
[2] Department of Engineering "Enzo Ferrari", University of Modena
and Reggio Emilia, Via Vignolese 905/b, 41125 Modena, Italy
{marcello.pietri,stefania.tosi,riccardo.lancellotti}@unimore.it

Abstract. Current monitoring solutions are not well suited to monitoring large data centers in different ways: lack of scalability, scarce representativity of global state conditions, inability in guaranteeing persistence in service delivery, and the impossibility of monitoring multi-tenant applications. In this paper, we present a novel monitoring architecture that strives to address these problems. It integrates a hierarchical scheme to monitor the resources in a cluster with a distributed hash table (DHT) to broadcast system state information among different monitors. This architecture strives to obtain high scalability, effectiveness and resilience, as well as the possibility of monitoring services spanning across different clusters or even different data centers of the cloud provider. We evaluate the scalability of the proposed architecture through an experimental analysis and we measure the overhead of the DHT-based communication scheme.

Keywords: Monitoring architecture · Cloud Computing · Large-scale · Scalability · Multi-tenancy

1 Introduction

Cloud Computing is the most adopted model to support the processing of large data volumes using clusters of commodity computers. According to Gartner, Cloud Computing is expected to grow 19 % in 2012, becoming a $109 billion industry compared to a $91 billion market last year. By 2016, it is expected to be a $207 billion industry. This esteem compares to the 3 % growth expected in the overall global IT market. Several companies such as Google [1], Microsoft [2], and Yahoo [3] process tens of petabytes of data per day coming from large data centers hosting several thousands nodes. According to [4], from 2005 to 2020, the digital universe will grow by a factor of 300, from 130 EB to 40000 EB, or 40 trillion GB (more than 5200 GB per person in 2020). From now until 2020, the digital universe will about double every two years.

In order to satisfy service level agreements (SLAs) and to keep a consistent state of the workflows in this tangled layout, such growing large infrastructures

© Springer International Publishing Switzerland 2015
M. Helfert et al. (Eds.): CLOSER 2014, CCIS 512, pp. 100–116, 2015.
DOI: 10.1007/978-3-319-25414-2_7

are usually monitored through a multitude of services that extract and store measurements regarding the performance and the utilization of specific hardware and software resources. These monitoring tools are operated by cloud providers and offered to the services' owners, but also ad-hoc monitoring solutions are designed in order to satisfy the requirements of big companies which own their private cloud infrastructures. For example, Sony uses the closed-source Zyrion Traverse database [5] to claim the monitoring of over 6000 devices and applications over twelve data centers across Asia, Europe and North America. The virtual data layer within the solution collects half a million resource data streams every five minutes.

This scenario requires the design of an advanced monitoring infrastructure that satisfies several properties:

1. **Scalability.** It must cope with a large amount of data that must be collected, analyzed, stored and transmitted at real-time, so as to take timely corrective actions to meet SLAs.
2. **Effectiveness.** It must provide an effective view of the system state conditions that can be used for management purposes and to identify the causes of observed phenomena. It must also adapt its monitoring functions to varying conditions in order to accommodate variable resources, system errors, and changing requirements.
3. **Resilience.** It must withstand a number of component failures while continuing to operate normally, thus ensuring service continuity. Single points of failure must be avoided for providing persistence of service delivery.
4. **Multi-tenancy.** It must be able to monitor applications distributed over different data centers in order to better perform troubleshooting activities in dynamic environments such as cloud scenarios.

We state that none of the existing solutions fulfills all these requirements. In this paper we overcome state-of-the-art limits with a novel open-source monitoring infrastructure. We propose a hybrid architecture for a quasi real-time monitoring of large-scale, geographically distributed network infrastructures spread across multiple data centers, designed to provide high scalability, effectiveness and resilience. Here, the term *hybrid* refers to the use of two different communication schemes: a *hierarchical* one and a *P2P-based* one. Each data center is equipped with its own decoupled monitoring infrastructure; each monitor adopts a hierarchical scheme that ensure scalability with respect to the number of monitored resources, in a subset of the whole architecture. Communications between data centers are performed through the root managers, software modules responsible for orchestrating the whole process. The root managers of every decentralized monitor are connected through a custom communication module that implements the P2P Pastry DHT routing overlay [6]. In this way, a service distributed across several data centers can be jointly monitored through the appropriate root managers. The internal operations of the monitor are geared towards effectiveness objectives. We provide real-time access to single performance samples or graphs, as well as more sophisticated analysis that aim at identifying system or application states for anomaly detection, capacity planning, or other management studies. Every single component in the infrastructure is designed to be resilient to failures. Whenever possible, we enrich the existing software modules with redundancy and failover mechanisms. Otherwise, we automatically restart the modules in case of failure.

The rest of this paper is organized as follows. Section 2 evaluates the current state-of-the-art in the area of large-scale system monitoring. Section 3 describes the design decisions supporting the described requirements, provides a high level architecture of the entire monitoring infrastructure, motivates the choice of the software components and discusses various implementation details. Section 4 investigates the theoretical scalability limits of the proposed architecture figured out from experimental scenarios. Finally, Sect. 5 concludes the paper with some remarks and future work.

2   Related Work

Current state-of-the-art monitoring tools do not guarantee scalability, effectiveness, resilience and multi-tenancy objectives. Fully centralized monitors cannot scale to the desired number of resource data streams. For example, the prototype system introduced in [7], which uses Ganglia [8] and Syslog-NG to accumulate data into a central MySQL database, shows severe scalability limits at only 64 monitored nodes, each one collecting 20 resource data streams every 30 s. Here, the main bottleneck is related to the increasing computational overhead occurring at high sampling frequencies. On the other hand, lowering the sampling frequency (commonly, once every five minutes) can make it difficult to spot rapidly changing workloads which in turn may entail the violation of SLAs [9].

Concerning resilience, the vast majority of both open-source and commercial monitoring infrastructures like OpenNMS [10], Zabbix [11], Zenoss [12] and Cacti [13] are not adequate or designed to address failures, especially if combined with the ability to gather and support millions of resource data streams per second.

In terms of effectiveness, most open-source monitoring tools only partially address this aspect. For example, Graphite [14] and Cacti provide only trending analyses, Nagios [15] provides alerting, while Chukwa [16] and Flume [17] are designed exclusively to collect resource data streams or logs. Also current decentralized, per-data-center, hierarchical monitors such as Ganglia [18] are limited to efficiently compute averages of measures spanning over several nodes. However, the complexity of current workloads in modern data centers calls for more sophisticated processing, such as the identification of correlations among different resource data streams, or the detection of anomalies in the global system state.

Astrolabe [19] is a hybrid solution that combines a hierarchical scheme with an unstructured P2P routing protocol for distributed communications as our proposal does. While it is resilient and highly scalable in terms of data collection and storage, it lacks in effectiveness and its manageability is a complex task since it incurs a lot of network traffic. Unstructured systems do not put any constraints on placement of data items on peers and how peers maintain their network connections and this solution suffers from non-deterministic results, high network communication overload and non-scalability of bandwidth consumption [20].

While collection and network monitoring were addressed in many works with significant results [21–23], the state-of-the-art technology in multi-tenant monitoring is a very niche field. In fact, none of the previous works deals with a multi-tenant environment. At the best of our knowledge, the only open contribution in this sense is given by [24]: it extends monitoring based on data stream management systems (DSMS) with the ability to handle multiple tenants and arbitrary data; however it does not address resilience in terms of single points of failure, it has no implemented prototype, and it does not present any type of analysis to support the proposed architectural choices.

The fuzzy DHT algorithm proposed in this paper addresses the issue of joining the need for advanced lookup features with the need to preserve the scalability of DHTs. Other studies propose flexible queries. For example, Liu et al. propose a system to support range queries [25], other researchers propose keyword queries based on inversed indexes [26,27], while Tang *et al.* introduce semantic searches on the CAN DHT [28]. However, all these proposals require separate search services or introduce a completely new routing mechanism. Our approach is different from these proposals for three main reasons. First, the fuzzy DHT algorithm allows the deployment of novel services with only slight modifications to the existing overlay networks, thus allowing a simpler deployment of the fuzzy DHT based overlay. Second, the proposed algorithm is explicitly designed to provide multiple keyword-based searches, which are convenient for locating resources based on attributes. Finally, our algorithm is explicitly designed with efficiency as a primary goal.

3   Architecture

The early decisions that inspired the design of the proposed architecture share four important goals: (1) to dominate the complexity of the monitoring problem (*Scalability*), (2) to tune the monitoring activities according to different objectives (*Effectiveness*), (3) to avoid single points of failure (*Resilience*), and (4) to monitor services spanning across different clusters or data centers (*Multi-tenancy*). This section details the architecture design of our proposal, with particular emphasis to the design decisions that allow the achievement of the mentioned goals. Figures 1 and 2 present the high level architecture of the monitoring infrastructure. The interested reader can read a more detailed description in [29,30].

We propose a hybrid architecture using a hierarchical communication scheme to ensure scalability and a P2P-based communication scheme to allow multi-tenancy. In our opinion, a hybrid solution is the only viable alternative for scaling to an arbitrary number of data centers and the huge problem size makes it literally impossible to deploy any kind of centralized infrastructure. Even worse, service centralization would not be fault-tolerant. For these reasons, each cluster in our architecture is equipped with an independent monitoring infrastructure.

In order to scale to millions of data streams per sample interval, it is mandatory to shift preliminary computations (such as the sampling of a resource and

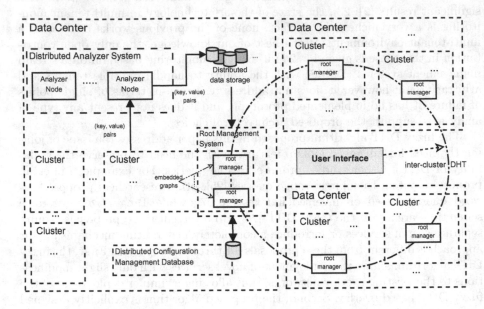

Fig. 1. Monitoring system architecture overview.

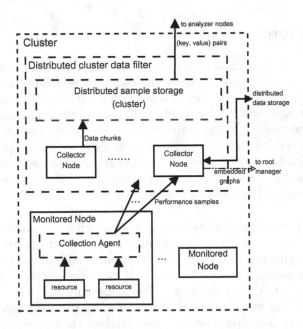

Fig. 2. Cluster architecture.

the performing of sanity checks on sampled data) as close as possible to the edge of the monitored infrastructure. Failure to do so would result in a system that unnecessarily processes potentially useless data. For this reason, collected resource data streams are initially filtered (or marked as invalid, anomalous) on the monitored nodes where a *collection agent* receives the samples from several probe processes. Probe processes are responsible for collecting periodically performance and/or utilization samples regarding a set of hardware and software resources. The collection agent performs preliminary validity checks on them, that are executed through dynamic, pluggable modules that receive in input the data stream and respond with TRUE or FALSE. If at least one check fails, the stream is tagged as invalid, but it is never discarded; this facilitates later debugging operations. The following checks are implemented now: missing value, value out of range, sequence of null values. Then, the collection agent updates the resource data streams and sends them to a set of associated collector nodes. We consider both the sending of uncoded (without compression) and coded (lossless compression) data. A detailed description of the collection agent has been presented by the authors in [31].

The collector node is the main component of the *distributed cluster data filter*. It receives the checked and coded resource data streams, performs the necessary decoding, applies low cost analyses on decoded data, and stores their results for a real-time plot or further analysis. In the former case, processing stops and the user is able to see immediately the behavior of the resource data streams. In order to support real-time analytics at large scale, at this level we adopt analytic approaches having linear computational complexity and adaptive implementation. Linear solutions permit to understand system behavior in real-time, so as to diagnose eventual problems and take timely corrective actions to meet service level objectives. Adaptivity allows analytic approaches to accommodate variable, heterogeneous data collected across the multiple levels of abstraction present in complex data center systems. Example analyses we implemented at this stage include:

1. computing moving averages of resource data streams, in order to provide a more stable representation of a node status;
2. aggregating (both temporally and spatially) node state representations to obtain global views of the cluster state conditions;
3. extracting trends for short-term prediction of resource consumption and of cluster state conditions;
4. detecting state changes and/or anomalies occurring in data streams for the erase of alarms and the adoption of recovering strategies;
5. correlating node state representations in order to identify dependencies among different nodes in the cluster and to exclude secondary flows.

Nodes and cluster state representations are then sent to two different storages: one for real-time plotting of the decoded and analyzed resource data streams, and one for non-real-time later processing at highest levels. The former storage for real-time plotting is handled by a modified version of OpenTSDB [32] that is able to plot a real-time short-term prediction of the resources trend. This analysis is performed using a linear regression and a Gaussian kernel. The latter storage for non-real-time processing, called *data sink*, receives data destined to further processing performed by the distributed analyzer described shortly. This solution reduces the number of files generated from one per node per unit time to a handful per cluster [33]. To enhance the performance of the storage engine, we chose to pack the resource data streams (few bytes per each) in larger chunks (64 KB by default) and to write them asynchronously to a distributed file system that can be scaled to the appropriate size by easily adding back-end nodes. In order to provide a homogeneous software layer (eg., Hbase coupling) and an open-source platform, and in order to support a map-reduce paradigm, the best possible choice is the Hadoop Distributed File System (HDFS). It allows extremely scalable computations, it is designed to run on commodity hardware, it is highly fault-tolerant, it provides high throughput access to application data, and it is suitable for applications that have large data sets.

In the latter case, data is made available to the *distributed analyzer system*. Its purpose is to compute more sophisticated analyses on the resource data streams, such as aggregation of information coming from different clusters, identification of correlated components in the system, anomaly detection and capacity planning. The data streams resulting from these analyses are persistently stored in the *distributed data storage*. Here, data is available as (key, value) pairs, where "key" is a unique identifier of a measure and "value" is usually a tuple of values describing it (e.g., timestamp, host name, service/process, name of the monitored performance index, actual value). The distributed analyzer system is composed by a set of analyzer nodes. Each analyzer node runs arbitrary batch jobs that analyze the state representation data streams of nodes and clusters. At this stage, we admit the implementation of more computational expensive analyses with respect to those applied at the cluster level. Now, analyses are applied only to small sets of representative information (i.e., nodes and cluster state representations) from which we require to obtain relevant information for management with high levels of accuracy. For example, analyses implemented at data center level are:

1. aggregation of cluster state representations to obtain global views of the data center state conditions;
2. long-term prediction of clusters and data center state conditions computed at different temporal scales and with different prediction horizons;
3. detection of changes and anomalous events in data center state conditions with the identification of which node(s) in the different clusters is the culprit.

We choose the Pig framework for the implementation of the analysis scripts [34]. Pig offers richer data structures over pure map-reduce, for example multivalued and nested dictionaries. Each Pig script is compiled into a series of equivalent map-reduce scripts that process the input data and write the results in a parallel way. Our scripts implement the analyses mentioned above. Further analyses can be easily supported by our architecture and implemented to satisfy more sophisticated requests.

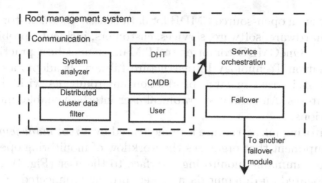

Fig. 3. The root management system.

Both the reduced streams representing the system state and the resource data streams processed by OpenTSDB must be written into a data storage. For the sake of performance, it is possible to avoid the reuse of the same structured storage. As matter of facts, the data storage:

- must scale with an increasing number of data streams;
- must be fault tolerant;
- should be designed towards the data management.

In this context, we choose Apache HBase [35] also because of the fact that it includes the homogeneity and the reuse of components. In our architecture, the HBase storage is responsible to preserve all the analyzed information about nodes, clusters and data center. Apache HBase is a distributed column-oriented database built on top of HDFS, designed from the ground-up to scale linearly just by adding nodes. It is not relational and it does not support SQL, but thanks to the proper space management properties, it is able to surpass a traditional RDBMS-based system by hosting very large and sparsely populated tables on clusters implemented on commodity hardware.

The information regarding the data center asset is stored in a *distributed configuration database*. In this way, we strive to avoid possible inconsistencies mainly due to a service being migrated or receiving more resources. The monitoring infrastructure associates data streams to the identifiers of the corresponding monitored resource. The configuration database is needed to store all information related to the asset of a cluster. Asset-related information includes a description of the resource metadata (name, id), placement (IP of the hosting node or virtual machine), sampling period, and a description of the time interval during which the resource is supposed to be assigned to a service. We think that it is a good idea to use off-the-shelf Configuration Management DataBase Systems (CMDBs). A CMDB is a repository of information related to all the components of an information system, and contains the details of the configuration items in the IT infrastructure. However, the majority of CMDBs is not natively fault tolerant. We address this shortcoming by replicating both its Web front-end and DB back-end. The configuration management database of our choice is

OneCMDB. It is an open-source CMDB for data centers that can store configurations such as hardware, software, services, customers, incidents, problems, RFCs and documents. OneCMDB conforms to IT Management best practice declared by the Information Technology Infrastructure Library. It adopts a client-server paradigm and it is used in large production environments with thousands of configuration items. An enhanced graphical user interface enables more effective system operations.

Each monitoring infrastructure is orchestrated by a *root management system*, a software component that organizes the workflow of monitoring operations and provides a programmable monitoring interface to the user (Fig. 3). All the root managers dislocated on different data centers are interconnected by an efficient DHT overlay routing network. In this first version of our prototype, the other main task carried out by a root manager is to forward early notifications of anomalies in the internal state of some resources to other interested, subscribed root managers. In this way, it is possible to anticipate the performance degradation of services depending on these failing resources.

The orchestration module is the heart of the monitoring system since it orchestrates the operations of the other aforementioned components (collector, data filter, analyzer). One of its main tasks is to trigger and to abort the execution of batch jobs in the distributed cluster data filter and in the analyzer nodes. The communication module is a simple messaging system used to interact with the other components of the monitoring architecture in order to communicate relevant information (such as anomalies in some resource state) to other monitoring systems dislocated in different data centers. The root manager node also receives commands from the user interface; these commands are forwarded to and processed by the orchestration module. The user interface is basically a Web-based application running on any selected node. It manages the resources owned by an application and provides a programmable dashboard with figures of merit, diagrams and configuration parameters (monitored nodes, resources, performance indexes, sampling intervals). Each cluster and each monitored process is represented using embedded OpenTSDB graphs, while the system view is represented using a similar but customized interface that supports also long-term predictions, aggregation analysis, detection and capacity planning. The failover module ensures fault tolerance by identifying which root managers are compromised and by restoring a safe state. To this purpose, each root manager runs part of the replica of the other root managers in the same data center. If a root manager fails, the replica becomes the master until the former one is restored.

When a service is installed on the nodes, the collection and analysis processes supply this information to the root management system, which stores it into the distributed configuration database. At each application deployment, a list of the involved nodes is defined. A unique key is associated to this list; both the key and the list are shared through the DHT with each root management system. The root management system responsible for the largest number of involved nodes selects its best root manager on the basis of multiple configurable metrics. Finally, the selected root manager becomes the service leader.

Each data center is composed by a set of root manager nodes connected through a Pastry-based Distributed Hash Table (DHT) called *fuzzy DHT*, which has been presented and simulated in [30]. We chose Pastry [6] because it is a generic, scalable and efficient substrate for P2P applications that forms a decentralized, self-organizing and fault-tolerant overlay network. Pastry provides efficient request routing, deterministic object location, and load balancing in an application-independent manner. Furthermore, it provides mechanisms that support and facilitate application-specific object replication, caching, and fault recovery. For example, it is possible to efficiently lookup all CPU utilization time series in a given cluster (or a replica if the origin source is unavailable). The DHT communication module implements all the needed overlay routing functions. The root management system is built upon a set of custom Python and Java modules. The DHT is implemented through the freepastry libraries. The publish-subscribe mechanism used to broadcast alerts to the interested root managers is implemented through Scribe [36]. We previously discussed these aspects from a security point-of-view in [37].

We used exclusively open-source tools that can be modified and adapted for our goals. We used GNU/Linux Debian, Ubuntu and Fedora OSs in different experimental testbeds, enhanced with the software packages from the Cloudera repository (CDH4). The languages used for the deployment of our modules are Bash (v4.2.36), Python (v2.7), Java (v1.6), JavaScript and C (where efficiency is needed, such as in our modified monitor probes). The batch processing framework is Hadoop, version 2.0. Our choice is motivated by the dramatic scalability improvement with respect to traditional RDBMS-based data storage architectures under random, write-intensive data access patterns [38]. To avoid single points of failure and to ensure service continuity, we enforce redundancy of every component of the monitoring architecture. Whenever possible, we deploy our solution using software that can be easily replicated. In other cases, we wrap the component through custom scripts that detect failures and restart it, in case.

We implemented the user interface using the Django MVC framework and the JQuery library to enhance the presentation of data. The responsiveness of the application is improved through the adoption of AJAX-based techniques and the Web server Apache v.2.2.

4 Analysis

We perform experimental analyses for evaluating the ability of the proposed monitoring architecture in satisfying all requirements of scalability, effectiveness, resiliency and multi-tenancy. Due to the limited space, in this section we only report analysis results about the scalability of our solution. We evaluate the scalability of the proposed architecture in terms of number of monitored resource data streams. In particular, we aim to find out:

- how many resource data streams can be monitored per node (intra-node scalability);
- how many nodes can be monitored in a cluster (intra-cluster scalability).

Highest level scalability (intra-data center scalability) is left for future extensions and strongly depends on both resource behaviors and aggregation results obtained through analytics computed in the distributed analyzer system. In this paper, we used the Amazon EC2 IaaS platform. In the considered infrastructure, the backing storage is shared across the instances (EBS), and the theoretical network connectivity is up to 1Gbps. The virtual machines are running instances of the TPC-W and RUBiS benchmark suites. MapReduce jobs queries are used for data distribution and analysis. We perform Map-Reduce versions of several performance analyses having different computational costs, including the moving average and the Principal Component Analysis (PCA) over more than 1 h of data collected from 2048 monitored nodes. We emphasize that the results are strongly influenced by the resource consumption of the TSDB component, and the tuning of this trade-off is out of the scope of this paper. However, we measure that the PCA (i.e., the most computational expensive analysis) requires an average of 5 min when computed over 8 collector nodes using around the 85 % of CPU (the 12.5 % was used for collector process). This result shows that the behavior of a single cluster during the collection of over more than 6M of resource data streams per second can be analyzed (in batches) within quasi real-time constraints.

In each monitored node, one probe is dedicated to system-related performance monitoring through the output of the vmstat and sar monitors. The remaining probes are process-related through pidstat and nethogs2 monitors. This system probe collects 25 different performance indexes, while each process probe collects 23 different resource data streams. The sampling interval is configured at 1 s for each probe in order to emulate the most challenging scenario.

4.1   Intra-node Scalability

In the first experimental testbed, we evaluate how many resource data streams can be handled for each monitored node. We use one collector node and one analyzer node running a single script that computes the moving average for every resource data stream. The detail of the resources of the monitored node is the following: micro instance, 613 MB memory, up to 2 EC2 Compute Units (Dual-Core AMD Opteron (tm) Processor 2218 HE, cpu 2.6 GHz, cache size 1,024 KB), EBS storage, dedicated network bandwidth of theoretically 100 Mbps per node.

Table 1 reports the average resource consumption (percentage of CPU, memory (RAM) and network (NET) utilization) of the collection agent as a function of the number of monitored resource data streams. We performed tests on both uncoded (*without compression*) and coded (*lossless compression*) data in order to evaluate the impact of compression on the scalability of the different resources. Then, we evaluate how the use of the *Adaptive algorithm* that we proposed in [39] improves the scalability of our architecture. The Adaptive algorithm is able to adapt the frequency of sampling and data updating to minimize computational and communication costs, while guaranteeing high accuracy of monitored information. From these tests, we see that at intra-node level, sending data streams has a negligible impact on the network bandwidth, despite the fact that it is reduced of about 50 % by using lossless compression and more than 80 % by

Table 1. Average resource utilization of the collection agent.

#probes	#resource data streams	Without compression			Lossless compression			Adaptive algorithm		
		CPU (%)	RAM (%)	NET (%)	CPU (%)	RAM (%)	NET (%)	CPU (%)	RAM (%)	NET (%)
1	25	0.0	0.4	0.005	0.3	0.4	0.002	0.1	0.5	0.001
2	48	0.1	0.5	0.009	0.5	0.5	0.004	0.1	0.5	0.002
4	94	0.1	0.6	0.019	1.1	0.6	0.009	0.2	0.7	0.004
8	186	0.1	1.0	0.041	1.8	0.9	0.019	0.3	1.0	0.008
16	370	0.3	1.4	0.085	2.9	1.4	0.041	0.4	1.4	0.016
32	738	0.5	2.5	0.173	4.1	2.6	0.083	0.6	2.7	0.032
64	1474	0.6	4.7	0.352	6.0	4.8	0.162	0.8	4.6	0.069
128	2946	0.9	9.4	0.681	9.8	9.3	0.337	1.2	9.5	0.127
256	5890	2.5	18.7	1.392	23.1	18.3	0.641	3.1	18.8	0.266

using the Adaptive algorithm. We see also that the most used resource without data compression or with Adaptive algorithm is the memory, while with lossless compression the most used resource is the CPU. At 128 probes, both the CPU and memory utilizations are less than 10 %. This threshold is commonly used as the largest fraction of resource utilization that administrators are comfortable devoting to monitoring. We have adopted this threshold as our target maximum resource utilization for the monitoring system. Hence, on each monitored node, we can collect up to 128 probes for a total of 2,946 resource data streams per second. We recall that a period of one second is much shorter than commonly adopted sampling periods that typically do not go below one minute.

4.2 Intra-cluster Scalability

In the following set of experiments, we consider nodes within a cluster, monitored with the same probe setup. We measure the resource consumption of the collector at cluster level with or without compression efforts and with the Adaptive algorithm.

Table 2 reports the average resource consumption of the collector node as a function of the number of monitored nodes. From this table, we see that without compression the most used resource is the network that allows the monitoring of at most 64 nodes (or 188,544 resource data streams) in a cluster. On the contrary, compressing data strongly impacts the CPU utilization. Despite that, the compression of data allows to monitor more than 128 nodes or $2,946 \cdot 128 = 377,088$ resource data streams per second. By using the Adaptive algorithm we are able to monitor up to 512 nodes per collector, meaning 1.5M resource data streams per second.

Table 2. Average resource utilization of the collector in the distributed cluster data filter.

#monitored nodes	#resource data streams	Without compression		Lossless compression		Adaptive algorithm	
		CPU (%)	NET (%)	CPU (%)	NET (%)	CPU (%)	NET (%)
1	2946	0.1	0.971	0.6	0.450	0.1	0.189
2	5892	0.1	1.943	0.9	0.899	0.1	0.355
4	11784	0.2	3.838	2.0	1.797	0.2	0.748
8	23568	0.4	7.763	3.6	3.594	0.4	1.463
16	47136	0.9	15.421	8.1	7.186	0.9	3.001
32	94272	1.9	31.055	17.1	14.374	1.9	5.872
64	188544	3.2	61.980	33.6	28.751	3.2	11.711
128	377088	-	-	69.9	57.539	6.1	23.404
256	754176	-	-	-	-	12.5	47.096
512	1508352	-	-	-	-	23.7	93.691

Table 3. Average resource utilization of a collector process.

#monitored nodes	#resource data streams	Collector		
		#nodes	CPU (%)	NET (%)
256	754176	1	12.5	47.096
512	1508352	2	12.8	48.327
1024	3016704	4	12.2	46.851
2048	6033408	8	12.4	46.908

As further result, we add collector nodes and increment the number of monitored hosts to evaluate the scalability of the distributed cluster data filter. Table 3 reports the average resource utilization across the collector nodes. We keep adding collectors up to 2,048 monitored nodes. We also add more HDFS and HBASE nodes to support the write throughput when the number of nodes becomes higher than 256. We keep 256 as limit in the number of nodes since overcoming the 50 % of incoming network bandwidth of the collector node means overcoming the 100 % of outcoming bandwidth. In this scenario, by using the Adaptive algorithm we are able to monitor about 6M resource data streams by using an average 12.5 % of CPU and 47.3 % of network bandwidth.

This analysis on scalability reveals that the proposed architecture is able to collect and process:

- more than 2900 resource data streams per second, from 128 probes, on a single monitored node, with a resource utilization <10 %;

Table 4. Average resource utilization of a TSDB process over the distributed cluster data filter.

#graphs	#resource data streams	CPU (%)	NET In (%)	NET Out (%)
10	4500	10,3	0,077	0,131
25	11250	25,1	0,163	0,265
50	22500	49,8	0,329	0,538
100	30000	66,4	0,432	0,714
100	45000	98,2	0,671	1,099

- more than 754000 resource data streams per second, from 256 different monitored nodes using a single collector node;
- more than 6000000 resource data streams per second per cluster.

By using the TSDB component, every collector node provides the real-time plotting. In Table 4, we report the resource consumption of this process. In this testbed we request an increasing number of graphs (from 10 to 100) and we set a refresh rate of 15 s for each graph. As for the collector process, the memory consumption of the TSDB component is negligible with respect to the CPU consumption. The TSDB process uses about the 66 % of CPU while plotting 100 graphs (i.e. 30000 resource data streams) for each collector node every 15 s. Moreover, Table 4 shows that both the incoming and outcoming network bandwidth consumptions are negligible if compared to the network consumptions of the collector process. By using the 12.5 % and the 66.4 % of CPU for the collector and TSDB respectively, more than the 20 % of spare CPU can be used for other purposes like the execution of the Distributed sample storage jobs.

4.3   DHT Scalability

In the last section we evaluate the efficiency of the DHT-based communication mechanism. Table 5 shows the average number of exchanged messages per lookup process as a function of the number of root managers in the monitoring infrastructure. We compare our implementation with two other popular P2P communication schemes: a flood-based system (like the one provided by the Gnutella file sharing network) and a probabilistic flood-based one. We observe that every algorithm shows an increment in the traffic generated with each query. However, the overhead growth of the flood-based and probabilistic flood algorithms is much more evident than the overhead growth of the fuzzy DHT algorithm. The main reason of this overhead lies in the fact that, for every lookup performed, the number of nodes to visit is much higher. The probabilistic flood-based algorithm can randomly decide to not forward queries across nodes; this explains the reduced overhead with respect to the pure flood-based solution. On the other hand, the better scalability of fuzzy DHT is due to its ability to route queries only to a reduced fraction of nodes that have an high probability of hosting the requested resource.

Table 5. Number of exchanged messages as a function of overlay network size.

Root managers	Messages fuzzy DHT	Messages flood-based	Messages probabilistic flood-based
1	1	1	1
2	2	2	1
4	2	4	2
8	3	7	5
16	4	15	13
32	5	31	26
64	6	62	48

5 Conclusions

In this paper, we proposed a novel hybrid architecture for monitoring large-scale, geo-graphically distributed network infrastructures spread across multiple data centers. Architectural choices are made in order to satisfy scalability, effectiveness, resiliency and multi-tenancy requirements. These choices are mandatory when you have to support gathering and analysis operations of huge numbers of data streams coming from cloud system monitors. The proposed architecture is already integrated with on-line analyzers working at different temporal scales. Our preliminary experiments show the potential scalability limits of the monitoring system: more than 6M of resource data streams per cluster, per second. All these operations of data streams are carried out within real-time constraints in the order of seconds thus demonstrating that huge margins of improvement are feasible.

References

1. Dean, J., Lopes, J.: MapReduce: simplified data processing on large clusters. In: OSDI 2004, 6th Symposium on Operating Systems Design and Implementation, USENIX Association (2004)
2. Calder, B., et al.: Windows Azure storage: a highly available cloud storage service with strong consistency. In: SOSP 2011, 23rd ACM Symposium on Operating System Principles. ACM (2011)
3. Shvachko, K., et al.: The hadoop distributed file system. In: MSST 2010, 26th Symposium on Massive Storage Systems and Technologies. IEEE Computer Society (2010)
4. Gantz, J., Reinsel, D.: The digital universe in 2020: big data, bigger digital shadows, and biggest growth in the far east (2012). http://www.emc.com/leadership/digital-universe/iview/big-data-2020.htm
5. Traverse: distributed, scalable, high-availability architecture (2010–2013). http://www.zyrion.com/company/whitepapers

6. Rowstron, A., Druschel, P.: Pastry: scalable, decentralized object location, and routing for large-scale peer-to-peer systems. In: Guerraoui, R. (ed.) Middleware 2001. LNCS, vol. 2218, pp. 329–350. Springer, Heidelberg (2001)
7. Litvinova, A., Engelmann, C., Scott, S.L.: A proactive fault tolerance framework for high-performance computing. In: PDCN 2010, 9th IASTED International Conference on Parallel and Distributed Computing and Networks (PDCN2010). ACTA Press (2010)
8. Massie, M.L., Chun, B.N., Culler, D.E.: The Ganglia distributed monitoring system: design, implementation, and experience. Parallel Comput. **30**, 817–840 (2004)
9. Keller, A., Ludwig, H.: The WSLA framework: specifying and monitoring service level agreements for web services. J. Netw. Syst. Manag. **11**, 57–81 (2003)
10. Surhone, L.M., Tennoe, M.T., Henssonow, S.F.: OpenNMS. Betascript Publishing, Mauritius (2011)
11. Olups, R.: Zabbix 1.8 Network Monitoring. Packt Publishing, Birmingham (2010)
12. Badger, M.: Zenoss Core Network and System Monitoring. Packt Publishing Ltd., Birmingham (2008)
13. Kundu, D., Lavlu, S.: Cacti 0.8 Network Monitoring. Packt Publishing, Birmingham (2009)
14. Davis, C.: Graphite - Scalable Realtime Graphing (2013). http://graphite.wikidot.com
15. Josephsen, D.: Building a Monitoring Infrastructure with Nagios. Prentice Hall, Upper Saddle River (2007)
16. Rabkin, A., Katz, R.: Chukwa: a system for reliable large-scale log collection. In: LISA 2010, 24th International Conference on Large Installation System Administration. USENIX Association (2010)
17. Hoffman, S., Souza, S.D.: Apache Flume: Distributed Log Collection for Hadoop. Packt Publishing, Birmingham (2013)
18. Sacerdoti, F.D., Katz, M.J., Massie, M.L., Culler, D.E.: Wide area cluster monitoring with Ganglia. In: Proceedings of Cluster Computing (2003)
19. Renesse, R.V., Birman, K.P., Vogels, W.: Astrolabe: a robust and scalable technology for distributed system monitoring, management, and data mining. ACM Trans. Comput. Syst. **21**, 164–206 (2003)
20. Lv, Q., Cao, P., Cohen, E., Li, K., Shenker, S.: Search and replication in unstructured peer-to-peer networks. In: ICS 2002, 16th International Conference on Supercomputing. ACM (2002)
21. Babu, S., Subramanian, L., Widom, J.: A data stream management system for network traffic management. In: NRDM 2001, 1st Workshop on Network-Related Data Management (2001)
22. Cranor, C., Johnson, T., Spataschek, O.: Gigascope: a stream database for network applications. In: SIGMOD 2003, 2003 ACM SIGMOD International Conference on Management of Data. ACM (2003)
23. Voicu, R., Newman, H., Cirstoiu, C.: MonALISA: an agent based, dynamic service system to monitor, control and optimize distributed systems. Comput. Phys. Commun. **180**, 2472–2498 (2009)
24. Hasselmeyer, P., d'Heureuse, N.: Towards holistic multi-tenant monitoring for virtual data centers. In: NOMS 2010, 2010 IEEE/IFIP Network Operations and Management Symposium Workshops. IEEE Computer Society (2010)
25. Liu, B., Lee, W.C., Lee, D.L.: Supporting complex multi-dimensional queries in p2p systems. In: Proceedings of 25th IEEE International Conference on Distributed Computing Systems (ICDCS 2005), Columbus, OH (2005)

26. Reynolds, P., Vahdat, A.: Efficient peer-to-peer keyword searching. In: Endler, M., Schmidt, D.C. (eds.) Middleware 2003. LNCS, vol. 2672, pp. 21–40. Springer, Heidelberg (2003)
27. Joung, Y.J., Fang, C.T., Yang, L.W.: Keyword search in dht-based peer-to-peer networks. In: Proceedings of 25th IEEE International Conference on Distributed Computing Systems (ICDCS 2005), Columbus, OH (2005)
28. Tang, C., Xu, Z., Mahalingam, M.: psearch: information retrieval in structured overlays. SIGCOMM Comput. Commun. Rev. **33**, 89–94 (2003)
29. Andreolini, M., Pietri, M., Tosi, S., Balboni, A.: Monitoring large cloud-based systems. In: CLOSER 2014, 4th International Conference on Cloud Computing and Services Science. SCITEPRESS Digital Library (2014)
30. Andreolini, M., Lancellotti, R., Yu, P.S.: A flexible and efficient lookup algorithm for peer-to-peer systems. In: IPDPS 2009, 23rd IEEE International Parallel and Distributed Processing Symposium. IEEE Computer Society (2009)
31. Andreolini, M., Colajanni, M., Pietri, M.: A scalable architecture for real-time monitoring of large information systems. In: NCCA 2012, 2nd IEEE Symposium on Network Cloud Computing and Applications. IEEE Computer Society (2012)
32. Sigoure, B.: OpenTSDB, a distributed, scalable Time Series Database (2010). http://opentsdb.net
33. Andreolini, M., Colajanni, M., Tosi, S.: A software architecture for the analysis of large sets of data streams in cloud infrastructures. In: CIT 2011, 11th IEEE International Conference on Computer and Information Technology. IEEE Computer Society (2011)
34. Olston, C., et al.: Pig Latin: a not-so-foreign language for data processing. In: SIGMOD 2008, 2008 ACM SIGMOD International Conference on Management of Data. ACM, New York (2008)
35. George, L.: HBase: The Definitive Guide. O'Reilly Media, Sebastopol (2011)
36. Castro, M., Druschel, P., Kermarrec, A.M., Rowstron, A.: Scribe: a large-scale and decentralized application-level multicast infrastructure. IEEE J. Sel. Areas Commun. (JSAC) **20**, 1489–1499 (2002)
37. Marchetti, M., Colajanni, M., Messori, M.: Selective and early threat detection in large networked systems. In: CIT 2010, 10th IEEE International Conference on Computer and Information Technology. IEEE Computer Society (2010)
38. Leu, J.S., Yee, Y.S., Chen, W.L.: Comparison of map-reduce and SQL on large-scale data processing. In: ISPA 2010, 1st International Symposium on Parallel and Distributed Processing with Applications. IEEE Computer Society (2010)
39. Pietri, M., Tosi, S., Andreolini, M., Colajanni, M.: Real-time adaptive algorithm for resource monitoring. In: CNSM 2013, 9th International Conference on Network and Service Management, Zurich, Switzerland, CNSM (2013)

A Data Location Control Model for Cloud Service Deployments

Kaniz Fatema[1]([⊠]), Philip D. Healy[1], Vincent C. Emeakaroha[1],
John P. Morrison[1], and Theo Lynn[2]

[1] Irish Centre for Cloud Computing and Commerce,
University College Cork, Cork, Ireland
kafatema@ucc.ic
[2] Irish Centre for Cloud Computing and Commerce,
Dublin City University, Dublin, Ireland

Abstract. A data location control model for Cloud services is presented.
The model is intended for use by Cloud SaaS providers that collect
personal data that can potentially be stored and processed at multiple geographic locations. It incorporates users' location preferences into
authorization decisions by converting them into XACML policies that are
consulted before data transfer operations. The model also ensures that
the users have visibility into the location of their data and are informed
when the location of their data changes. A prototype of the model has
been implemented and was used to perform validation tests in various
Cloud setups. These scenarios serve to demonstrate how location control
can be integrated on top of existing public and private Cloud platforms.
A sketch is also provided of an architecture that embeds location control
functionality directly into the OpenStack Cloud platform. We further
propose an enhancement to the model that alters its behaviour from
being restrictive to prescriptive so that Cloud providers can copy data
to a non-preferred locations in case of emergency. Under this approach,
the number of authorized vs unauthorized transfers can be made publicly
available by the provider as an assurance measure for consumers.

Keywords: Authorization system · Access control · Data location ·
XACML · Cloud computing

1 Introduction

Cloud Computing offers a new style of computing that allows consumers to pay
only for the services used and frees them from the management overhead of
the underlying infrastructure. Although Cloud Computing has gained significant traction in recent years, surveys have consistently shown that consumers'
concerns around security and loss of control over data are hindering adoption
[7,23]. Additionally, the physical location of data can have an impact on its vulnerability to disclosure and can have implications for service quality and legal

M. Helfert et al. (Eds.): CLOSER 2014, CCIS 512, pp. 117–133, 2015.
DOI: 10.1007/978-3-319-25414-2_8

consequences [1,13]. Many regulations such as HIPAA and the EU Data Protection Directive impose restrictions on the movement of data between geographical locations. Data location therefore represents a sensitive issue for Cloud service providers. Existing and potential customers seek assurance that Cloud service providers will act as faithful stewards of information entrusted to them, and the provider itself wishes to avoid falling foul of data protection rules and other regulations.

However, these concerns must be balanced against the Cloud provider's desire to maintain redundancy and operational efficiency. There are a number of valid reasons for copying data to geographically dispersed locations such as risk mitigation, reduce operational expenditure, maintenance and localised caching for a better performance. Enterprises that offer Cloud services must therefore balance the benefits of migrating data against concerns relating to trustworthiness in the eyes of users and regulatory compliance.

Users' concerns about how their data are disseminated and used can be addressed by allowing them to specify policies about how they wish their data to be used and assuring them of the enforcement of this policy. In the context of data location, this assurance can be provided in two ways (a) with a transparency mechanism that allows users to view the locations where their data are being stored and (b) with a notification mechanism that informs them when there is a change to the *status quo*. If the users' policies are to carry any weight then they must be consulted before operations are performed that would result in movement or remote duplication so that violations can be avoided.

A means of addressing this challenge is to implement an authorization system that inputs queries relating to data relocation and returns results that indicate the permissibility of the proposed actions. Of course, such a system is of little value unless it is appropriately integrated into the service provider's internal processes and mechanisms. As such, there is a residual trustworthiness issue in that the users must trust that this integration has taken place and that the decisions of the authorization system are being honoured. These issues could be addressed through independent verification mechanisms such as trustmarks, audits and assurance services [17].

Although the basic concept of an authorization system [9,15] is to protect access to secured resources, it may play an important role in Cloud data management since Cloud service delivery can involve significant amounts of data transmission and storage. SaaS providers offering services, such as web applications, may accumulate a large amount of personal data like names, addresses, medical records, purchase history and so on during the operation of the service. The management, processing and storage of such data while considering customers' data location choices is challenging. This paper describes a mechanism for SaaS providers, who might in turn be using services from IaaS and PaaS layers, to incorporate the location choices of their customers while managing and storing data in Clouds. The ISO/IEC 10181-3:1996 standard access control framework is used as the technological foundation. The following issues are addressed:

1. Capturing users' location preferences as policies that can be automatically consulted, providing an authorization mechanism for data movement decisions that takes user-specific policies into account, providing users with visibility into the location of their data and ensuring that users are informed when the location of their data changes.
2. Testing the validity of the model by deploying it into various Cloud setups.
3. A proposal to allow prescriptive as well as restrictive behaviour to allow data transfers in case of emergency while quantifying the location assurance provided by the provider.

The remainder of this paper is organized as follows: Sect. 2 presents an analysis of related work. Section 3 provides background information on authorization systems and how they can play a role in Cloud data management. Section 4 presents the design of the proposed location control model, while Sect. 5 provides the technical details and Sect. 6 provides the results of validation tests. Finally, Sect. 7 concludes the paper and suggests future research directions.

2 Related Work

The Data Location Assurance Service proposed by Noman *et al.* is based on an approach where the Cloud service provider sends regular updates to enterprises about the location of their data [20]. The enterprise in turn provides location assurance to users by providing information on whether the data are in their preferred location in a simple yes/no format. This approach relies heavily on the trustworthiness of the Cloud service provider. Massonet *et al.* describe how negotiation can be used to integrate service providers' policies with those of infrastructure providers in a federated Cloud environment [18]. The infrastructure provider's security policy states the availability of logging facilities, logging type and monitoring, while the service provider's policy states its security requirements. A virtual machine is migrated to a site only if its security policy matches with the security requirements of the service provider. An audit log is created from the collaboration of between service provider and infrastructure provider. The location of data is identified through the presence of data centre's certificate in the audit log. Neither of these systems allow for detailed location preferences, such as multiple preferred geographic regions, to be collected from end users and enforced automatically.

Numerous implementations of policy-based authorization have been proposed in order to protect access to sensitive data in the Cloud [4,6,14]. A distributed authorization system architecture for Cloud services was proposed by Almutairi *et al.* where each Cloud layer has a virtual resource manager that protects access to the virtualized resources of its layer using an access control module [2]. Ries *et al.* proposed a policy-based approach to location issues [21]. However, information on how to incorporate location into policy or how to enforce policies is missing there.

In contrast to other policy languages, such as P3P [8], EPAL [3], PERMIS [5] and FlexDDPL [22], XACML (an OASIS standard) provides both a policy language and an access control decision request/response language and also specifies

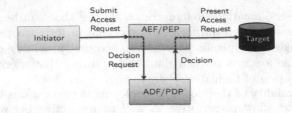

Fig. 1. ISO/IEC 10181-3 access control framework (ACF).

a policy evaluation engine. Chadwick *et al.* have modified the XACML model to allow multiple policy languages and multiple policies of independent authorities to be supported by the model, making it suitable for use in Cloud scenarios [6]. We chose to adopt XACML for our location control model due to its standardised format and built-in enforcement mechanism. It is also the most widely used language for defining security policy [24].

3   Background Information

In this section, we present some background information on authorization systems and how the location control model can be integrated with Cloud deployments. We further specify the scope and constraints of our solution.

3.1   Authorization Systems

Access control/authorization is a process of determining whether a request to access (*e.g.* read, write, delete, copy, etc.) a resource object (*e.g.* file, database, program, system component) by a subject (*e.g.* user, system or process) should be granted or denied. The access control/authorization system can grant or deny the request based on whether or not certain policy constrains have been satisfied. ISO/IEC 10181- 3:1996 [15] defines a generic access control framework (ACF) as shown in Fig. 1. It consists of four components: (i) initiators (subjects), (ii) targets (resource objects), (iii) access control enforcement functions (AEFs) – commonly known as policy enforcement points (PEPs) – and (iv) access control decision functions (ADFs) – commonly known as policy decision points (PDPs). The initiators submit access requests (also known as user requests) that specify the operation to be performed on the target. The AEF transforms the request into one or more decision requests (also known as authorization queries) and sends these to the ADF. The ADF decides whether a decision request should be granted or denied based on the provided policies and sends the decision back to the AEF.

An access decision can contain obligations, such as sending e-mail to the data subject or recording the permitted access in a log. These obligations are enforced by the PEP while executing the access decision.

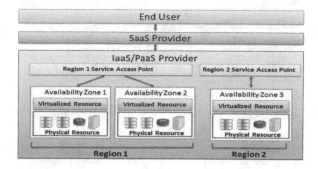

Fig. 2. Location aware Cloud usage model.

3.2 Use Case

Figure 2 shows an overview of our system model and how it integrates with Cloud deployments. The model considers interactions among three different groups of stakeholders: (i) Cloud IaaS/PaaS providers, (ii) Cloud SaaS providers and (iii) End users.

Cloud IaaS/PaaS Providers – For the purposes of this use case, we assume that the Cloud service providers are either IaaS or PaaS providers who offer virtualized resources/environment to the enterprises (*i.e.*, the SaaS providers) as services. The services are offered in separate regions, as shown in Fig. 2. They deploy resource instances and data according to the instructions of their customers and do not move data without being instructed by the customers. For example, Amazon EC2 provisioning currently works in this manner. Each region is identified by a unique name and is accessed via specified access points that act as a gateways to the service. Each region may consist of a number of availability zones, as shown in Fig. 2, where the instances and data can be copied to provide better availability in the event of a failure. Customers can choose one or more availability zones where their data and service instances can be replicated.

Cloud SaaS Providers – Cloud SaaS providers are the customers of IaaS and PaaS services. They compose their SaaS services over the IaaS or PaaS services to offer them to the end users. These services may be designed to collect and process the end users' personal data. Depending on their organizational needs, a SaaS provider can choose to put their services in more than one regions and a number of availability zones in each region. SaaS providers are typically enterprises that manage the customers' data and are responsible for instructing the Cloud IaaS/PaaS providers correctly about which data are to be stored in which regions.

End Users/Data Owners – End users are the persons who are consuming the service. SaaS providers may collect personal data from end users which are later stored and processed in the Cloud environment. The end users who are sharing their personal data are referred to as *data owners*.

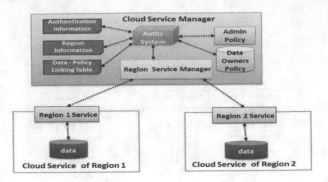

Fig. 3. The Cloud service manager (CSM) manages services and data in different Cloud regions.

This model assumes data to be of any format which should have two properties: (i) it should be identified by one uniquely identifiable name, *DataID*, and (ii) it is expected to be treated as one unit while actions (*e.g.* copy, read, write) are performed on it. The idea of having a unique identifier within a Cloud is not an impractical assumption as each Cloud user has a unique account which can be used or combined to form the unique identifier. In federated scenarios involving multiple participants a number of Cloud and identifier linking mechanisms can be used to create a globally unique identifier.

The granularity of data depends on the application scenario. It can be applied to a file or a set of files grouped under one folder, or a database entry. The unique identifier of the data, DataID, and the identifier of the policy, PolicyID, that is applicable for protecting the data, are linked together by the model. This linking will allow the policy that is relevant for that data to be evaluated while a request for performing an action (*e.g.* copy, read, write) on data is received. As policy is linked to a DataID regardless of the format of data the model will protect the access of any type of data based on the relevant policy.

4   Data Location Control

This section presents the technical details of the model and how its functionality can be extended to make it a prescriptive model from a restrictive one. The core of our approach is a Cloud service manager (CSM) that manages access to all Cloud data and services using an authorization system. The authorization system evaluates two types of policies when making an access decision based upon an access request. The first is the organizational administrative policy that specifies the enterprise roles and their attributed actions on services or data (*e.g.*, a marketing officer can execute a service, read the data and so on) or the roles of other external services to perform actions on their protected data. This administrative policy is executed for all access requests. The second type of policy consulted is the data owner's specific policy. All the data owners' policies are stored in the data owners' policy store. The service manager also includes a user authentication information table for managing user authentications, a region information table that details the regions where each data set, identified by a DataID is stored and a data-policy linking table that correlates each PolicyID to a DataID in order to retrieve the correct policy of the data owner for a specific data set. Figure 3 depicts how the region service manager receives instructions from the authorization system on where to store or retrieve data.

4.1   Intra-Service Interaction Strategy

This section discusses the interaction strategy used to manage data locations within a SaaS deployment. The discussion is partitioned into four catagories: inputting data, accessing data, updating data location and checking location.

Data Input – To use the SaaS, the end users first need to register for it. During the registration process, the user specifies authentication information (typically a user name and password or credentials) that is stored by the service provider to identify the user. The authentication information provided by each user is associated with a *DataID* that identifies the data of this user. The user provides a policy expressing her preferred primary location for storing the data. It also specifies alternative locations where data can be moved for different reasons, for example, to achieve better performance or cheaper cost. The data owner's policy is provided with a PolicyID, which is also linked to the DataID in the data-policy linking table as shown in Fig. 3. Each DataID is linked to a region information table that contains the current locations of the data identified by the DataID. This information is updated whenever the data location changes.

Accessing Data – All the requests for accessing data (*e.g.* reading the data or processing the data) goes to the CSM's authorization system. The CSM first gets the data owner's PolicyID in the data-policy linking table and retrieves the policy from the data owners' policy store. The administrative policy and the data owner's policy are evaluated against the access request. If the policies evaluations are successful, the requested access is granted. The authorization system can be configured with various static conflict resolution strategies [12] or can obtain the conflict resolution strategy dynamically [19] to resolve the conflicts between the administrative policy and data owner's policy.

Updating Data Location – The Cloud service administrator continuously monitors the performance of the services. If there is a need to copy the data to another location, she places a permission request to the CSM authorization system. The CSM accesses the data owner's policy and the administrative policy to evaluate them as described previously. If the policy allows for copying to the new location, then the data are copied and the region information table is updated to reflect these changes. If the user requires notification upon data location change, then the authorization system enforces this through the obligation enforcer.

Checking Location – When a user wants to query the location of her data, she first logs in to the service with her access credentials so that the service can identify the data she owns. To allow the user access the region information, either the administrator's policy or the data owner's policy has to allow it as the authorization system evaluates these policies to determine the access right. If any of the policies return "Grant" then the user is given the requested information.

4.2 Inter-cloud Data Outsourcing

To achieve better efficiency and scalability, SaaS providers may need to outsource the processing of end users' data. To realise this strategy, the SaaS provider maintains an external Cloud information table to store the information of the external Cloud services with copies of the data for each DataID. This table is linked with the region information table that contains the information of regions where the SaaS provider host its own service and originally stores the data, as seen in Fig. 4.

The SaaS provider's administrative policy expresses which external services are allowed to access their protected data and each data owner's policy specifies the allowed locations where his/her data can be copied. When an external service requests permission from the CSM's authorization system to transferring data to a certain location of their Cloud, the administrative policy along with each data owner's policy are evaluated. If the administrative policy or the data owner policy does not allow data transfer to the specified locations, then the permission is denied. If the request is accepted, the data along with the policy of the data owner are sent to the external service. A Service Level Agreement (SLA) negotiation process may take place between the SaaS provider and the external service provider in order to ensure that the data owner policy is respected upon any access request to the data. The external service provider may use the same PolicyID and DataID or may assign new IDs according to its organizational format. When assigning new IDs, there must be a link to the old ones for traceability. The external service provider maintains the outsourced data location similar to the approach described in Sect. 4.1. However, in this case access is granted based on the data owner's policy since the external service provider might have a different administrative policy.

A scheme similar to that for viewing location information as mentioned in Sect. 4.1 is provided to allow data owners to view their data location entries in the external Cloud information table. To view the data location information, there are two options. The end user (data owner) can access this information through the default SaaS originally hosting her data. The default SaaS provider is then responsible for acquiring this information from the external service provider. The external service provider's administrative policy can be written in a way to allow this access. This can be specified in the SLA document with the external service provider. Alternatively, since the external service provider evaluates the data owners policy upon receipt of an access request for a user's data, the data owner's policy can be used to allow the necessary access to the data location information. Figure 4 shows how data location can be controlled by the CSM's authorization systems for two different service managers.

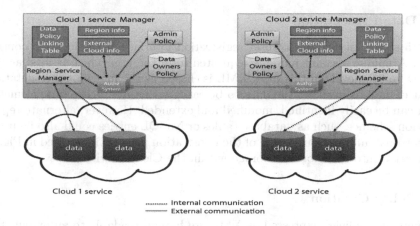

Fig. 4. Controlling data location across multiple Clouds.

4.3 Quantifying Location Assurance

The location control model was originally designed as a purely restrictive measure to prevent the copying of users' data to non-preferred locations [11]. However, the model could alternatively be integrated into a Cloud service in a fashion that does not preclude the provider from copying data in emergency situations (such as natural disasters or power outages) to a location that may not be the users' preferred location. Hence rather than being prescriptive, the model can be used to recommend to the administrator whether a location is preferred by the user or not. In this case the CSM will copy data to a location if a "Permit" decision is obtained from the authorization system. A "Deny" decision from the authorization system will inform the Cloud provider that the location is not preferred by the user. The Cloud provider might still continue to copy the data to a non-preferred location in case of emergency provided that the obligation to e-mail the user is executed. The location control model can use this information to quantify the provider's level of compliance. The compliance level is calculated as the proportion of authorized vs unauthorized transfer, and can be expressed as a percentage, $l = (a/t) * 100$, where l is the level of location assurance, a is the number of authorized transfers and t is the total number of transfers made. Furthermore, this facility can help the provider to maintain a balance between operational need and users' location preferences.

5 Implementation

This section presents the technical details required for a practical implementation of the proposed location control model.

5.1 Data Presentation

Figure 5 shows an example of user registration interface of the location control model. A unique account name is requested from the user which is used as the DataID and PolicyID in this case. XML is chosen as the internal representation format of data as it allows the data to be easily structured in separate elements which can be easily identified, modified and extended. However, alternate representation schemes, such as database tables or NoSQL entries could also be used. The personal information section of the registration page, as illustrated in Fig. 5, is converted into XML before storage within the Cloud service.

5.2 Policy Creation

Although the policies expressed as XML are human readable to an extent, the format is not particularly user-friendly. In our model, the data owner is presented with a web interface, see Fig. 5 (implemented with PHP) for indicating location preferences. The interface works like a template for policy; the policy document is created automatically based on the locations that the user selects. The prototype implementation of the interface can be found online[1]. After the customer's location preferences have been entered, the resulting XACML request context containing user's policy (as PolicyContents element) is generated where *Location* is defined as an Environment attribute in our XACML policy. This request context is then sent to the authorization system via a SOAP call.

5.3 Visibility for Data Owners

As described in Sect. 4, the location information for each user's data is referenced in the region information table of the CSM. As the policies that are evaluated against an access request to decide whether or not the access request should be granted, there needs to be a policy to allow the data owner to access the entries in the region information table for his/her data. This can be placed either inside the Cloud administrative policy set or the data owner's policy set. When it is stored in the Cloud Administrator's policy set, it has to be written in a generic way without requiring each individual user's credential to be specified in the policy. An example of such a policy is: If the credential of the requester matches the data owner's credential then allow access to the Region Information of that specific data. The result of such a generic policy is that there will exist only one policy for this purpose in the system. This policy will match the credential of the data owner, which is passed to the authorization system from the Authentication Information table, with the credential presented by the requester while making an access request to the service.

Alternatively, the policy to allow data owners to access the region information of their data can be placed in the data owners' policy sets. The policy would allow the requester presenting the appropriate credential to access region information

---

[1] http://143.239.71.90:8013/data_location/User_registration.html.

for his/her data. A drawback with this approach is that the size of policy for each data owner will be increased which may lead to significant growth in the size of the overall policy store. On the other hand, a benefit of this approach is that it would ease the process of distributed enforcement of the data owner's policy in a remote Cloud as the data owner's policy will be passed to the remote Cloud service and no extra mechanism will be needed to identify the data owner.

With the first approach, the user credential and the administrative policy would also need to be passed to the remote service in order to allow the user to access location information from an external Cloud. The remote service would need to make sure that these user credentials are stored correctly and passed to the request contexts and would also need to integrate the received administrative policy with its own administrative policy. We therefore chose the second approach to ease the distributed enforcement of our location control model.

5.4 CSM Implementation

The CSM prototype was implemented using PHP. It in turn uses an open source authorization system that is implemented in Java as a web service and is available online[2]. This authorization system receives requests as *XACMLAuthzDecision-Query* elements of the SAML profile of XACML and returns decisions in the form of *XACMLAuthzDecisionStatementType* elements. The system can store policy that comes with the request context and allows the policy of the data owner to be stored. It maintains the data-policy linking table for the provided DataID and PolicyID. It can return obligations if configured appropriately in the policy and can retrieve policy for a relevant DataID which is passed by the CSM to remote authorization systems via SOAP calls. The remote authorization system receiving a request based on its policy either accepts the request and stores the policy or rejects the request. The authorization system can be configured to use various conflict resolution rules for combining the decisions of administrative policy and data owners' policy. The details of the conflict resolution rules can be found in [10]. In this instance, the deny-overrides conflict resolution rule is used. The rationale behind this choice is that it will ensure that if either the administrative policy or the data owner's policy returns a "Deny" the final decision will be a "Deny". The final decision will be a "Grant" only if one of the policies returns a "Grant" but no other policy has returned a "Deny".

We have implemented the Authentication Information table and Region Information table as MySQL tables.

6 Validation

A number of tests were performed to validate the model using various Cloud setups. These validation tests verified the correctness of various functional aspects of the model, including: the translation of data owners' location preferences into policy, the storage of the data and policy in the desired locations, the

---

[2] http://sec.cs.kent.ac.uk/permis/downloads/Level3/standalone.shtml.

execution of the policies and obligations, the surfacing of location information to the user.

This testing was performed using two Cloud setups. The first was a vSphere private Cloud and the other was a public Cloud. This section describes how the model performed under these scenarios and also provides a guideline for implementing a location aware OpenStack Cloud so that the model can be used to control the data location there.

The location control model can be used to control the locations of users' data in any Cloud environment provided that the following requirements are met: the Cloud should be organized into number of regions and each region should have a distinguished access point/endpoint, there should be a server or VM where the CSM can be installed and this should be used to control access to the data in the Cloud regions, each data and policy should have a unique ID (which is already being maintained by the CSM implementation).

Controlling Data Location in vSphere Private Cloud. The prototype implementation of the location control model was initially deployed on a virtual machine running in a vSphere private Cloud with ESXi host. The virtual machine was configured with one virtual core Intel Xeon E5620 CPU running at 2.4 GHz with 2 GB of memory. Another virtual machine with an identical configuration was used to mimic a remote storage location. Different directories of the remote storage location were used to denote different regions which were distinguished by the unique directory paths. The model copied data to locations by connecting to the remote storage via SSH and transferring a file containing an XML representation of a user's data of size less than 1KB via the SCP protocol. All of the functionality described above was found to operate correctly in both of the private and public Cloud setups.

An additional objective was to determine the performance overhead of the system. By averaging over the response times of 100 requests in total in the vSphere Cloud setup it was found that it takes approximately 0.04 s in order to process a transaction that (a) identifies the correct data location and actions to perform on that data; and (b) queries the authorization system, obtains a response and updates the database accordingly; which indicates that at least 25 requests can be handled per second by the current implementation of the model. In contrast, a 0.2 s overhead was observed for connecting to the remote storage via SSH and transferring a file containing an XML representation of a loyalty card of size less than 1KB via SCP. Therefore, for this particular scenario the overhead of using the location control model was found to be negligible compared to the overall cost of performing remote data transfers.

Controlling Data Location in a Public Cloud. The prototype implementation of the model was used to control the location of data in a public Cloud using Amazon S3. Amazon has published the end point for each its regional services which is used to call the services at a specific location. A bucket was created in each region of the Amazon Cloud which can be reached only through

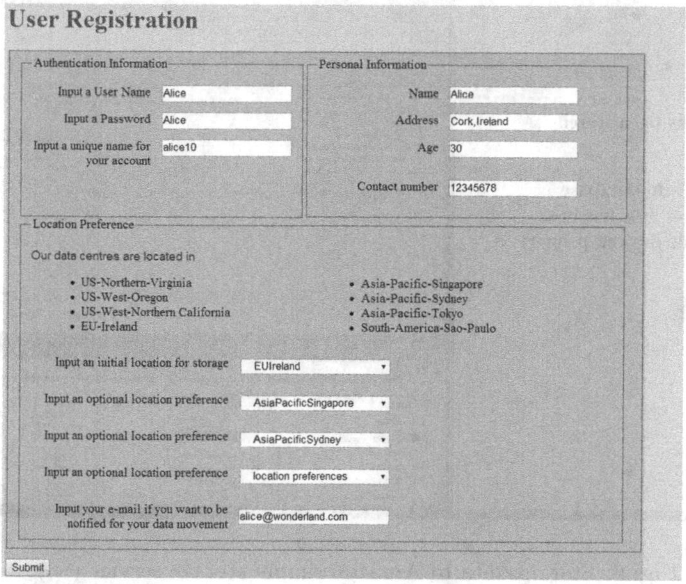

Fig. 5. Location control model interface for user registration.

the unique endpoint of that region. The CSM was installed in a machine with an Intel core i7-2670QM CPU running at 2.2 GHz with 6 GB memory. Each user's data item was copied as an S3 object to the bucket of a region based on his/her policy. The Location Preference section of Fig. 5 shows how the options were provided to users for choosing data location preferences in Amazon Cloud regions in the form of combo-box. Every time a data item was copied to a region the data location table of the CSM was updated and the location information was e-mailed to the user (if requested). However, to verify whether the data item was copied in the desired location of the public Cloud we used an S3 browser which gives visibility into all the buckets and S3 objects in each bucket. The left window of Fig. 6 shows the output of the model when a data storage request was successful, the lower right window shows the files that have been generated for a unique account name 'alice10'. The file 'alice10_Request.xml' contains the XACML request context that has been generated based on the location preferences of the user, the file 'alice10_Response.xml' contains the response that was obtained from the authorization system (these two files are kept in local storage only for verification purpose) and the file 'alice10.txt' is the data file that is stored in the Cloud which we can see in the upper right window in the S3 browser that is has been stored in the EU West region (Ireland).

Guideline for Implementation in OpenStack. Here we sketch how to integrate location awareness into open Cloud platforms such as OpenStack. The deployment of the location control model in OpenStack requires that the

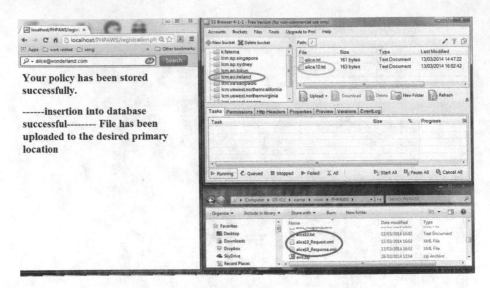

Fig. 6. Storing data to Amazon simple storage service (S3).

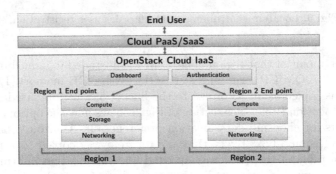

Fig. 7. Location aware Cloud usage model.

OpenStack Cloud should to be deployed into a number of regions. Each region should have its own API endpoints. In the simplest approach, in one of the virtual machine the location control model will be installed and this VM will work as a controller for data access/copy. This VM will also be responsible for storing users' policies and linking the policies to the data by the DataID.

For OpenStack, obvious integration points include: Horizon, the web-based dashboard that controls all OpenStack components; Keystone, which manages the authentication and authorization of services and users; Swift, which provides object store functionality; and Cinder, which provides block storage. OpenStack supports the concepts of geographically dispersed regions with separate endpoints [16], providing a good fit with the data location control model described in Sect. 4. Under this scenario, as seen in Fig. 7, one Keystone and Horizon is shared between the regions to provide a common access control and dashboard, while distributed Swift and Cinder components allow for complete separation of storage by region. The object storage functionality provided by Swift provides an easier starting point for the integration of location control compared to Cinder as it deals with named, atomic units of data. A first step would be to assign a Swift object to each user to keep data. Since a data set is identified by a DataID in the Location Control Model we assume that the user's Swift object ID can be used as DataID if it can identify the same object in all regions.

Based on the preferences of the user the location control model will execute instructions for storing Swift objects in the desired region by calling the appropriate API endpoint. The copy instruction will be executed by finding the desired object from its current region and then copying it to a desired region by using the appropriate region API endpoint and Swift object ID for data.

7 Conclusions and Future Work

The data location control model presented here allows SaaS providers to manage the location of end users' data based on their preferences. It also empowers users with the ability to get up-to-date location information for their data and the assurance that they will be notified when their data change location. A drawback of this approach is that it relies on the trustworthiness of the provider who must be trusted to integrating requests to the authorization system into their software and procedures and honour the resulting output. Hence, end users cannot verify that location information provided to them is actually true. However, these issues could be addressed by trustmarks and other third-party verification methods. Crytographic techniques could also be used to enhance the trustworthiness of the model. For example, the data could be encrypted using a key that can must be obtained through a request to the authorization system.

Our prototype stored the data as files in XML format. However, the model could also be used to protect access to collections of files, such as medical records composed of a variety of files in various formats. Future work will focus on improving the granularity of policies to allow for selective disclosure of data. This granularity could be extended to database entries where one single row can be identified by DataID and selective disclosure can be provided for various items represented by columns of that row. Future work will examine the issues around running the authorization system in a federated Cloud scenario, how well do the region boundaries of each provider correlate with those of the others?

Acknowledgements. The research work described in this paper was supported by the Irish Centre for Cloud Computing and Commerce, an Irish national Technology Centre funded by Enterprise Ireland and the Irish Industrial Development Authority.

References

1. Albeshri, A., Boyd, C., Nieto, J.G.: Geoproof: proofs of geographic location for cloud computing environment. In: 2012 32nd International Conference on Distributed Computing Systems Workshops (ICDCSW), pp. 506–514 (2012)

2. Almutairi, A., Sarfraz, M., Basalamah, S., Aref, W., Ghafoor, A.: A distributed access control architecture for cloud computing. IEEE Softw. **29**(2), 36–44 (2012)
3. Ashley, P., Hada, S., Karjoth, G., Powers, C., Schunter, M.: Enterprise privacy authorization language (EPAL 1.2). Submission to W3C (2003)
4. Basescu, C., Carpen-Amarie, A., Leordeanu, C., Costan, A., Antoniu, G.: Managing data access on clouds: a generic framework for enforcing security policies. In: 2011 IEEE International Conference on Advanced Information Networking and Applications (AINA), pp. 459–466 (2011)
5. Chadwick, D., Zhao, G., Otenko, S., Laborde, R., Linying, S., Nguyen, T.A.: PERMIS: a modular authorization infrastructure. Concurrency Comput. Pract. Experience **20**(11), 1341–1357 (2008)
6. Chadwick, D.W., Fatema, K.: A privacy preserving authorisation system for the cloud. J. Comput. Syst. Sci. **78**(5), 1359–1373 (2012)
7. Chen, D., Zhao, H.: Data security and privacy protection issues in cloud computing. In: 2012 International Conference on Computer Science and Electronics Engineering (ICCSEE), vol. 1, pp. 647–651. IEEE (2012)
8. Cranor, L.F.: P3P: making privacy policies more useful. IEEE Secur. Priv. **1**(6), 50–55 (2003)
9. De Capitani di Vimercati, S., Samarati, P., Jajodia, S.: Policies, models, and languages for access control. In: Bhalla, S. (ed.) DNIS 2005. LNCS, vol. 3433, pp. 225–237. Springer, Heidelberg (2005)
10. Fatema, K., Chadwick, D.W., Lievens, S.: A multi-privacy policy enforcement system. In: Fischer-Hübner, S., Duquenoy, P., Hansen, M., Leenes, R., Zhang, G. (eds.) Privacy and Identity Management for Life. IFIP AICT, vol. 352, pp. 297–310. Springer, Heidelberg (2011)
11. Fatema, K., Healy, P., Emeakaroha, V.C., Morrison, J.P., Lynn, T.: A user data location control model for cloud services. In: International Conference on Cloud Computing and Services Science, CLOSER 2014 (2014)
12. Godik, S., Anderson, A., Parducci, B., Humenn, P., Vajjhala, S.: Oasis extensible access control 2 markup language (XACML) 3. Technical report OASIS (2002)
13. Gondree, M., Peterson, Z.N.J.: Geolocation of data in the cloud. In: Proceedings of the Third ACM Conference on Data and Application Security and Privacy, pp. 25–36. ACM (2013)
14. Iskander, M.K., Wilkinson, D.W., Lee, A.J., Chrysanthis, P.K.: Enforcing policy and data consistency of cloud transactions. In: 2011 31st International Conference on Distributed Computing Systems Workshops (ICDCSW), pp. 253–262. IEEE (2011)
15. ISO. Information technology - open systems interconnection - security frameworks for open systems: Access control framework (1996)
16. Jackson, K.: OpenStack Cloud Computing Cookbook. Packt, Birmingham (2012)
17. Lynn, T., Healy, P., McClatchey, R., Morrison, J., Pahl, C., Lee, B.: The case for cloud service trustmarks and assurance-as-a-service. In: International Conference on Cloud Computing and Services Science CLOSER 2013 (2013)
18. Massonet, P., Naqvi, S., Ponsard, C., Latanicki, J., Rochwerger, B., Villari, M.: A monitoring and audit logging architecture for data location compliance in federated cloud infrastructures. In: 2011 IEEE International Symposium on Parallel and Distributed Processing Workshops and Ph.D. Forum (IPDPSW), pp. 1510–1517 (2011)
19. Mohan, A., Blough, D.M.: An attribute-based authorization policy framework with dynamic conflict resolution. In: Proceedings of the 9th Symposium on Identity and Trust on the Internet, pp. 37–50. ACM (2010)

20. Noman, A., Adams, C.: DLAS: data location assurance service for cloud computing environments. In: 2012 Tenth Annual International Conference on Privacy, Security and Trust (PST), pp. 225–228. IEEE (2012)
21. Ries, T., Fusenig, V., Vilbois, C., Engel, T.: Verification of data location in cloud networking. In: 2011 Fourth IEEE International Conference on Utility and Cloud Computing (UCC), pp. 439–444. IEEE (2011)
22. Spillner, J., Schill, A.: Flexible data distribution policy language and gateway architecture. In: 2012 IEEE Latin America Conference on Cloud Computing and Communications (LATINCLOUD), pp. 1–6. IEEE (2012)
23. Subashini, S., Kavitha, V.: A survey on security issues in service delivery models of cloud computing. J. Netw. Comput. Appl. **34**(1), 1–11 (2011)
24. Turkmen, F., Crispo, B.: Performance evaluation of XACML PDP implementations. In: Proceedings of the 2008 ACM workshop on Secure web services, pp. 37–44. ACM (2008)

From Regulatory Obligations to Enforceable Accountability Policies in the Cloud

Walid Benghabrit[1], Hervé Grall[1], Jean-Claude Royer[1], Mohamed Sellami[5(✉)],
Monir Azraoui[2], Kaoutar Elkhiyaoui[2], Melek Önen[2],
Anderson Santana De Oliveira[3], and Karin Bernsmed[4]

[1] Mines Nantes, 5 rue A. Kastler, 44307 Nantes, France
{walid.benghabrit,herve.grall,
jean-claude.royer}@mines-nantes.fr
[2] EURECOM, Les Templiers,
450 Route des Chappes, 06410 Biot, Sophia Antipolis, France
{monir.azraoui,kaoutar.elkhiyaoui,melek.onen}@eurecom.fr
[3] SAP Labs France, 805 avenue du Dr Donat Font de l'Orme,
06250 Mougins, Sophia Antipolis, France
anderson.santana.de.oliveira@sap.com
[4] SINTEF ICT, P.O. Box 4760, Sluppen, 7465 Trondheim, Norway
Karin.Bernsmed@sintef.no
[5] ISEP, 10 rue de Vanves, 92130 Issy Les Moulineaux, France
mohamed.sellami@isep.fr

Abstract. The widespread adoption of the cloud model for service delivery triggered several data protection issues. As a matter of fact, the proper delivery of these services typically involves sharing of personal/business data between the different parties involved in the service provisioning. In order to increase cloud consumer's trust, there must be guarantees on the fair use of their data. Accountability provides the necessary assurance about the data governance practices to the different stakeholders involved in a cloud service chain. In this context, we propose a framework for the representation of accountability policies. Such policies offer to end-users a clear view of the privacy and accountability clauses asserted by the entities they interact with, as well as means to represent their preferences. Our framework offers two accountability policy languages: (i) an abstract language called AAL devoted for the representation of preferences/clauses in an human readable fashion, and (ii) a concrete one for the implementation of enforceable policies.

Keywords: Accountability · Data protection · Framework · Policy language · Policy enforcement

1 Introduction

According to [1], accountability regards the data stewardship regime in which organizations that are entrusted with personal and business confidential data are

© Springer International Publishing Switzerland 2015
M. Helfert et al. (Eds.): CLOSER 2014, CCIS 512, pp. 134–150, 2015.
DOI: 10.1007/978-3-319-25414-2_9

responsible and liable for processing, sharing, storing and otherwise using the data according to contractual and legal constraints from the time it is collected until when the data is destroyed (including onward transfers to third parties). Obligations associated to such responsibilities can be expressed in an accountability policy, which is a set of rules that defines the conditions under which an accountable entity must operate.

Today, there is neither an established standard for expressing accountability policies nor a well defined way to enforce these policies. Since cloud services often combine infrastructure, platform and software applications to aggregate value and propose new cloud applications to individuals and organizations, it is fundamental for an accountability policy framework to enable "chains of accountability" across cloud services addressing regulatory, contractual, security and privacy concerns.

In the context of the EU FP7 A4Cloud project[1] we are currently working on defining a framework where accountability policies will be enforceable across the cloud service provision chain by means of accountability services and tools. Accountable organizations will make use of these services to ensure that obligations to protect personal data and data subjects' rights[2] are observed by all who store and process the data, irrespective of where that processing occurs. Under the perspective of the concept of accountability, we have elicited the following types of accountability obligations that must be considered while designing our policy framework:

- Access and Usage Control rules - express which rights should be granted or revoked regarding the use and the distribution of data in cloud infrastructures, and support the definition of roles as specified in the Data Protection Directive, e.g. data controller and data processor.
- Capturing privacy preferences and consent - to express user preferences about the usage of their personal data, to whom data can be released, and under which conditions.
- Data Retention Periods - to express time constraints about personal data collection.
- Controlling Data Location and Transfer - clear whereabouts of location depending on the type of data stored and on the industry sector processing the data (subject to specific regulations) must be provided. Accountability policies for cloud services need to be able to express rules about data localization, such that accountable services can signal where the data centers hosting them are located. Here we consider strong policy binding mechanisms to attach policies to data.
- Auditability - Policies must describe the clauses in a way that actions taken upon enforcing the policy can be audited in order to ensure that the policy was adhered to. The accountability policy language must specify which events have to be audited and what information related to the audited event have to be considered.

---

[1] The Cloud Accountability Project: http://www.a4cloud.eu/.
[2] This work mainly focus on the European Data Protection directive [2].

- Reporting and notifications - to allow cloud providers to notify end-users and cloud customers in case of policy violation or incidents for instance.
- Redress - express recommendations for redress in the policy in order to set right what was wrong and what made a failure occur.

In this paper we provide a cloud accountability policy representation framework designed while considering the aforementioned requirements. We define an abstract yet readable language, called AAL, for accountability clauses representation in a human readable fashion. We also define a concrete policy enforcement language, called A-PPL, as an extension of the PPL [3] language. The proposed framework, offers the means for a translation from abstract clauses expressed in AAL to concrete policies in A-PPL.

The rest of this paper is organized as follows. Section 2 describes related work. Section 3 gives an overview on the main components of our policy representation framework. We present the abstract accountability policy language we propose in Sect. 4 and the concrete one in Sect. 5. Section 6 describes a realistic use case as a proof of concept to our work. Section 7 discusses our work and presents directions for future work.

2   Related Work

In the following, we provide an overview of related work in the field. We organize this section along the following categories that relate to our contribution in this paper: accountability in computer science, obligations in legal texts and directives, enforcement and policy languages.

2.1   Accountability

There is a recent interest and active research for accountability which overlap several domains like security [4–6], language representation [7,8], auditing systems [9,10], evidence collection [11,12] and so on. However, only few of them consider an interdisciplinary view of accountability taking into account legal and business aspects. We particularly emphasize the work from [6,9] since they provide a general, concrete view and yet an operational approach.

Regarding tool supports and frameworks we can find several proposals [12–14], but none of them provides a holistic approach for accountability in the cloud, from end-user understandable sentences to concrete machine-readable representations. In [11], authors propose an end-to-end decentralized accountability framework to keep track of the usage of the data in the cloud. They suggest an object-centered approach that packs the logging mechanism together with users' data and policies.

2.2   Obligations in Regulations

There is an international trend in protecting data, for instance in Europe with Directive 95/46/EC [2], the HIPAA rules [15] in the USA and the FIPPA act [16] in Canada. As an example, Directive 95/46/EC states rules to protect personal data in case of processing or transferring data to other countries. There exist some attempts to formalize or to give rigorous analyses of this kind of rules. In [7] the authors present a restricted natural language SIMPL (SIMple Privacy Language) to express privacy requirements and commitments. In [17] the authors describe a general process for developing semantic models from privacy policy goals mined from policy documents. In [18], the authors develop an approach where contracts are represented by XML documents enriched with logic metadata and assistance with a theorem prover. In [8] the authors provide a formal language to express privacy laws and a real validation on the HIPAA and GLBA [19] sets. These works either are not end-to-end proposals, only cover data privacy not accountability or are only formal proposals without an enforcement layer.

2.3   Enforcement and Policies

A number of policy languages have been proposed in recent years for machine-readable policy representation. We reviewed several existing policy languages (see [20] for details). We present here the results of our analysis of existing policy languages. Rather than designing a new policy language for accountability, we leverage a concrete existing language that covers most of the accountability obligations listed in Sect. 1. We aim at extending it with features that enable the expression of accountability policies.

The first step of our analysis is to check to which extent the selected policy languages can express the accountability obligations. None of the languages we reviewed enables the expression of all these obligations. However, they may focus on one or several of the accountability obligations. For example, PPL [3] can be used to express access and usage control rules, privacy preferences and policies and it enables the notifications. From this first analysis, we classify our selected policy languages into four categories: (i) *Access Control:* eXtensible Access Control Markup Language (XACML, [21]); (ii) *Privacy:* The Platform for Privacy Preferences (P3P, [22]), the Primelife Policy Language (PPL, [3]) and SecPal for Privacy (SecPal4P, [23]); (iii) *Policy specification for security:* Conspec [24] and Ponder [25]; (iv) *Service Description:* The Unified Service Description Language (USDL, [26]), SLAng [27] and WS-Policy [28,29]. Note that one language can belong to several categories. We also argue that we cannot define from our selected set of languages an additional category *Accountability language.* In particular, most of the languages do not provide means to express logging, reporting and audit obligations that are essential to support accountability. Therefore, the design of the accountability language we propose in the following sections represents an unprecedented attempt to express accountability obligations via a policy language.

In a second step, we analyze the extensibility of the reviewed languages in order to extend one of the languages with accountability features. We focus on XML-based languages, since XML [30] provides many extension points to extend the language. In addition, XML is a standard and well documented.

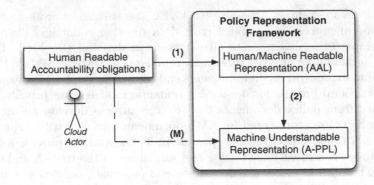

Fig. 1. Overview on the accountability policy representation framework.

Thus adding extension to an XML-based language is fairly simple. Languages such as XACML, P3P and PPL use XML to define policies related to access control and privacy. In our work we consider PPL since it provides elements that capture the best accountability obligations.

As a result of this survey, we focus our effort on the extension of PPL. Extending PPL for accountability has also been investigated on other papers, concurrently and independently from our work. Contemporaneous work by Butin et al. [31] leverages PPL to design logs for accountability. They identify the lack of expressiveness of PPL as far as the creation of logs for accountability is concerned. They also discuss the fact that the PPL does not allow to specify the content of the notification in a data handling policy. Similarly, Henze et al. [32] identify location of storage and duration of storage as the two main challenges in cloud data handling scenarios. They propose to use PPL to specify *data annotations* that contain the data handling obligations (e.g. "delete after 30 days"). Without giving more details, they propose to extend PPL with an attribute that specifies a maximum and a minimum duration of storage and with an element that restricts the location of stored data. Our proposed language also addresses these two challenges and we give in Sect. 5 the details of the extensions that solve these issues.

3   The Cloud Accountability Framework

In this section, we provide an overview of our proposed policy representation framework. Such framework must allow end-users to easily express their accountability clauses and preferences and even be complete and rigorous enough to be run by a policy execution engine. Hence we are faced with the following dilemma: the policy must be written by an end-user, which does not necessarily have skills in a certain policy language and the policy must be machine understandable at the same time. Machine understandable means that sentences can be read, understood and executed by a computer.

In this context, we propose a policy representation framework (see Fig. 1) that allows a user, step (1) in Fig. 1, to express his accountability needs in a human readable fashion and (2) offers the necessary means to translate them (semi-)automatically[3] to a machine understandable format.

Accountability as it appears in legal, contractual and normative texts about data privacy make explicit four important roles that we consider in our proposal:

- Data subject: this role represents any end-user which has data privacy concerns, mainly because he outsourced some of its data to a cloud provider.
- Data processor: this role is attributed to any computational agent which processes some personal data. It should act under the control of a data controller.
- Data controller: it is legally responsible to the data subject for any violations of its privacy and to the data protection authority in case of misconduct.
- Auditor: it represents data protection authorities which are in charge of the application of laws and directives.

3.1 Step (1). Human/Machine Readable Representation

To express accountability clauses we define an Abstract Accountability Language (AAL), which is devoted to expressing accountability clauses in an unambiguous style and which is close to what the end-user needs and understands. As this is the human readable level, this language should be simple, akin to a natural logic, that is a logic expressed in a subset of a natural language.

For instance, a simple access control clause to state that "the data d cannot be read by all agents" will be formulated in a human/machine readable fashion using our accountability language as "DENY ANY:Agent.READ(d:Data)". Details on the AAL syntax are provided in Sect. 4.

3.2 Step (2). Machine Understandable Representation

In this step (called the mapping), the accountability clauses expressed in AAL are (semi-)automatically translated into a machine understandable policy. We target a policy language that is able to enforce classic security means (like access or usage controls) but also accountability clauses. Such automatic translation may need several passes, due to the high level of abstraction of AAL.

As analyzed in Sect. 2, the PrimeLife Policy Language (PPL) [3] seems the most convenient language for privacy policies representation. It can be extended to address specific accountability obligations such as auditability, notification or logging obligations. Hence, we propose an extension to PPL, A-PPL for accountable PPL, which supports such obligations. The details of this extension are described in Sect. 5.

---

[3] Here "semi" means that sometimes human assistance could be needed.

4   Abstract Language

We introduce in this section AAL (Abstract Accountability Language), which is devoted to expressing accountability clauses in an unambiguous human readable style. The AAL concepts are presented in Sect. 4.1, its syntax in Sect. 4.2 and we provide an outlook on our approach for a machine understandable representation of AAL policies in Sect. 4.4.

4.1   AAL Concepts

As explained in [9] an accountable system can be defined with five steps: prevention, detection, evidence collection, judgment and punishment. We follow this line for the foundation of our accountability language. In AAL, usage control expressions represent the preventive description part. Audit expressions encompass the detection, evidence collection and judgment parts. Finally, rectification expressions represent the punishment description part. We use the term rectification since these expressions don't cover only punishment, but also remediation, compensation, sanction and penalty. Thereby, an AAL sentence is a property (more formally a distributed system invariant) expressing usage control, auditing and rectification. The general form of an AAL sentence is: `UsageControl Auditing Rectification` and the informal meaning is: *try to ensure the usage control, in case of an audit, if a violation is observed then the rectification applies.* The reader should also note that there are two flavors of AAL sentences:

– User preferences: expressing the clauses a data subject wants to be satisfied, for instance he does not want its data to be distributed over the network or only used for statistics by a given data processor, and so on.
– Processor clauses: these are the clauses the data processor declares to ensure regarding the data management and processing.

Finally, as many policy representation languages, we consider permission, obligation and prohibition in AAL. They occur in various approaches, like in PPL, or in the ENDORSE project[4]. Permission, obligation and prohibition are respectively expressed in AAL sentences with these keywords: `PERMIT`, `MUST` and `MUSTNOT/ DENY`, as advocated by the IETF RFC 2119 [33].

4.2   AAL Syntax

Figure 2 shows the syntax of AAL using a Backus-Naur Form (BNF) [34] like syntax. AAL allows the expression of `Clauses` representing actions that have to be met either in an accountability policy or preference. A `Clause` has one usage expression and optionally an audit and a rectification expression: `ActionExp ('AUDITING' ActionExp)? ('IF_VIOLATED_THEN' ActionExp)?`. The expression `ActionExp` of a clause can be either atomic or composite.

---

[4] http://ict-endorse.eu/.

Listing 1.1. AAL Syntax.

```
1   Clause         ::= CLAUSE Id ':' (Quant*)? Usage (Audit Rectification)?
2   Usage          ::= ActionExp
3   Audit          ::= AUDITING (ActionExp THEN)? agent.audit'['agent']' '()'
4   Rectification  ::= IF_VIOLATED_THEN ActionExp
5   ActionExp      ::= Action | NOT ActionExp | Modality ActionExp | Author | Condition
6                    | ActionExp (AND|OR|ONLYWHEN) ActionExp | IF ActionExp THEN ActionExp
7   Exp            ::= Variable | Constant | Variable.Attribute
8   Condition      ::= (NOT)? Exp | Exp ('==' | '!=') Exp | Condition (AND|OR) Condition
9   Author         ::= (PERMIT | DENY) Action
10  Action         ::= agent.service ('['[agent]']')? '('Exp')' (Time)? (Purpose)?
11  Quant          ::= (FORALL | EXISTS) Var [WHERE Condition]
12  Variable       ::= Var ':' Type
13  Modality       ::= MUST | MUSTNOT | ALWAYS
14  Type, var, val, attr Id, agent, Constant, Purpose ::= literal
```

Fig. 2. Excerpt of the AAL Syntax.

As an example, consider the user preference of a data subject who grants read access to an agent A on its data D. This usage control is a permission, which can be expressed as follows.

```
PERMIT A.READ(D:Data)
```

But the full accountability sentence does imply that an auditor B will audit the system and, in case of violations, can sanction the data controller C.

```
PERMIT A.READ(D:Data)
AUDITING MUST B.AUDIT(C.logs)
IF_VIOLATED_THEN MUST B.SANCTION(C)
```

Further examples of user preferences and clauses expressed in AAL are provided in Sect. 6.

4.3 Semantics and Verification

We define formal semantics for AAL based on a pure temporal logic approach. However, since we need data and agent quantification we precesiley rely on a first-order linear temporal logic [35]. The translation is rather straightforward, except that the audit process introduces a new modality with a specific formal interpretation (see [36] for details). From this interpretation it is possible to check the consistency of an AAL formula or the compliance of two AAL clauses using a logical prover. This last feature is explicitly suitable to match user preferences and processor clauses. Furthermore, principles for abstract component design have been defined and can be checked with a model-checker. We present these design principles in [37], how to translate them in the μ-calculus and how to verify AAL clauses with the mCRL2 toolset [38].

4.4 Machine Understandability

Generating machine understandable policies from accountability preferences and clauses written in AAL can be easily done when dealing with usage control clauses. However, this mapping is less obvious for clauses with temporal modalities and with auditing. The main issue for such mapping is the gap between the AAL language, which is property-oriented, and the machine understandable language, which is operational. To fill this gap we need more artifacts, Fig. 3 provides an overview on our proposed mapping process.

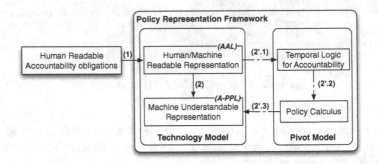

Fig. 3. Overview on the machine understandable translation of AAL.

According to this figure, we can see that going from a human/machine readable representation in AAL to a machine understandable representation of the accountability preferences/clauses (arrow numbered (2) in Fig. 3) is done through three steps:

- **(2'.1).** First, a temporal logic is used to make more concrete AAL sentences as temporal logic properties. Indeed, in an accountability policy we should represent the notions of permission, obligation and prohibition. In addition, there is a need to express conditions and various logical combinations. Furthermore, one important thing is to have time, at least logical discrete time, for instance to write: "X writes some data and then stores some logs". Our target is a temporal logic with time, one concrete candidate is mCRL2 [38].
- **(2'.2).** Second, a policy calculus is used to describe the operational semantics associated to the concrete properties defined in (2'.1). This calculus is based on the concept of reference monitor [39] for both the agents and the data resources. It relies on a previous work for distributed agent communicating via messages [40]. This operational semantics provides means for abstractly executing the temporal logic expressions. This process is known as "program synthesis", starting from a property it generates a program ensuring/enforcing the property.
- **(2'.3).** Finally, the generated policy using our policy calculus is (semi-) automatically translated to a machine understandable policy based on predefined transformation rules. Our target is the A-PPL extension of PPL which is described in the next section.

5   Concrete Language

Our accountability policy representation framework maps AAL clauses to concrete and operational machine understandable policies. As already mentioned in Sect. 2.3, in order not to define yet another completely new language to map accountability obligations to machine-understandable policies, we conducted a preliminary study on existing languages and among all the possible candidates, PPL seems the one that best captures the accountability concepts. Therefore, in this section, we present how A-PPL extends PPL to address accountability obligations.

PPL implicitly identifies three roles: the data subject, data controller, third-party data controller and data processor roles. Besides, PPL defines an obligation as a set of triggers and actions. Triggers are events related to the obligation that are filtered by a condition and that trigger the execution of actions. Therefore, PPL defines markups to declare an obligation. Inside the obligation environment, one can specify a set of triggers and their related actions.

5.1   Extension of Roles

To address accountability concerns in a cloud environment, it might be necessary to include in the policy a reference to the role of the subject to which the policy is applied to. For instance, in PPL, it was not possible to identify the data controller. We therefore suggest adding to the PPL <Subject> element a new attribute, `attribute:role`, for this purpose. Furthermore, in addition to the four roles PPL inherently considers (data subject, data controller, downstream data controller, data processor), A-PPL extends PPL with one additional role. We add the auditor role that is considered as a trusted third-party that can conduct independent assessment of cloud services, information systems operations performance and security of the cloud implementation. This new role is important to catch accountability specific obligations such as auditability, reporting notification and possibly redress.

5.2   Extension of Actions and Triggers

We add to PPL a set of new A-PPL actions and triggers in order to map accountability obligations. We introduce two new triggers that relate to access control. We propose `TriggerPersonalDataAccessPermitted` and `TriggerPersonal-DataAccessDenied`. They fire actions based on the result of an access decision taken on a piece of data. In other words, if the evaluation of the access control on the targeted data results is Permit, `TriggerPersonalDataAccessPermitted` may trigger an action specified in the policy. Symmetrically, `TriggerPersonal-DataAccessDenied` triggers actions when an access on a piece of data is denied. We also enhance the action of logging `ActionLog` and notification `ActionNotify` that already exist in PPL. For instance, while PPL currently enables notification thanks to the `ActionNotifyDataSubject`, A-PPL defines a new and more general `ActionNotify` action in which one can define the recipient of the notification thanks to a newly defined parameter `recipient`. Moreover, the additional notification `type` parameter defines the purpose of the notification which can be, for example, policy violation, evidence or redress notification. On the other hand, the current `ActionLog` action in PPL fails to capture accountability obligations. The new `ActionLog` action in A-PPL introduces many additional parameters to provide more explicit information on the logged event. For example, `timestamp` defines the time of the event, and `Resource location` identifies the resource the action was taken on. We also create two actions related to auditability: `ActionAudit` that creates an evidence request and `ActionEvidenceCollection` that collects requested evidence. In addition, auditability requires the definition of two new triggers related to evidence: `TriggerOnEvidenceRequestReceived` that occurs when an audited receives an evidence request and `TriggerOn EvidenceReceived` that occurs when an auditor receives the requested evidence. Similarly, when an update occurs in a policy or in a user preference, the update may trigger a set of actions to be performed. Thus, we create two additional triggers: `TriggerOnPolicyUpdate` and `TriggerOnPreferenceUpdate`. Finally, to handle complaints that a data subject may file in the context of remediability, we define the trigger `TriggerOnComplaint` that triggers a set of specific actions to be undertaken by an auditor or/and a data controller.

6   Validation

In this section we validate our policy representation framework by extracting obligations from one of the use cases documented in the A4Cloud public deliverable DB3.1 [41] and illustrate their representation in AAL and A-PPL.

6.1   The Health Care Use Case

This use case concerns the flow of health care information generated by medical sensors in the cloud. The system, which is illustrated in Fig. 4, is used to support diagnosis of patients by the collection and processing of data from wearable sensors. Here, we investigate the case where medical data from the sensors will be exchanged between patients, their families and friends, the hospital, as well as between the different Cloud providers involved in the final service delivery.

In this use case the patients are the data subjects from whom personal data is collected. The hospital is ultimately responsible for the health care services and will hence act as one of the data controllers for the personal data that will be collected. The patients' relatives may also upload personal data about the patients and can therefore be seen as data controllers (as well as data subjects, when personal data about their usage of the system is collected from them). As can be seen in Fig. 4, the use case will involve cloud services for sensor data collection and processing (denoted cloud provider "X"), cloud services for data storage (denoted cloud provider "Y") and cloud services for information sharing

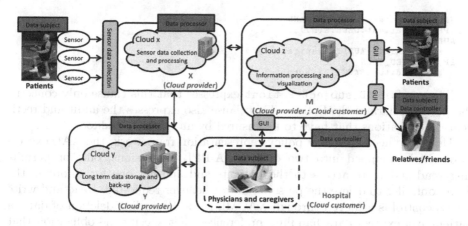

Fig. 4. An overview over the main actors involved in the health care use case.

(denoted cloud provider "M"), which will be operated by a collaboration of different providers. Since the primary service provider M, with whom the users will interface, employs two sub-providers, a chain of service delivery will be created. In this particular case, the M platform provider will be the primary service provider and will act as a data processor with respect to the personal data collected from the patients. Also the sub-providers, X and Y, will act as data processors. The details of the use case are further described in [41].

6.2   Obligations for the Use Case

We have identified a number of obligations for this use case, which needs to be handled by the accountability policy framework. Here we list three examples and we explain how they will be expressed in AAL and mapped into A-PPL. Note that the complete list of obligations is much longer, but we have chosen to outline those that illustrate the most important relationships between the involved actors. Due to space limitations we do not include the complete A-PPL policies here; the reader is referred to the project documentation [20] to see the full policy expressions.

Obligation 1: The Data Subject's Right to Access, Correct and Delete Personal Data. According the Data Protection Directive [2], data subjects have (among others) the right to access, correct and delete personal data that have been collected about them. In this use case it means that the hospital must allow read and write grant access to patients as well as relatives with regard to their personal data that have been collected and stored in the cloud. There must be also means to enforce the deletion of such data.

The AAL expression catching the clauses associated to the patient is:

```
FORALL D:Data WHERE d.subject = Patient
(PERMIT Patient.READ(D)   AND
```

```
  PERMIT Patient.WRITE(D) AND
  PERMIT Patient.DELETE(D))
AUDITING
  MUST Auditor.AUDIT(hospital.logs)
IF_VIOLATED_THEN
  MUST Auditor.SANCTION(hospital)
```

The condition D.subject=Patient expresses that this clause only concerns the personal data of the Patient. This clause also expresses the audit and rectification obligations that have to be ensured by an external Auditor.

Using the accountability policy representation framework, the AAL expression will be mapped into two different A-PPL expressions; one for permitting read and write access to the patients and another one for enforcing the data controller to delete the personal data whenever requested. Read and write access control is achieved through XACML rules. Regarding deletion of data, a patient can express data handling preferences that specify the obligation that the data controller has to enforce to delete the personal data. This obligation can be expressed using the A-PPL obligation action ActionDeletePersonalData, which will be used by the patient to delete personal data that has been collected about him.

An explicit audit clause implies that information related to the usage control property are logged (the amount and the nature of this information is not discussed here). Thus the audit clause is translated into an AuditAction which is responsible to manage the interaction with the auditor. This runs an exchange protocol with the auditor which ends with two responses: either no violation of the usage has been detected or a violation exists. In the latter, some rectification clauses should be specified.

In the sequel we only consider usage control clauses since the translation process for audit and rectification is similar to the previous example.

Obligation 2: The Data Controller Must Notify the Data Subjects of Security or Personal Data Breaches. This obligation defines what will happen in case of a security or privacy incident. In AAL it will be expressed by the hospital as:

```
FORALL pRelatives:Agent IN Patient.relatives
IF hospital.VIOLATEPOLICY() THEN
 MUST hospital.NOTIFY[Patient]("incident") AND
 MUST hospital.NOTIFY[pRelatives]("incident")
```

In A-PPL, such notification is expressed through the obligation action ActionNotify. It takes as parameters, the recipient of the notification (here, the data subject) and the type of the notification (here, security breach).

Obligation 3: The Data Processor Must, upon Request, Provide Evidence to the Data Controller on the Correct and Timely Deletion of Personal Data. To express the timely deletion of personal data, which in addition will be logged to be used as evidence, the following AAL expression can be used by the provider M:

```
MUST M.DELETE(D:Data) THEN
MUST M.LOGS("deleted", D, currentDate)
```

In A-PPL, the obligation trigger `TriggerPersonalDataDeleted` combined with the obligation action `ActionNotify` will notify the data subject of the deletion of its data. In addition, if necessary, the obligation action `ActionLog` will allow the provider M to log when personal data have been deleted.

The three examples that we have provided in this section represent a snapshot of the full power of AAL and A-PPL. In [41] we outline more examples of obligations for the health care use case, which among other things demonstrate how informed consent can be gathered from the patients before their data is being processed, how the purpose of personal data collection can be specified and controlled, how the data processor M can inform the hospital of the use of sub-processors and how the data processors can facilitate for regulators to review evidence on their data processing practices.

7   Conclusions

Dealing with personal data in the cloud raises several accountability and privacy issues that must be considered to promote the safety usage of cloud services. In this paper we tackle the issue related to accountability clauses and preferences representation. We propose a cloud accountability policy representation framework. This framework enables accountability policy expression in a human readable fashion using our abstract accountability language (AAL). Also, it offers the means for their mapping to concrete enforcement policies written using our accountability policy language (A-PPL). Our framework applies the separation of concerns principle by separating the abstract language from the concrete one. This choice makes both contributions, i.e. AAL and A-PPL, self-contained and allows their independent use. The ability of our framework to represent accountability clauses/preferences was validated through a realistic use case.

Our future research work will focus on the mapping from AAL to A-PPL. As part of our implementation perspectives, we are currently working on two prototypes. An AAL editor that assists end-users in writing their preferences/-clauses and implements the required artifacts to map them to concrete policies in A-PPL. We also started the development of an A-PPL policy execution engine that will be in charge of interpreting and matching A-PPL policies and preferences

Acknowledgements. This work was funded by the EU's 7th framework A4Cloud project.

References

1. Pearson, S., Tountopoulos, V., Catteddu, D., Südholt, M., Molva, R., Reich, C., Fischer-Hübner, S., Millard, C., Lotz, V., Jaatun, M.G., Leenes, R., Rong, C., Lopez, J.: Accountability for cloud and other future internet services. In: CloudCom, pp. 629–632. IEEE (2012)

2. Directive, E.U.: Directive 95/46/EC of the European Parliament and of the Council of 24 October 1995 on the protection of individuals with regard to the processing of personal data and on the free movement of such data (1995). http://ec.europa.eu/justice/policies/privacy/docs/95--46-ce/dir1995-46_part1_en.pdf

3. Ardagna, C.A., Bussard, L., De Capitani Di Vimercati, S., Neven, G., Paraboschi, S., Pedrini, E., Preiss, S., Raggett, D., Samarati, P., Trabelsi, S., Verdicchio, M.: Primelife policy language (2009). http://www.w3.org/2009/policy-ws/papers/Trabelisi.pdf

4. Weitzner, D.J., Abelson, H., Berners-Lee, T., Feigenbaum, J., Hendler, J., Sussman, G.J.: Information accountability. Commun. ACM 51, 82–87 (2008)

5. Xiao, Z., Kathiresshan, N., Xiao, Y.: A survey of accountability in computer networks and distributed systems. Secur. Commun. Netw. 5, 1083–1085 (2012)

6. Pearson, S., Wainwright, N.: An interdisciplinary approach to accountability for future internet service provision. Int. J. Trust Manag. Comput. Commun. 1, 52–72 (2013)

7. Le Métayer, D.: A formal privacy management framework. In: Degano, P., Guttman, J., Martinelli, F. (eds.) FAST 2008. LNCS, vol. 5491, pp. 162–176. Springer, Heidelberg (2009)

8. DeYoung, H., Garg, D., Jia, L., Kaynar, D., Datta, A.: Experiences in the logical specification of the HIPAA and GLBA privacy laws. In: 9th Annual ACM Workshop on Privacy in the Electronic Society (WPES 2010), pp. 73–82 (2010)

9. Feigenbaum, J., Jaggard, A.D., Wright, R.N., Xiao, H.: Systematizing "accountability" in computer science. Technical report YALEU/DCS/TR-1452, University of Yale (2012)

10. Jagadeesan, R., Jeffrey, A., Pitcher, C., Riely, J.: Towards a theory of accountability and audit. In: Backes, M., Ning, P. (eds.) ESORICS 2009. LNCS, vol. 5789, pp. 152–167. Springer, Heidelberg (2009)

11. Sundareswaran, S., Squicciarini, A., Lin, D.: Ensuring distributed accountability for data sharing in the cloud. IEEE Trans. Dependable Secure Comput. 9, 556–568 (2012)

12. Haeberlen, A., Aditya, P., Rodrigues, R., Druschel, P.: Accountable virtual machines. In: 9th USENIX Symposium on Operating Systems Design and Implementation, OSDI, pp. 119–134 (2010)

13. Wei, W., Du, J., Yu, T., Gu, X.: Securemr: a service integrity assurance framework for mapreduce. In: Proceedings of the 2009 Annual Computer Security Applications Conference, pp. 73–82. IEEE Computer Society, Washington, DC (2009)

14. Zou, J., Wang, Y., Lin, K.J.: A formal service contract model for accountable SaaS and cloud services. In: International Conference on Services Computing, pp. 73–80. IEEE (2010)

15. US Congress: Health insurance portability and accountability act of 1996, privacy rule. 45 cfr 164 (2002). http://www.access.gpo.gov/nara/cfr/waisidx_07/45cfr164_07.html

16. Legislative Assembly of Ontario: Freedom of information and protection of privacy act (r.s.o. 1990, c. f.31) (1988)

17. Breaux, T.D., Anton, A.I.: Deriving semantic models from privacy policies. In: Sixth IEEE International Workshop on Policies for Distributed Systems and Networks (POLICY 2005), pp. 67–76 (2005)

18. Kerrigan, S., Law, K.H.: Logic-based regulation compliance-assistance. In: International Conference on Artificial Intelligence and Law, pp. 126–135 (2003)

19. US Congress: Gramm-leach-bliley act, financial privacy rule. 15 usc 6801–6809 (1999). http://www.law.cornell.edu/uscode/usc_sup_01_15_10_94_20_I.html

20. Garaga, A., de Oliveira, A.S., Sendor, J., Azraoui, M., Elkhiyaoui, K., Molva, R., Önen, M., Cherrueau, R.A., Douence, R., Grall, H., Royer, J.C., Sellami, M., Südholt, M., Bernsmed, K.: Policy Representation Framework. Technical report D:C-4.1, Accountability for Cloud and Future Internet Services - A4Cloud Project (2013). http://www.a4cloud.eu/sites/default/files/D34.1%20Policy%20representation%20Framework.pdf
21. OASIS Standard: eXtensible Access Control Markup Language (XACML) Version 3.0. 22, January 2013. http://docs.oasis-open.org/xacml/3.0/xacml-3.0-core-spec-os-en.html
22. Marchiori, M.: The platform for privacy preferences 1.0 (P3P1.0) specification. W3C recommendation, W3C (2002). http://www.w3.org/TR/2002/REC-P3P-20020416/
23. Becker, M.Y., Malkis, A., Bussard, L.: S4p: A generic language for specifying privacy preferences and policies. Technical report MSR-TR-2010-32, Microsoft Research (2010)
24. Aktug, I., Naliuka, K.: ConSpec - a formal language for policy specification. Electron. Notes Theor. Comput. Sci. **197**, 45–58 (2008)
25. Damianou, N., Dulay, N., Lupu, E.C., Sloman, M.: The ponder policy specification language. In: Sloman, M., Lobo, J., Lupu, E.C. (eds.) POLICY 2001. LNCS, vol. 1995, pp. 18–38. Springer, Heidelberg (2001)
26. Barros, A., Oberle, D.: Handbook of Service Description: USDL and Its Methods. Springer Publishing Company, Incorporated, New York (2012)
27. Lamanna, D.D., Skene, J., Emmerich, W.: SLAng: a language for defining service level agreements. In: Proceedings of the The Ninth IEEE Workshop on Future Trends of Distributed Computing Systems, pp. 100–106. IEEE Computer Society, Washington, DC (2003)
28. OASIS Web Service Security (WSS) TC: Web Services Security: SOAP Message Security 1.1 (2006). https://www.oasis-open.org/committees/download.php/16790/wss-v1.1-spec-os-SOAPMessageSecurity.pdf
29. OASIS Web Services Secure Exchange (WS-SX) TC: WS-Trust 1.4 (2012). http://docs.oasis-open.org/ws-sx/ws-trust/v1.4/errata01/os/ws-trust-1.4-errata01-os-complete.html
30. Bray, T., Paoli, J., Sperberg-McQueen, C.M., Maler, E., Yergeau, F.: Extensible markup language (XML). World Wide Web J. **2**, 27–66 (1997)
31. Butin, D., Chicote, M., Le Métayer, D.: Log design for accountability. In: IEEE CS Security and Privacy Workshops (SPW), pp. 1–7 (2013)
32. Henze, M., Großfengels, M., Koprowski, M., Wehrle, K.: Towards data handling requirements-aware cloud computing. In: 2013 IEEE International Conference on Cloud Computing Technology and Science (CloudCom) (2013)
33. Bradner, S.: IETF RFC 2119: Key words for use in RFCs to Indicate Requirement Levels. Technical report (1997)
34. Knuth, D.E.: Backus normal form vs. backus naur form. Commun. ACM **7**, 735–736 (1964)
35. Fisher, M.: Temporal representation and reasoning. In: van Harmelen, F., Lifschitz, V., Porter, B. (eds.) Handbook of Knowledge Representation, pp. 513–550.
Elsevier, Amsterdam (2008)
36. Benghabrit, W., Grall, H., Royer, J.-C., Sellami, M., Bernsmed, K., De Oliveira, A.S.: Abstract accountability language. In: Zhou, J., Gal-Oz, N., Zhang, J., Gudes, E. (eds.) IFIPTM 2014. IFIP AICT, vol. 430, pp. 229–236. Springer, Heidelberg (2014)

37. Benghabrit, W., Grall, H., Royer, J.C., Sellami, M.: Accountability for abstract
    component design. In: 40th EUROMICRO Conference on Software Engineering
    and Advanced Applications, SEAA, Verona, Italia (2014)
38. Cranen, S., Groote, J.F., Keiren, J.J.A., Stappers, F.P.M., de Vink, E.P.,
    Wesselink, W., Willemse, T.A.C.: An overview of the mCRL2 toolset and its
    recent advances. In: Piterman, N., Smolka, S.A. (eds.) TACAS 2013 (ETAPS 2013).
    LNCS, vol. 7795, pp. 199–213. Springer, Heidelberg (2013)
39. Schneider, F.B.: Enforceable security policies. ACM Trans. Inf. Syst. Secur. **3**,
    30–50 (2000)
40. Allam, D., Douence, R., Grall, H., Royer, J.C., Südholt, M.: Well-Typed Services
    Cannot Go Wrong. Rapport de recherche RR-7899, INRIA (2012)
41. Bernsmed, K., Felici, M., Oliveira, A.S.D., Sendor, J., Moe, N.B., Rübsamen, T.,
    Tountopoulos, V., Hasnain, B.: Use case descriptions. Deliverable, Cloud Account-
    ability (A4Cloud) Project (2013)

Context-Aware Provisioning and Management of Cloud Applications

Uwe Breitenbücher[1]([✉]), Tobias Binz[1], Oliver Kopp[2], Frank Leymann[1],
and Matthias Wieland[2]

[1] Institute of Architecture of Application Systems,
University of Stuttgart, Stuttgart, Germany
{breitenbuecher,binz,leymann}@informatik.uni-stuttgart.de
[2] Institute for Parallel and Distributed Systems,
University of Stuttgart, Stuttgart, Germany
{kopp,wieland}@informatik.uni-stuttgart.de

Abstract. The automation of application provisioning and management is one of the most important issues in Cloud Computing. However, the steadily increasing number of different services and software
components employed in composite Cloud applications leads to a high
risk of unintended side effects when different technologies work together
that bring their own proprietary management APIs. Due to unknown
dependencies and the increasing diversity and heterogeneity of employed
technologies, even small management tasks on a single component may
compromise the whole application functionality for reasons that are neither expected nor obvious to non-experts. In this paper, we tackle these
issues by introducing a method that enables detecting and correcting
unintended effects of provisioning and management tasks in advance
by analyzing the context in which the tasks are executed. We validate
the method practically and show how context-aware expert management
knowledge can be applied fully automatically to provision and manage
running Cloud applications.

Keywords: Application management · Provisioning · Context ·
Automation · Cloud computing

1 Introduction

Cloud Computing enables enterprises to outsource their IT efficiently due to
properties such as pay-on-demand computing [25]. To exploit these properties
for their offerings, Cloud providers have to automate their processes for application provisioning and management. Therefore, a lot of tools and management
technologies have been developed. However, due to specific requirements on
employed Cloud services and software components, proprietary systems of different providers often have to be combined in *Complex Composite Cloud Applications* [20]. Unfortunately, automating the provisioning and management of such

© Springer International Publishing Switzerland 2015
M. Helfert et al. (Eds.): CLOSER 2014, CCIS 512, pp. 151–168, 2015.
DOI: 10.1007/978-3-319-25414-2_10

applications is a difficult challenge because their management technologies typically provide proprietary and heterogeneous management APIs, security mechanisms, and data formats which need to be integrated, too [8]. This leads to a high risk of unexpected side effects when a task unintentionally affects multiple parts of an application. Thus, managing such applications requires (i) a deep technical insight in each technology and (ii) an overall understanding of the system. In many cases, only experts are able to execute management tasks correctly. However, they also reach their limits when a management task has to be executed on a complex application whose exact structure and runtime state are not documented: Unknown relations and dependencies between components that directly influence each other's functionality lead to a serious management challenge. Thus, if the *context*, in which a management task is executed, is not explicitly known, understood, and considered, there is a high risk of unintended side effects. In addition, as manually executing management task in large systems is slow, costly, and error prone, Cloud application management must be automated [14,20,30].

In this paper, we present an approach that enables applying expert management knowledge for provisioning and management tasks in a certain context automatically to running applications. We introduce an abstract (i) *Context-Aware Application Management Method* and (ii) present a fully automated realization of this method for the provisioning and management of applications to validate its practical feasibility. The method introduces *Declarative Management Description Models* (DMDM) to describe management tasks declaratively including their context in a formal model. This enables experts to detect unintended impacts and side effects of management tasks through analyzing them in the context in which they are executed. We show that an individual context analysis is often required due to the heterogeneous nature of the involved components and management technologies—which is not possible using imperative approaches such as workflows or scripts. The automated realization of the method validates the method's practical feasibility. It enables organizations to operate a variety of different applications consisting of heterogeneous components without the need to employ or educate specialized experts that have the required technical knowledge. This paper is an extended version of a former work [10] we presented at the *4th International Conference on Cloud Computing and Services Science (CLOSER 2014)*. While the former paper considers only application management, we show in this paper how the method can be used also for the provisioning of applications by introducing *Automated Provisioning Patterns*.

In the next section, we describe limitations of existing management automation approaches and present a motivating scenario in Sect. 3. Section 4 presents the method, which is automated in Sect. 5. In Sect. 6, we present the paper's new contribution: We apply the method to application provisioning and introduce Automated Provisioning Patterns. In Sect. 7, we describe related work. Section 8 concludes the paper and gives an outlook on future work.

2   Limitations of Imperative Management Approaches

To automate application management, the execution of management tasks is often described imperatively using executable processes implemented as workflows [26], scripts, or programs. If an application is crucial to the business of an enterprise, errors that possibly result in system downtime are not acceptable. Therefore, often only the robust and reliable workflow technology can be used that provides features such as fault handling and compensation mechanisms [26]. Nevertheless, before executing such workflows, they must be verified to ensure a correct implementation. Unfortunately, the context, in which the management tasks are executed, is not explicitly described and, thus, not visible in such processes. As a result, management processes cannot be analyzed by experts in consideration of the management tasks' context as only operation calls, service invocations, or script executions on the *directly* affected components are described in workflows, but not the surrounding environment: Experts see only the directly affected part of the application, not the whole application structure. Thus, other application components that may be affected indirectly, too, cannot be considered in this analysis. For example, if the database of a Web-based application shall be replaced by a database from a different vendor, the application's Web Server may require a certain database connector to be installed for connecting to the new database. If this dependency is not considered and handled by the management workflow that replaces the database through installing the required connector, too, the application cannot connect to its database anymore. This quickly results in system downtimes caused by errors that are neither easy to find nor to fix. Thus, the most important requirement to enable context-aware management is a formal model that describes both the management tasks as well as their context.

3   Motivating Scenario

In this section, we describe the motivating scenario that is used to explain the proposed method and its realization. The scenario describes a business application that consists of a PHP-based Web frontend and a PostgreSQL database. The frontend shall be migrated from one Cloud to another. Because the application evolved over time, it is currently hosted on two Clouds: The PHP frontend is hosted on Microsoft's public Cloud offering "Windows Azure", the PostgreSQL database on Amazon's PaaS offering "Relational Database Service (RDS)". The PHP frontend runs on an Apache HTTP Server (including PHP-module) which is installed on an Ubuntu Linux operating system that runs in a virtual machine hosted on Azure. The management task that has to be executed is migrating the PHP frontend to Amazon's IaaS offering "Elastic Compute Cloud (EC2)" to reduce the number of employed Cloud providers. This migration results in two issues that compromise the application's functionality if they are not considered in advance: (i) Missing database driver and (ii) missing configuration of the database service. To migrate the PHP frontend, we have to create a new virtual machine on Amazon EC2, install the Apache HTTP Server and the PHP-module, and deploy the corresponding PHP files. This works without further configuration issues. However, connecting the PHP application to the database is not as easy as it seems to be: Simply defining the database configuration of the PHP frontend by setting the database's endpoint, username, and password is not sufficient. Here, a technical detail of the underlying infrastructure needs to be considered: The PHP-module of the Apache HTTP Server needs different database drivers to connect to different types of databases. Thus, if the Post-greSQL driver gets not installed explicitly on the server, the PHP frontend is not able to connect to the database. However, this is not easy to recognize as applications often employ MySQL databases whose drivers are typically installed together with the PHP-module. Thus, installing the required driver for Post-greSQL might be forgotten. The second issue is even more difficult to foresee if the administrator is not an expert in Amazon RDS: Databases running on Amazon RDS are per default not accessible from external components. To allow connections, a so-called "Security Group" must be defined to configure the firewall. This group specifies the IP-addresses which are allowed to connect to the database. Both issues result in breaking the application's functionality as the frontend can not connect to the database. The reason for both problems lies in ignoring the context in which the tasks are executed: (i) If an application shall connect to a certain database, the application's runtime environment must support this kind of database. (ii) Accessing a database hosted on Amazon RDS requires also more than simply writing endpoint information into a configuration file as the firewall of the service has to be configured, too. Thus, for these tasks, the context in the form of the infrastructure that hosts the database and the database type has to be considered to recognize the problems. However, both problems cannot be detected if the migration is implemented using traditional approaches such as management workflows or scripts: A wrong process possibly models only the steps for (i) shutting down the old virtual machine on Azure, (ii) creating the new virtual machine on Amazon EC2, (iii) installing the Apache Web Server and the PHP-module, (iv) deploying the frontend, and (v) setting the database's IP-address, name, port, username, and password in the frontend's configuration. However, this process neither provides information about the database's type nor which infrastructure is employed. Thus, the context, in which the management tasks are executed, is not described and the problems can not be detected.

4   Context-Aware Application Management Method

The *Context-Aware Application Management Method* provides a means to consider the context in which management tasks on application components or relations are executed. The method is shown in Fig. 1 and separates between a declarative description of the management tasks to be executed and the final executable management process. In the following subsections, we explain each step in detail.

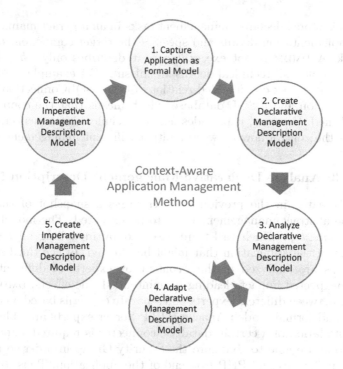

Fig. 1. Context-Aware application management method.

4.1 Step 1: Capture Application as Formal Model

First, the application to be managed is described as a formal model. This model captures the application structure and its state, i.e., (i) all components such as Web Servers, virtual machines, or installed applications, (ii) the relations between them, e.g., database connections, and (iii) their runtime information. The semantics of these *model elements* are described using types, e.g., a component may be of type "ApacheHTTPServer", a relationship of type "SQLConnection". To enable a precise definition of the elements, types can be inherited: The "ApacheHTTPServer" type is a subtype of "HTTPServer". Runtime information is described as element properties, e.g., the "ApacheHTTPServer" has the properties "IP-Address" and "Port" that specify its endpoint. Their schema is defined by the type of the element. This formalization of the running application provides a detailed, structured, and machine readable means to document a current snapshot of the application structure and all runtime information.

4.2 Step 2: Create Declarative Management Description Model

In the second step, the desired management tasks are described based on the formal model. Therefore, we introduce the *Declarative Management Description Model* (DMDM) that extends the formal model captured in Step 1 by a declarative description of the management tasks to be executed on components and relations. This model declares management tasks in an abstract manner without technical implementation details and specifies the target component or relation of each task. A DMDM is not executable as it describes only *what* has to be done, but not *how*—all technical details are missing. For example, a DMDM may declare a "Create" task on an added relation of type "SQLConnection" between a PHP application and a SQL database, which means that the connection has to be established. However, it provides neither technical implementation details nor specifies the control flow between multiple different management tasks.

4.3   Step 3: Analyze Declarative Management Description Model

The DMDM created in the previous step captures a snapshot of the application and the abstract management tasks to be executed. The model describes the whole *context* in which tasks are executed by modelling all components and relations of the application that might be affected. In the third step, management tasks are analyzed in their context by experts of different domains to detect unexpected impacts leading to unintended side effects. DMDMs enable cooperation between different experts and separate concerns based on a uniform, structured, and formal model: Apache HTTP Server experts are able to detect that the installation of a certain database connector is required, experts of the Amazon Cloud are able to configure the Security Group in order to allow connections from the external PHP frontend of the application. Thus, DMDMs can be analyzed by multiple experts of different domains in a cooperative manner.

4.4   Step 4: Adapt Declarative Management Description Model

After the expert analysis, found problems have to be resolved to achieve the desired management goals. Therefore, the DMDM is adapted in this step by the respective experts to enable a correct execution of the tasks: Components, relations, and tasks of the DMDM may be added or reconfigured. For example, the missing database connector found in the analysis of the previous step is resolved by adding the task to install the required connector on the Web Server. Thus, each task was verified in its respective context in the previous step and gets corrected if necessary in this step. However, if tasks are added or reconfigured, all tasks have to be analyzed again for correctness as the context changes through this adaptation. This may lead to new problems and unintended side effects on other components or relations that have to be found. Therefore, Step 3 and Step 4 are repeated until no new problems are found and all tasks were considered in the final context. This ensures that also the adaptations are checked.

4.5   Step 5: Create Imperative Management Description Model

The verified and adapted Declarative Management Description Model resulting from the previous step describes the tasks to be performed declaratively in an abstract manner—only *what* management tasks have to be performed, but not *how*. Thus, the model is not executable as the technical realization is not described. Therefore, an executable process model that implements the management tasks declared in the DMDM must be created. As this process model *imperatively* describes how the tasks have to be executed, we call these management processes *Imperative Management Description Models* (IMDM). An IMDM can be executed using an appropriate process engine and describes also the control flow and data handling between the management tasks. The IMDM has to implement exactly the semantics of the management tasks described by the adapted Declarative Management Description Model resulting from the previous step.

4.6   Step 6: Execute Imperative Management Description Model

In the last step, the IMDM is executed to perform the desired management tasks on the real running application. Therefore, a process engine is employed to run the process. As a result, the changes described by the tasks are applied to the running application in consideration of the context.

5   Realization and Validation

The presented method enables combining *declarative* management descriptions, which include all relevant context information to verify the tasks, and *imperative* processes, which are employed to actually perform the tasks on running applications. Thus, it combines two different types of Management Description Models which enables benefiting from advantages of both worlds. Therefore, the presented method provides the basis for enabling automated context-aware application provisioning and management. In this section, we validate the proposed method by showing a fully automated implementation using existing frameworks. We describe our prototypical realization for all steps of the method in the following.

5.1   Formalizing Applications Using Enterprise Topology Graphs

In Step 1, the application structure and runtime information have to be captured as formal model. We use *Enterprise Topology Graphs* (ETG) [5] as model language as they are a common way to formalize such information. ETGs are directed graphs that describe the application's structure as topology model that contains each component as typed node and each relation as typed edge. Runtime information is captured as properties of the respective model element. Thus, ETGs can be used to model the context in which a management task is executed. As ETGs support the XML-format, they are machine readable. On the left of Fig. 2, the ETG of the motivating scenario is shown. Binz et al. showed that ETGs of running applications can be discovered fully automatically using the ETGs *Discovery Framework* [3]. Thus, the first step of formalizing the application to be managed can be automated by using this framework.

5.2 Automating the DMDM Creation

Capturing application snapshots as ETG models provides a means to describe the context in which a management task is executed. Therefore, to create the DMDM in Step 2, we use the discovered ETG and annotate the management tasks to be executed directly at the affected components and relations of the ETG. In Breitenbücher et al. [6], we introduced so-called *Desired Application State Models*, which provide exactly this type of model for describing tasks to be executed declaratively in the context in which they have to be executed based on ETGs. Figure 2 shows the Desired Application State Model that describes our migration motivating scenario (rendered using *Vino4TOSCA* [11]). The colored circles with the symbols inside represent the management tasks to be executed in the form of so-called *Management Annotations* [6]. A Management Annotation describes a task to be performed in a declarative way: It defines only the type of the task and possible configuration properties, but not how to execute it. The green colored "Create-Annotations" with the star inside declare that the corresponding elements have to be created, whereas the red colored "Destroy-Annotations" with the "x" inside declare that the elements have to be destroyed. Management Annotations can be also bound declaratively to non-functional requirements in the form of policies that must be fulfilled when executing the task [9,13]. Annotating management tasks to ETGs, i.e., creating a DMDM, can be automated, too: Desired Application State Models can be generated by applying so-called *Automated Management Patterns* to ETGs [6]. An Automated Management Pattern consists of a (i) Topology Fragment and a

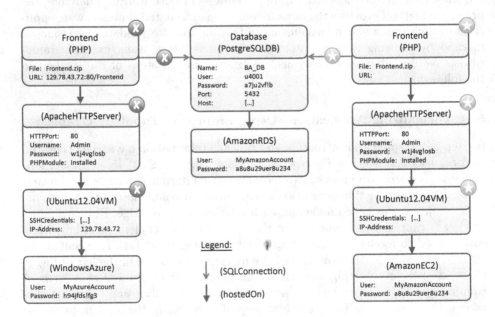

Fig. 2. Desired Application State Model after applying the idiom (simplified).

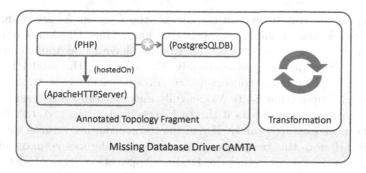

Fig. 3. CAMTA that recognizes the problem of missing PostgreSQL database connector.

(ii) Topology Transformation. The *Topology Fragment* describes the application structure to which the pattern can be applied. Thus, the pattern can be applied to all ETGs that match this fragment. The *Topology Transformation* implements the pattern's solution as executable transformation that automatically annotates the Management Annotations to be executed to the input ETG. We distinguish between *Semi-Automated Management Patterns*, which provide an abstract solution of a pattern that must be refined for concrete use cases manually, and *Fully-Automated Management Idioms*, which provide an already refined solution [7]. For example, the Desired Application State Model shown in Fig. 2 is the result of applying the "Migrate PHP Application to Amazon EC2 Idiom". Thus, the only manual step is selecting a Fully-Automated Management Idiom.

5.3 Context-Aware Task Analyzer

After the Desired Application State Model was created automatically by applying an Automated Management Pattern, it has to be analyzed by experts in Step 3 and adapted if necessary in Step 4. As we aim for automating the whole method realization, also these two steps need to be automated. Therefore, we introduce the concept of *Context-Aware Management Task Analyzers* (CAMTA) that provides a means to capture context-aware expert management knowledge in a form that enables a fully automated application to the Desired Application State Model resulting out of the previous step. The notion of CAMTAs is detecting and correcting problems by analyzing the tasks in their context and adapting the model if necessary fully automatically without manual interaction. Therefore, a CAMTA consists of two parts: (i) An *Annotated Topology Fragment* and a (ii) *Transformation*, similarly to Automated Management Patterns. The Annotated Topology Fragment is a small topology that specifies the management tasks in a certain context for which the CAMTA is able (i) to analyze correctness and (ii) to provide expert management knowledge required to adapt the model if necessary. The fragment is used for matchmaking of CAMTAs and Desired Application State Models: If the CAMTA's fragment matches elements and Management Annotations in the model, the Context-Aware Management Task Analyzer is able to analyze exactly that part. Thus, the Annotated Topology Fragment is used to select the CAMTAs that have to be applied to analyze the DMDM in Step 3 fully automatically. For adapting the model in Step 4, each CAMTA implements a context-aware transformation that transforms the input Desired Application State Model fully automatically if necessary. Therefore, the transformation checks if the tasks specified in the CAMTA's Topology Fragment can be executed safely: If yes, the transformation returns the unmodified model. If not, the transformation adds or configures components, relationships, or tasks for correcting the Desired Application State Model. Figure 3 shows a CAMTA that analyzes the tasks of establishing a SQL connection from a PHP application hosted on an Apache HTTP Server to a PostgreSQL database. The shown CAMTA is able to analyze if establishing a SQLConnection in the context of a PHP Application running on the Apache HTTP Server to a PostgreSQL database is possible. This is expressed by its Annotated Topology Fragment on the left. The transformation shown on the right analyzes the Desired Application State Model, finds out whether the PostgreSQL connector driver is missing, and adds the corresponding model elements and tasks to the model if necessary. Thus, based on two CAMTAs, the Desired Application State Model, which results from applying a Fully-Automated Management Idiom, gets adapted fully automatically to resolve the issues of the missing database connector and Security Group configuration. The respective CAMTAs insert two different Management Annotations into the Desired Application State Model: (i) A "ConfigureSecurityGroup-Annotation" that is attached to the Amazon-RDS node and an "InstallDriver-Annotation" attached to the Apache HTTP Server node. The ConfigureSecurityGroup-Annotation configures the Amazon-RDS instance in a way that the database is accessible by the Apache HTTP Server. The InstallDriver-Annotation declares that the required connector for PostgreSQL databases must be installed. As Desired Application State Models typically specify multiple tasks to be executed in the form of Management Annotations that need to be analyzed in their context, multiple different CAMTAs are needed to check the correctness of the whole model. As they may change the model, all CAMTAs need to be applied every time after one CAMTA transformed the model to ensure that all Management Annotations are validated in the current context. As soon as input and output model do not change anymore after applying all matching CAMTAs, Step 4 is finished.

5.4   Management Plan Generation

After the DMDM was analyzed for correctness and adapted in the previous steps, the resulting model is not executable as it describes the tasks to be performed only declaratively, i.e., without implementation and control flow: The DMDM has to be transformed into an executable imperative model in Step 5. Therefore, we employ the Management Planlet Framework presented in Breitenbücher et al. [6] that employs *Management Planlets* to translate Desired Application State Models fully automatically into executable BPEL workflows. Management Planlets

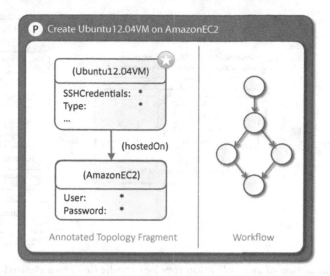

Fig. 4. Management Planlet that creates an Ubuntu12.04 virtual machine on Amazon's infrastructure service Elastic Compute Cloud (EC2).

provide the low-level imperative management logic to execute the declarative Management Annotations used in Desired Application State Models and support defining functional as well as non-functional requirements [9,13]. They serve as generic management building blocks that can be orchestrated to implement a higher-level management task. A Management Planlet consists of two parts: (i) *Annotated Topology Fragment* and (ii) a *workflow*. The fragment exposes the Planlet's functionality and is used to find Planlets that are capable of executing the specified management tasks in the respective context. For example, the Planlet shown in Fig. 4 is capable of executing the Create-Annotation attached to an Ubuntu12.04VM node if this node has to be hosted on AmazonEC2. The Planlet's workflow implements exactly the management logic required to create this virtual machine on EC2. Based on these fragments, Planlets can be orchestrated to an overall management plan that performs all annotations defined in the Desired Application State Model. Therefore, the framework employs a Plan Generator that transforms Desired Application State Models into executable workflows.

6 Context-Aware Cloud Application Provisioning

In this section, we present the new contribution of this paper that focuses on the context-aware provisioning of applications. We show how the Context-Aware Application Management Method presented in Sect. 4 can be used also for context-aware provisioning and show afterwards how this variant of the method can be automated by introducing the concept of *Automated Provisioning Patterns*.

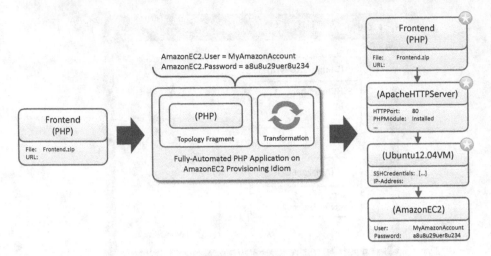

Fig. 5. Transformation of an application topology model (left) to a Desired Application State Model (right) by applying a Fully-Automated Provisioning Idiom.

6.1 Provisioning Variant of the Method

The original method for management consists of six steps and starts with capturing the application to be managed as formal model describing the application's structure and state. This model provides the entry point to define the management tasks to be executed. In our realization, all following steps are based on the original ETG that provides the basic context. In terms of provisioning, such an instance model does not exist as no ETG is available for non-provisioned applications. Therefore, the first step has to be removed if the method shall be applied to application provisioning. Thus, the method directly starts with creating the DMDM. As a result, we define Step 1 of the method as optional to enable using the method for both application provisioning as well as executing management tasks—the following steps are identical. However, to automatically create the DMDM for the provisioning in the form of a Desired Application State Model, this requires a special kind of pattern since Automated Management Patterns and Idioms require an input ETG to be transformed. Therefore, we introduce Automated Provisioning Patterns in the following subsection.

6.2 Automated Provisioning Patterns and Provisioning Idioms

We distinguish also for the provisioning between patterns and idioms by introducing (i) Semi-Automated Provisioning Patterns and (ii) Fully-Automated Provisioning Idioms. Both consist of a (i) Topology Fragment and a (ii) Topology Transformation, similar to the management approach. However, their input is not the ETG of a running application but an *application topology model* of the desired application. This model is either empty or describes single nodes and relations of the desired application deployment—but without runtime information.

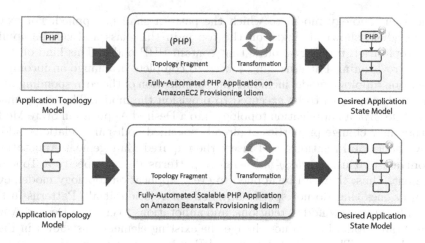

Fig. 6. Two classes of Automated Provisioning Patterns/Idioms: topology-dependent (top) and topology-independent (bottom).

The Topology Fragment is matched against the topology model and the transformation works on the matching elements. *Semi-Automated Provisioning Patterns* generate Desired Application State Models that need to be refined afterwards, i.e., they insert nodes or relations of abstract types that must be refined to a concrete type manually. In addition, added Management Annotations may need to be configured or additional annotations may need to be added. For example, an inserted abstract "InfrastructureService" node must be refined manually to a concrete node type, e.g., "AmazonEC2". *Fully-Automated Provisioning Idioms* generate already refined Desired Application State Models that can be used directly for the plan generation. For example, Fig. 5 shows an idiom for hosting a PHP application on EC2. The idiom consumes the application topology, which was created manually by an administrator in Step 2, and requests user and password of the Amazon account as input. The topology model contains only a PHP node describing the files to be deployed. The idiom's transformation inserts concrete infrastructure nodes, relations, and Management Annotations that are already refined for this concrete use case. Thus, the resulting Desired Application State Model can be used directly for the plan generation. In Step 2, multiple provisioning patterns and idioms can be applied to build complex applications.

6.3   Topology-Dependent and Topology-Independent Patterns

In this section, we present two different classes of Automated Provisioning Patterns: (i) Topology-dependent and (ii) topology-independent. We do not distinguish between patterns and idioms in this section because this difference is not important for the following considerations. Therefore, we refer to both as Automated Provisioning Patterns. The first class of *topology-dependent* patterns specify a Topology Fragment that must match corresponding elements in an application topology model to which the pattern shall be applied. For example, the idiom shown in Fig. 6 on the top is in this class and can be applied to all application topology models that contain PHP nodes. This kind of Automated Provisioning Patterns can be used to complete or change an incomplete application topology model including the specification of the corresponding Management Annotations to be executed to provision the model. Thus, they might really *transform* an application topology into a Desired Application State Model, i.e., they may change properties of already specified nodes and relations, add or remove nodes and relations, and insert the required Management Annotations. In contrast to this, *topology-independent* patterns do not specify a Topology Fragment. Thus, they can be applied to every application topology model, even to empty ones that do not specify any node or relation at all. Patterns in this class only *insert* new nodes, relations, and annotations to create a Desired Application State Model but do not change the existing elements, as shown in Fig. 6 on the bottom. This kind of Automated Provisioning Patterns can be used to capture complete application architecture templates that can be inserted at once without transforming the original topology model elements. For example, a complete scalable LAMP (Linux, Apache, MySQL, PHP) stack hosted on a certain Cloud provider can be implemented as Fully-Automated Provisioning Idiom.

7 Related Work

Context-aware systems adapt their functionality and behaviour using context information about the environment. An often used definition for context was given by Dey [15]: "Context is any information that can be used to characterize the situation of an entity, where an entity can be a person, place, physical or computational object". An important type of context information, which is often neglected, is the state and structure of an application to be managed. In this paper, we use this type of context information to verify, configure, and execute management tasks on applications and their infrastructure. The automated realization of the presented management method provides, therefore, the basis to implement Context-aware Cloud Application Management Systems.

To model and manage context information, many frameworks have been developed in the past years. There are simple, widget-like frameworks for sensor information such as the Context Toolkit [16] and systems that support smart environments like Aura [23] or Gaia [31]. Different types of development frameworks, e.g., the framework of Henricksen and Indulska [22], and context management platforms, e.g., the Nexus Platform [21], were developed that aim at efficient provisioning of context information within a global scope. These frameworks use *Context Models* as an abstraction layer between applications and the technical infrastructure that gathers the context data. However, there is no framework that manages context information for application management in the form of the Declarative Management Description Models introduced in this paper, which provide a kind of Context Model that (i) enables capturing the environment in which management tasks are executed and (ii) the management tasks themselves described in a declarative fashion. In the realization, the context is captured in a domain-specific data structure in the form of ETGs. Furthermore, no sensors integration has to be achieved because the context is detected on the fly using the ETG Discovery Framework [3]. Thus, the context is always up to date and does not have to be stored or managed using additional tooling.

There are several approaches that enable describing application topologies including runtime information and dependencies. Scheibenberger and Pansa [32] present a generic meta model to describe resource dependencies among IT infrastructure components. They separate the static view, which captures functional and structural aspects, from the dynamic operational view, which captures runtime information. In contrast to the employed concept of ETGs in the validation, their approach enables to model dependencies between component properties. The method's realization may be extended to capture also such fine-grained dependencies if necessary that may help experts to analyze possible impacts of a certain management task. The *Common Information Model* (CIM) [17] is a standard that provides an extensible, object-oriented data model used to capture information about different parts of an enterprise. It also provides a specification to describe application structures including dependencies. However, all these works may be used to formalize the application structure, dependencies, and runtime information, but they provide no means to model also the management tasks to be executed as required to implement a DMDM.

There are several frameworks that employ declarative descriptions to generate workflows such as Eilam et al. [18], Maghraoui et al. [28], and Keller et al. [24]. The first two focus mainly on provisioning of applications whereas the third also considers application management. In general, the proposed method can be adapted and applied to all approaches that transform declarative descriptions into imperative processes. However, it must be ensured that the declarative descriptions (i) provide the whole context and (ii) that the management tasks to be executed are described by this model somehow. In a former work [12], we showed how declarative provisioning descriptions can be transformed automatically into imperative workflows based on the TOSCA standard [4,29]. The application to be provisioned is described as topology model describing all application components and relations. As the tasks to be executed are obvious and the whole context of the provisioning is provided by this model in the form of the topology, the method can be adapted for this standards-based provisioning approach, too.

There are several pattern-based approaches that focus on the automation of application provisioning and deployment. For example, Lu et al. [27] use patterns to automate the deployment of applications. However, they employ *model-based patterns* that are different from the kind of patterns and idioms we consider in this paper. Their patterns are defined as topology models that are used to associate or derive the corresponding logic required to deploy the combination of nodes and relations described by the topology, similarly to our concept of Management Planlets. Fehling et al. [19] show how architectural Cloud patterns can be applied using a provisioning tool. However, all available approaches do not generate models that declaratively specify the abstract management tasks to be executed following a concept such as Management Annotations. Nevertheless, as the context is typically provided by the employed models, the general idea of the method can be applied to most of these approaches, too.

The model-driven SOA deployment platform presented by Arnold et al. [1,2] supports formally capturing topology-based deployment models at different levels of abstraction—ranging from abstract models, which they call *patterns*, to *concrete* models. This classification is similar to our approach of differentiating patterns and idioms and enables non-expert administrators to safely compose and iteratively refine deployment patterns, which results in fully-specified topologies with bindings to concrete resources. However, in contrast to our automated patterns and idioms, their patterns and concrete models capture only the structure and constraints of a composite solution and do not specify the management or provisioning tasks to be executed. In Arnold et al. [2], they present an approach how these patterns can be realized automatically and introduce *Parameterized Reconfiguration Patterns* that are conceptually similar to our Automated Provisioning Patterns: They define preconditions in the form of existing model elements and specify new elements to be provisioned. Similarly, Parameterized Reconfiguration Patterns also define input parameters that are used to configure the provisioning. The result of applying such patterns are models specifying the desired application state, but without the tasks to be executed. Nevertheless, the general idea of the method can be applied to this approach, too.

8 Conclusions

In this paper, we introduced an abstract Context-Aware Application Management Method that enables applying context-aware provisioning and management expertise. We showed that separating models for context-aware analysis and management task execution provides a powerful means to benefit from advantages of both worlds. Therefore, we employed abstract Declarative Management Description Models for describing the context as well as the management tasks to be executed themselves that are transformed into Imperative Management Description Models. The presented method is validated by an automated prototypical realization for application provisioning and management using the Management Planlet Framework. We plan to integrate non-functional requirements into the method and its realization and to apply both to the OASIS standard TOSCA.

Acknowledgements. This work was partially funded by the BMWi project Cloud-Cycle (01MD11023).

References

1. Arnold, W., Eilam, T., Kalantar, M., Konstantinou, A.V., Totok, A.A.: Pattern based SOA deployment. In: Krämer, B.J., Lin, K.-J., Narasimhan, P. (eds.) ICSOC 2007. LNCS, vol. 4749, pp. 1–12. Springer, Heidelberg (2007)

2. Arnold, W., Eilam, T., Kalantar, M., Konstantinou, A.V., Totok, A.A.: Automatic realization of SOA deployment patterns in distributed environments. In: Bouguettaya, A., Krueger, I., Margaria, T. (eds.) ICSOC 2008. LNCS, vol. 5364, pp. 162–179. Springer, Heidelberg (2008)
3. Binz, T., Breitenbücher, U., Kopp, O., Leymann, F.: Automated discovery and maintenance of enterprise topology graphs. In: SOCA 2013, pp. 126–134. IEEE, December 2013
4. Binz, T., Breitenbücher, U., Kopp, O., Leymann, F.: TOSCA: portable automated deployment and management of cloud applications. In: Bouguettaya, A., Sheng, Q.Z., Daniel, F. (eds.) Advanced Web Services, pp. 527–549. Springer, New York (2014)
5. Binz, T., Fehling, C., Leymann, F., Nowak, A., Schumm, D.: Formalizing the cloud through enterprise topology graphs. In: CLOUD 2012, pp. 742–749. IEEE, June 2012
6. Breitenbücher, U., Binz, T., Kopp, O., Leymann, F.: Pattern-based runtime management of composite cloud applications. In: CLOSER 2013, pp. 475–482. SciTePress, May 2013
7. Breitenbücher, U., Binz, T., Kopp, O., Leymann, F.: Automating cloud application management using management idioms. In: PATTERNS 2014, pp. 60–69. IARIA Xpert Publishing Services, May 2014
8. Breitenbücher, U., Binz, T., Kopp, O., Leymann, F., Wettinger, J.: Integrated cloud application provisioning: interconnecting service-centric and script-centric management technologies. In: Panetto, H., Dillon, T., Eder, J., Bellahsene, Z., Ritter, N., De Leenheer, P., Dou, D., Meersman, R. (eds.) ODBASE 2013. LNCS, vol. 8185, pp. 130–148. Springer, Heidelberg (2013)
9. Breitenbücher, U., Binz, T., Kopp, O., Leymann, F., Wieland, M.: Policy-aware provisioning of cloud applications. In: SECURWARE 2013, pp. 86–95. IARIA Xpert Publishing Services, August 2013
10. Breitenbücher, U., Binz, T., Kopp, O., Leymann, F., Wieland, M.: Context-aware cloud application management. In: CLOSER 2014, pp. 499–509. SciTePress, April 2014
11. Breitenbücher, U., Binz, T., Kopp, O., Leymann, F., Schumm, D.: Vino4TOSCA: a visual notation for application topologies based on TOSCA. In: Dillon, T., Rinderle-Ma, S., Dadam, P., Zhou, X., Pearson, S., Ferscha, A., Bergamaschi, S., Cruz, I.F., Meersman, R., Panetto, H. (eds.) OTM 2012, Part I. LNCS, vol. 7565, pp. 416–424. Springer, Heidelberg (2012)
12. Breitenbücher, U., et al.: Combining declarative and imperative cloud application provisioning based on TOSCA. In: IC2E 2014, pp. 87–96. IEEE, March 2014
13. Breitenbücher, U., et al.: Policy-aware provisioning and management of cloud applications. Int. J. Adv. Secur. 7(1&2), 15–36 (2014)
14. Brown, A.B., Patterson, D.A.: To err is human. In: EASY 2001, p. 5, July 2001
15. Dey, A.K., Abowd, G.D., Salber, D.: Managing Interactions in Smart Environments. A Context-Based Infrastructure for Smart Environments, pp. 114–128. Springer, London (2000)
16. Dey, A.K., Abowd, G.D., Salber, D.: A conceptual framework and a toolkit for supporting the rapid prototyping of context-aware applications. Hum. Comput. Interact. 16, 97–166 (2001)
17. Distributed Management Task Force: Common Information Model (2010)
18. Eilam, T., et al.: Pattern-based composite application deployment. In: Integrated Network Management, pp. 217–224. IEEE (2011)

19. Fehling, C., Leymann, F., Retter, R., Schumm, D., Schupeck, W.: An architectural pattern language of cloud-based applications. In: PLoP 2011. ACM, October 2011
20. Fehling, C., Leymann, F., Rütschlin, J., Schumm, D.: Pattern-based development and management of cloud applications. Future Internet 4(1), 110–141 (2012)
21. Großmann, M., et al.: Efficiently managing context information for large-scale scenarios. In: PerCom 2005. IEEE (2005)
22. Henricksen, K., Indulska, J.: A software engineering framework for context-aware pervasive computing. In: PerCom 2004. IEEE (2004)
23. Judd, G., Steenkiste, P.: Providing contextual information to pervasive computing applications. In: PerCom 2003. IEEE (2003)
24. Keller, A., Hellerstein, J.L., Wolf, J.L., Wu, K.L., Krishnan, V.: The CHAMPS system: change management with planning and scheduling. In: NOMS 2004, pp. 395–408. IEEE (2004)
25. Leymann, F.: Cloud computing: the next revolution in IT. In: The Photogrammetric Record, pp. 3–12, September 2009
26. Leymann, F., Roller, D.: Production workflow: concepts and techniques. Prentice Hall PTR, USA (2000)
27. Lu, H., Shtern, M., Simmons, B., Smit, M., Litoiu, M.: Pattern-based deployment service for next generation clouds. In: SERVICES 2013, pp. 464–471. IEEE, June 2013
28. El Maghraoui, K., Meghranjani, A., Eilam, T., Kalantar, M., Konstantinou, A.V.: Model driven provisioning: bridging the gap between declarative object models and procedural provisioning tools. In: van Steen, M., Henning, M. (eds.) Middleware 2006. LNCS, vol. 4290, pp. 404–423. Springer, Heidelberg (2006)
29. OASIS: Topology and Orchestration Specification for Cloud Applications Version 1.0, May 2013
30. Oppenheimer, D., Ganapathi, A., Patterson, D.A.: Why do internet services fail, and what can be done about it? In: USITS. USENIX Association, June 2003
31. Roman, M., Campbell, R.H.: Gaia: enabling active spaces. In: SIGOPS 2000, pp. 229–234. ACM (2000)
32. Scheibenberger, K., Pansa, I.: Modelling dependencies of it infrastructure elements. In: BDIM 2008, pp. 112–113. IEEE, April 2008

A Distributed Cloud Architecture
for Academic Community Cloud

Shigetoshi Yokoyama[✉] and Nobukazu Yoshioka

National Institute of Informatics, Tokyo, Japan
{yoko,nobukazu}@nii.ac.jp

Abstract. This study describes a new approach to cloud federation architecture for academic community cloud. Two basic approaches have been proposed to deal with cloud burst, disaster recovery, business continuity, etc., in community clouds: standardization of cloud services and multi-cloud federation. The standardization approach would take time; i.e., it would not be effective until there are enough implementations and deployments following the standard specifications. The federation approach places limitations on the functionalities provided to users; they have to be the greatest common divisor of the clouds' functions. Our approach is "cloud on demand", which means on-demand cloud extension deployments at remote sites for inter-cloud collaborations. Because we can separate the governance of physical resources for cloud deployment and the governance of each cloud by this approach, each organization can have full control on its cloud. We describe how the problems of the previous approaches are solved by the new approach and evaluate a prototype implementation of our approach.

Keywords: Inter-cloud · Community cloud · Cluster as a service · Bare-Metal provisioning · Academic cloud

1 Introduction

Private clouds get some benefit from the consolidations made possible by using virtualization technology. However an individual organization cannot reduce IT costs significantly through the use of its own private cloud because it must have on hand the maximum IT resources needed to deal with peak traffic.

In order to better utilize IT resources, a hybrid cloud solution is feasible in some situations. A hybrid cloud consists of a private cloud and public cloud; the private cloud deals with flat traffic and the public cloud covers peak traffic. However, when security matters, it is not feasible to send all the peak traffic to the public cloud.

It is important to think about sharing IT resources among private clouds to ensure better utilization and security at the same time. This idea can be viewed as a private cloud hosting service.

Table 1 describes the characteristics of public, private and hybrid clouds. Cloud users have to decide what kind of cloud they want to use, depending on their applications. A hybrid cloud integrates private and public clouds vertically. It assigns peak traffic of

© Springer International Publishing Switzerland 2015
M. Helfert et al. (Eds.): CLOSER 2014, CCIS 512, pp. 169–186, 2015.
DOI: 10.1007/978-3-319-25414-2_11

applications that do not necessarily need strong security to the public cloud. It cannot fit the situation in which all peak traffics have to be dealt with securely.

On the other hand, a community cloud is a way to keep clouds independent from one another while getting flexibility and security at the same time. In fact, there has been a lot of activity on ways to establish community clouds. The approaches can be categorized into two kinds. One is standardization of cloud services and the other is multi-cloud federation. The standardization approach would take time; i.e., it would not be effective until there are enough implementations and deployments following the standard specifications. The federation approach places limitations on the functionalities provided to users; they have to be the greatest common divisor of the clouds' functions.

We propose a new approach, called "cloud on demand", which integrates many private clouds horizontally and shares IT resources among them to accommodate peak traffic. By applying this solution, users can get good IT resource utilization like in a public cloud and have the level of security of a private cloud.

In this paper, we introduce our cloud on demand solutions called dodai and colony and describe a real cloud on demand service that was recently deployed as the research cloud of our research institute, National Institute of Informatics (NII).

This paper is organized as follows. Section 2 describes the previous approaches. Section 3 introduces the cloud on demand solution. Section 4 shows a prototype implementation. We summarize our evaluation of case studies in Sect. 5 and conclude in Sect. 6.

Table 1. Characteristics of cloud solutions.

	Cost	Security	Ease of Application Development
Public Cloud	Strong for peak traffic pattern	Depends on public cloud provider policy and management	Has public cloud architecture constraints
Private Cloud	Strong for flat traffic pattern	Depends on controllable private cloud management	Can choose application architecture
Hybrid Cloud	Strong for flat + peak traffic pattern	Depends on controllable deployment architecture and private cloud management	Has hybrid cloud architecture constraints
Community Cloud	Strong for small to big and flat to peak traffic	Depends on controllable private cloud management	Can choose application architecture

2   Previous Approaches

In this section, we describe the previous approaches, which are cloud standardization and cloud federation.

2.1   Cloud Standardization

One of the famous cloud standardization activities is the Global Inter-Cloud Technology Forum (GICTF) [4]. Its mission is as follows:

– Promote the development and standardization of technologies to use cloud systems.
– Propose standard interfaces that allow cloud systems to interwork with each other.
– Collect and disseminate proposals and requests regarding the organization of technical exchange meetings and training courses.
– Establish liaisons with counterparts in the U.S. and Europe, and promote exchanges with relevant R&D teams.

GICTF has produced a number of white papers, including "Use Cases and Functional Requirements for Inter-Cloud Computing", "Technical Requirements for Supporting the Inter-cloud Networking", "Inter-cloud Interface Specification Draft (Inter-cloud Protocol)" and "Inter-cloud Interface Specification Draft (Cloud Resource Data Model)."

There are other similar standardization activities like the Open Cloud Standards Incubator, Cloud Storage Technical Work Group, Open Cloud test bed and Open Cloud Computing Interface Working Group [7].

The use cases they deal with are as follows:

U1. Guaranteed performance during abrupt increases in load
U2. Guaranteed performance regarding delay
U3. Guaranteed availability in the event of a disaster or a large-scale failure
U4. Service continuity
U5. Market transactions via brokers
U6. Enhanced convenience by service cooperation.

The clouds maintain independence from one another and collaborate with each other through standard interfaces. This approach seems to be the ultimate solution for community clouds but it will take time to get a consensus from all the communities on the standard.

2.2   Cloud Federation

Cloud federation is the practice of interconnecting the cloud computing environments of multiple service providers for the purpose of loads balancing traffic and accommodating spikes in demand. Cloud federation requires one provider to federate the computing resources of the cloud providers. Cloud federation consists of the following components:

Application: a set of virtual machines and data volumes connected by a virtual network to be deployed at the IaaS level.

Portal: a common entry point for multiple cloud providers. A user submits an application to the portal. The portal selects providers to run the application. Usually, the portal can only offer functionalities that are the greatest common divisor of the providers.

This approach tries to cover use cases U1, U2, U3, U4 and U5. In contrast, we assume that the main purpose of establishing community clouds is to accommodate use cases U1, U2, U3 and U4. That is, our cloud on demand solution focuses on these use cases.

3   Cloud on Demand

Our approach is different from the previous ones. Figure 1 is an overview of our cloud on demand solution. There are two service components. One is called Cluster as a Service [9], and the other is called the inter-cloud object storage service [10, 11]. Cluster as a Service is a service by which users create clusters consisting of physical servers, and it can deploy software components for building an IaaS.

The inter-cloud object storage service lets users store objects, like machine images, as if they were using a local cloud object storage service. Physically, each cloud is connected to a high-speed wide area network, such as SINET-4 [8]. The network connections are made by using network functionalities like L2VPN and VPLS. The physical servers can be located in the same L2 network segment if the same VLAN–ID is assigned to them. The physical servers that are assigned different VLAN-IDs are securely separated from the other network segments.

Through this design, we can generate physical machine clusters in inter-cloud environments on which we can deploy IaaS software like OpenStack, Eucalyptus, and others in our favourite configurations for each.

In addition, we configure a distributed inter-cloud object storage service using open source software like OpenStack swift for storing machine images.

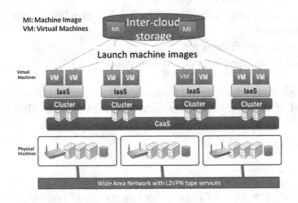

Fig. 1.   Architecture overview.

To allocate the application execution environments, we deploy an IaaS cluster on demand on physical servers and deploy the application virtual machine cluster on it. In this case, the IaaS cluster uses the inter-cloud object storage service to launch virtual machines from machine images that have been prepared for the application cluster. IaaS clusters themselves are not necessarily destroyed after each the application execution. The life cycle of the IaaS is independently controlled by the application execution environment managers.

3.1   Cluster as a Service (CaaS)

Cluster as a Service is designed as follows:

(1) Two-layer implementation

The lower layer takes care of physical machine cluster management. The upper layer handles virtual machine cluster management. Moreover, each layer is programmable with web APIs.

(2) The lower layer

The lower layer handles the operating systems of each node composing a cluster. Nodes can be allocated to clusters dynamically from software and securely separated by using network technology, like virtual LAN in the allocation.

(3) The upper layer

The upper layer deals with deploying IaaS software such as OpenStack and Eucalyptus. It also can deploy PaaS software. The layer has configuration management tools to ease deployment on the nodes of clusters.

An actual deployment example is depicted in Fig. 2.

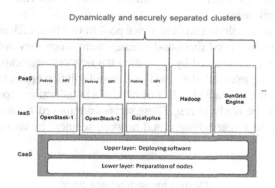

Fig. 2.   Cluster as a service.

3.2   Inter-cloud Object Storage Service

Figure 3 depicts the service from the user's view point. Users of these clouds can share objects, simply by dropping objects in inter-cloud-containers. Users explicitly specify the locations where they want to store objects.

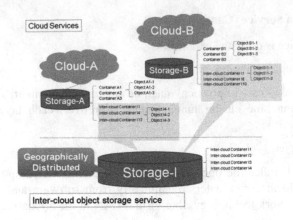

Fig. 3. Inter-cloud storage service.

4 Prototype

4.1 CaaS Overview

We developed Cluster as a Service by which a private cloud can be deployed from common computer resources.

The cloud on demand solution has a resource pool from which each private cloud allocates IT resources as they need them and releases them when they are not using them (Fig. 4). The security is guaranteed by separating the network segments for each private cloud. When servers are released, the cloud on demand solution erases the storage before it allocates it to the other private clouds. For rapid elastic allocation, some servers in the resource pool have to be ready to run. These servers are moved from the resource pool network segment to the target private cloud network segment by changing the network configuration.

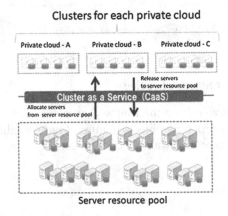

Fig. 4. Cluster as a Service.

4.2   Requirements of CaaS

Req. (1) Computer resources must be dynamically allocated to the clusters of different private clouds
Req. (2) Clusters must be securely separated.
Req. (3) Software components of the cloud must be easily deployed on the clusters.

4.3   Design of CaaS

CaaS is designed to satisfy these requirements:

(1) Two-layer implementation

The lower layer takes care of Req. (1) and Req. (2). The upper layer handles Req. (3). Moreover, each layer is programmable with web APIs.

(2) Lower layer

The lower layer handles the operating systems of each node composing a cluster for using machine images. Nodes can be allocated to clusters dynamically from software and securely separated by using network technology, like virtual LANs, in the allocation. The lower layer also deals with erasing storage when servers are released. A prototype of this layer is dodai-compute [2].

(3) Upper layer

The upper layer deals with deploying IaaS/PaaS software such as Hadoop, Grid Engine, OpenStack, and eucalyptus. Configuration management tools make it easy to deploy software on the nodes of clusters. A prototype of this layer is dodai-deploy [3].

4.4   Dodai-Compute

The lower layer dodai-compute is a system based on OpenStack nova to control operations (such as run instances from an image) on physical machines instead of VMs. Figure 5 illustrates the architecture of dodai-compute. The run instances, terminate instances, start instances, stop instances, reboot instances and associate address operations on physical machines can be done via EC2 APIs. The architecture of dodai-compute is as follows. Dodai-compute uses PXEboot via a cobbler library to bootstrap physical machines corresponding to run instance API calls. It also uses an OpenFlow controller to assign network segments to the physical machine. IPMI is used to control physical machines corresponding to the start instance, stop instance and reboot instance. The terminate instance operation is used to move physical machines to the machine pool network segment. The OpenFlow controller does this operation. The disks are physically cleaned up and become ready for the next launch. The associate address operation is done by an agent in each physical machine instance.

VLANs are used on some private clouds. When IaaS is deployed on them, we use OpenFlow technology, instead of VLAN, in order to separate network segments for each private cloud.

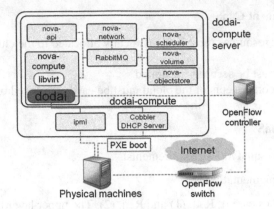

Fig. 5. Dodai-compute architecture.

4.5 Dodai-Deploy

The upper layer of dodai-deploy's specification and its prototype are described in this section. Dodai-deploy has the following functionalities:

(1) Installation configuration proposal creation

Dodai-deploy runs according to a user installation plan called a 'proposal.'

(2) Installation and un-installation

Software components are installed according to a proposal on target physical machine nodes and virtual machine nodes. Dodai-deploy can un-install software components, as well.

(3) Test installation result

Automatic testing of the deployed IaaS and PaaS is an important functionality of dodai-deploy. Users can use these functionalities through a Web GUI and CLI.

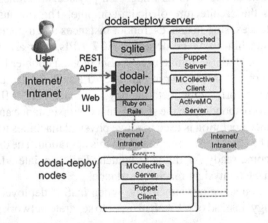

Fig. 6. Dodai-deploy architecture.

Figure 6 illustrates the architecture of dodai-deploy. The dodai-deploy server generates manifest files for the puppet configuration tool [6] when users submit proposals requesting installations. The architecture was designed with fast deployment in mind to cope with the growing number of target machines. Parallel deployment is the key to achieving this goal but dependencies among software components have to be used to make usable deployment strategies. The actual parallel deployment procedure uses MCollective [MCollective (2013)] to control many puppet clients.

4.6 Colony

We describe how to implement a geographically distributed inter-cloud storage service. Storage-I in Fig. 7 should be a network-aware object storage service in order to make the remote application deployment rapid. The prototype uses OpenStack Swift as the base software. A prototype of this inter-cloud storage service is colony [1].

OpenStack Object Storage (code-named Swift is open source software for creating redundant, scalable data storage using clusters of standardized servers to store peta-bytes of accessible data). It is not a file system or real-time data system, but rather a long-term storage system for large amounts of static data that can be retrieved, leveraged, and updated. Object Storage uses a distributed architecture with no central point of control, providing greater scalability, redundancy and permanence.

Objects are written to multiple hardware devices, with the OpenStack software responsible for ensuring data replication and integrity across the cluster. Storage clusters scale horizontally by adding new nodes. Should a node fail, OpenStack works to replicate its content from other active nodes. Because OpenStack uses software logic to ensure data replication and distribution across different devices, inexpensive commodity hard drives and servers can be used in lieu of more expensive equipment.

Swift has proxy nodes and auth nodes acting as the front-end and storage nodes acting as the back-end for accounts, containers, and object storage.

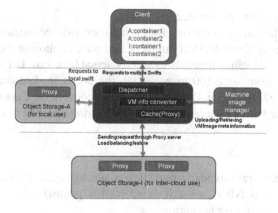

Fig. 7. Software components of colony.

The internal software components of the service are shown in Fig. 7. The caching component makes the machine image launch fast. The dispatcher selects the nearest object replica in object storage service-I, even if there is no copy in the local cache.

4.6.1 How the Original Swift Works

The basic mechanism of downloading and uploading objects in the original Swift is as follows:

(1) GET

The proxy server randomly chooses a replica from the ring and asks the storage server to send the object in which the replica resides.

(2) PUT

The proxy server knows the storage servers to which object replicas from the ring should be put and sends the objects to the all storage servers. The PUT operation ends when the all replica writes finish.

This implementation is based on an assumption that the replicas are concentrated in the network, for example, in the same data center. However, in our context, this assumption is not valid. Actually, if we apply the original OpenStack swift to storage-I, the GET and PUT operations take time when the randomly selected replica is far away. This is the reason why we have to make the Swift software network-aware.

4.6.2 Network-Aware OpenStack Swift

(1) How to make Swift network-aware

In the put operation, all replicas are written in the same site as the proxy server instead of writing them to the location the ring specifies. The replicas of the original positions are made asynchronously by the object replicator. After confirming the replication, the local copies corresponding to the replicas are deleted. In the get operation, the 'nearest' replica, instead of a random one, is chosen by the mechanism described in the next section. The proxy server works with the cache mechanism as well.

(2) How to measure network distance

We use the zone information in the ring for the network distance measurement. The zone information consists of fixed decimal numbers, and we can allocate them freely. Therefore, we can use these decimal numbers to specify actual locations. Let's say the nodes in data center #1 are from zone-100 to zone-199, the nodes in data center #2 are from zone-200 to zone-299, and so on. By using this sort of convention, the software can know the network distance without our having to modify the ring structure or code related to it.

5   Evaluation

In order to evaluate the prototype in a real context, we deployed and evaluated our cloud on demand solution as NII's research cloud (called gunnii). We also evaluated the prototype in a number of user scenarios.

5.1 Evaluation Environment

We deployed cloud on demand solution as our research cloud providing bare-metal cloud service to NII researchers on July, 2012. An overview of gunnii from the users' viewpoint is shown in Fig. 8. NII researchers can extend their existing research clusters to this research cloud on demand.

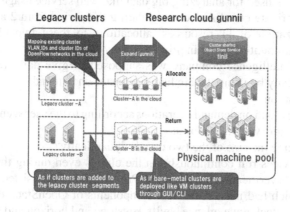

Fig. 8. Overview of the NII research cloud, gunnii.

Figure 9 shows how we use OpenFlow technologies with dodai-compute in this configuration. Dodai-compute provisions bare-metal clusters by using PXEboot and IMPI interfaces and allocates the bare-metal machines in OpenFlow closed networks, regions, on demand. It also connects these regions to corresponding existing closed networks of research groups, which are assigned individual VLAN-IDs by setting up suitable flow tables in OpenFlow switches.

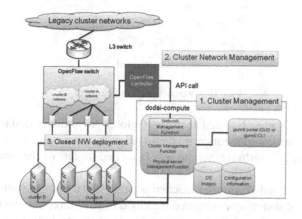

Fig. 9. Gunnii's architecture.

5.2 User Scenario According to U1 (Guaranteed Performance Against a Abrupt Increase of the Load)

We also set up two private clouds. One was an OpenStack [5] IaaS private cloud (private cloud-A), on which web services of a simulated e-commerce company were hosted. The other was a Hadoop PaaS private cloud of a business intelligence company (private cloud-B), which was used for analyzing big data like web service usage logs.

The traffic of private cloud-A decreased during the period from 2 am to 5 am. To increase the utilization of IT resources, allocations to these two clouds changed depending on the amount of traffic in private cloud-A.

The business intelligence company was supposed to give daily feedback to the e-commerce company by using the big hadoop cluster on demand.

(1) Cost evaluation

We verified the cloud on demand operations according to the user scenarios in gunnii. The verification points were as follows:

1. Can we change the size of the two clouds dynamically?
2. Can the services run continuously on the clouds even during the size change?

Figure 10 shows the verification environment. Private cloud-A consisted of two servers: a master node which had master software components of OpenStack diablo software and included OpenStack nova, glance, swift, keystone and horizon and slave software. The other server only had slave software like nova compute and swift object servers.

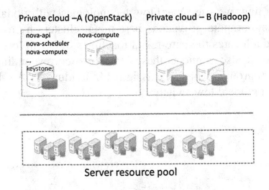

Private cloud –A (OpenStack)   Private cloud – B (Hadoop)

nova-api   nova-compute
nova-scheduler
nova-compute
...
keystone

Server resource pool

Fig. 10. Verification environment.

First, two servers were allocated to private cloud-A by using dodai-compute and OpenStack software components were deployed with dodai-deploy. In order to check verification point 2, a virtual machine was launched on one of the OpenStack nova-computes.

When private cloud-A's traffic reached a peak, dodai-compute allocated another server to it and dodai-deploy configured the cloud to have three servers (Fig. 11).

During this rerun, the application connection to the virtual machine was not interrupted. Nova-api and other software were continuously available to users. This was possible because dodai-deploy can notice that software components are deployed and services are running already on the two pre-existing servers. It deploys software

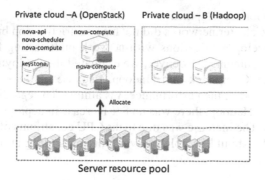

Fig. 11. Private cloud expansion.

components only to the newly allocated server. Moreover, through the OpenStack nova mechanism, the nova-scheduler automatically recognizes the new nova-compute.

On the other hand, when a bigger hadoop cluster is needed, private cloud-A should release a server. In this experiment, we released the most recently allocated server, because it was not the server on which the virtual machine was running. In a real situation, however, we would need to monitor the allocations of virtual machines by nova-compute and need to live migrate some of them to servers that will not be released (Fig. 12).

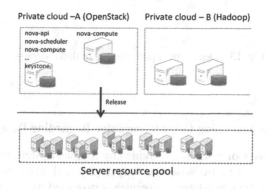

Fig. 12. Private cloud reduction.

In the experiment, the newly allocated server was released by using a dodai-compute terminate-instance call. OpenStack nova detected the loss of one server for nova-compute, and it did not try to launch virtual machines on that server later.

(1) Security

We verified that the network separation of the OpenFlow controller and the disk cleanup process in machine pool segment maintained the security of the user information. It was impossible to get into other clusters through the network and impossible to retrieve any information of the previous user from the physical machines.

(2) Ease of Application Development
We verified that the cluster networks did not have restrictions on broadcast or multicast. Users can develop applications with network multicasting functionalities on elastic private environments. Moreover, we evaluated the deployment performance of dodai-deploy for OpenStack and Hadoop. Because of the concurrent deployments to the target nodes, the performance was almost flat regarding the number of nodes. However, for Hadoop, there was an 8 % increase in deployment time in going from $n = 7$ to $n = 8$. The increase was due to the CPU constraints of the dodai-deploy server (Fig. 13). We should be able to avoid this by scaling up or scaling out the dodai-deploy server.

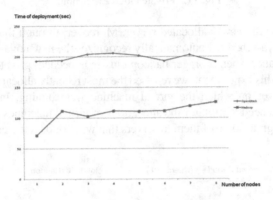

Fig. 13. Deployment performance of dodai-deploy.

5.3   User Scenario According to U2 (Guarantee Regarding Delay)

In this scenario, a user of a service provided by a cloud system goes on a business trip to a remote location. Because the longer physical distance causes a longer network delay from the site where the service is provided, the user may experience performance degradation as far as the response time goes.

(1) Extension to wide area network configuration
The evaluation environment of gunii was in a data center configuration. However, our cloud on demand solution architecture allows for an easy extension to a wide area network. Figure 14 shows how we can make this extension.

(2) Delay
The delay stays practically small because the cloud on demand solution can deploy the corresponding service in a data center nearer to the user.

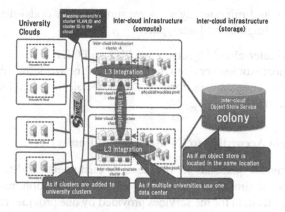

Fig. 14. Cloud on demand in a wide area network configuration.

5.4 User Scenario According to U3 (Guaranteed Availability in the Event of a Disaster or a Large-Scale Failure)

In this scenario, the cloud system of a municipality is damaged in a natural disaster and cannot continue to provide its services.

The disaster recovery operations used the resources of the remote municipalities (Such measures would be pre-arranged).

(1) Cloud migration

We developed a cloud migration tool which can migrate OpenStack IaaS from site-A to site-B by using dodai-compute, dodai-deploy and colony, and we demonstrated it in public. It stored the OpenStack user database and snapshots as well as configuration information for dodai regularly at site-A and restored them after reconstruction of the OpenStack at site-B using dodai (Fig. 15).

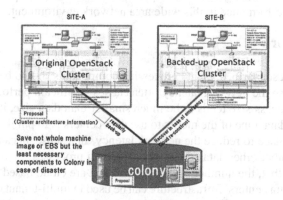

Fig. 15. Cloud migration.

Moreover, we could migrate any software supported by dodai-deploy, i.e., Open-Stack, Hadoop, GridEngine and Eucalyptus.

(2) Performance of inter-cloud object storage PUT and GET
By making the object storage service OpenStack swift network-aware, the inter-cloud object storage is almost equal in performance to local object storage for PUT and GET, which is described in [12].

5.5   User Scenario According to U4 (Service Continuity)

Normally, if a provider suspends its business, its customers need to re-register with different providers for similar services. To avoid such a situation, resources, applications, and customer ID data for the services provided by one provider can be transferred to the cloud systems of other providers in advance. Then, if its business is suspended, its consumers can use similar services provided by the other providers.

(1) Cloud migration
As described in the previous section, however it not necessary for dodai to regularly store a user database, snapshots, or configuration information.

(2) Performance of inter-cloud storage PUT and GET performance
Same as in the previous section.

6   Conclusions

We proposed a solution called cloud on demand and described a prototype implementation based on the dodai and colony projects. The cloud-on demand was proved to be feasible in the actual user scenarios in one data center. This architecture can be extended to wide area networks using SINET L2VPN and VPLS services if we plug the upper link from the OpenFlow switches into the SINET directly
    We are now constructing a new prototype of cloud on demand upon SINET, and we will evaluate its performance in this wide area network environment.

7   Future Work

In the BIG DATA scenario, data and processing components should be close enough to each other, because the network latency often causes significant performance degradation. Since the process size tends to be much smaller than data size, it is better for the process move to data. One of the merits to use data centers is to put the process and the data in the same place to reduce the network latency. In a sense, because the data have "gravity", data gather other data and those data attract processes.
    In addition to that, the number of data centers that are cloud based is getting bigger recently. These data centers' infrastructure can be used in multi-tenant context. Because of this multi-tenancy, effective management can be realized with software controlled infrastructures. We are expecting to have cloud based hyper-huge data centers because of this trend.

The scenario above works for the archive type data when the volume of BIG DATA matters. If we think about velocity of BIG DATA like real-time stream data processing, we have to slightly change the scenario. In this case, the network latency makes the process components move to the source of the data stream. This means we need to have distributed data center instead of centralized data center because the sources of the data streams are distributed. The distributed data centers have to be multi-tenant for effective resource usage as well as the centralize data centers do. This concludes that we need to have cloud based distributed data center, which is the definition of distributed cloud and its position can be seen in Fig. 16.

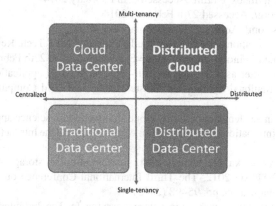

Fig. 16. The position of the distributed cloud.

In the context of distributed cloud discussion, there is comparison between few mega data centers versus many micro data centers [13]. If we want to satisfy both volume and velocity scenarios at the same time, we need to have the distributed cloud in the following sense.

Distributed cloud = Virtual cloud upon few mega DCs and many micro DCs

Virtual cloud providers allocate resource from real cloud providers as bare metal machines or virtual ones. Using those machines virtual the cloud providers deploy clusters for each tenant according to their requests as shown in Fig. 16.

The distributed cloud is an extension of the cloud federation architecture described in this paper (Fig. 17).

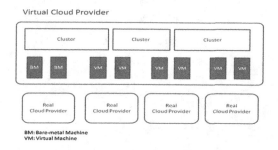

Fig. 17. Virtual Cloud Provider.

Acknowledgements. We would like to thank all the contributors to the dodai project, especially Shin-ichi Honiden, Yoshitaka Kuwata, Masashi Ochida, Osamu Habuka, Takahiro Shida, Guan Xiaohua, Motonobu Ichimura, Takahiko Yuzawa and Daishi Kimura.

References

1. https://github.com/nii-cloud/colony. Accessed 27th February 2014
2. https://github.com/nii-cloud/dodai-compute. Accessed 27th February 2014
3. https://github.com/nii-cloud/dodai-deploy. Accessed 27th February 2014
4. http://www.gictf.jp/index_e.html. Accessed 27th February 2014
5. http://openstack.org/. Accessed 27th February 2014
6. http://puppetlabs.com/. Accessed 27th February 2014
7. Sakai, H.: Standardization activities for cloud computing. NTT Tech. Rev. **9**(6), 1–6 (2011)
8. http://www.sinet.ad.jp/index_en.html?lang=English. Accessed 27th February 2014
9. Yokoyama, S.: Cluster as a Service for self-deployable cloud applications. In: 2012 12th IEEE/ACM International Symposium Cluster, Cloud and Grid Computing (CCGrid), pp. 703–704 (2012)
10. Yokoyama, S.: An academic community cloud architecture for science applications. In: 2012 IEEE/IPSJ 12th International Symposium on Applications and the Internet (SAINT), pp. 108–112 (2012)
11. Yokoyama, S., Yoshioka, N., Ichimura, M.: Intercloud object storage service: colony. In: CLOUD COMPUTING 2012, The Third International Conference on Cloud Computing, GRIDs, and Virtualization, pp. 95–98 (2012)
12. Yokoyama, S.: A network-aware object storage service. In: The 2nd International Workshop on Network-aware Data Management to be held in conjunction with SC12, pp. 556–561 (2012)
13. Hamilton, J.: On delivering embarrassingly distributed cloud services. In: HotNets (2008)

New Governance Framework to Secure Cloud Computing

Ahmed Shaker Saidah[(✉)] and Nashwa Abdelbaki

School of Information and Communication Technology,
Center for Informatics Science, Nile University, Cairo, Egypt
ahmed.shaker@nileu.edu.eg, nabdelbaki@nileuniversity.edu.eg

Abstract. Cloud computing is enabling proper, on-demand network access to a shared pool of computing resources that is elastic in reserve and release with minimal interaction from cloud service provider. As cloud gains maturity, cloud service providers are becoming more competitive, which increase the percentage of cloud adoption. But security remains the most cited challenge in Cloud. So, while we are progressing in cloud adoption, we have to define key elements of our cloud strategy and governance. Governance is about applying policies relating to used services. Therefore, it has to include the techniques and policies that measure and control how we manage cloud. In this paper, we develop an innovative governance model. We changed and tuned the Guo, Z., Song, M. and Song, J governance model from theoretical model into practical model using Cloud Control Matrix (CCM). But, governance model alone will not allow us to bridge the gap between control requirements, technical issues and business risks. As a result, we introduce a new Cloud governance framework using the processes on the new Cloud governance model and controls in CCM. The Framework focuses on using business drivers to guide cloud governance activities while considering cloud risks as part of the organization's risk management processes.

Keywords: Security framework · Governance model · Cloud computing

1 Introduction

Cloud Computing is a new term for an old service with new features. Many of us used to have an e-mail account during the last two decades. Data location, storage and processing are usually unknown to the user. In fact, this was a kind of Cloud service. Cloud was known as on demand infrastructure in the 90s and as Grid/Utility computing in the 2000s. Clouds and Grids are common in their vision, architecture and technology, but they differ in security, programming model, business model, compute model, data model and applications [1]. Earlier in these days, it was too risky to store our data outside organization premises; safety was a concern.

Data is the most valuable asset in any organization. It can be categorized as PI (personal information) or organizations' data. Nowadays, all Internet users intensively process and store data on the Cloud. Cloud Computing depends on sharing of resources to gain economies of scale. It focuses on maximizing the effectiveness of the shared

© Springer International Publishing Switzerland 2015
M. Helfert et al. (Eds.): CLOSER 2014, CCIS 512, pp. 187–199, 2015.
DOI: 10.1007/978-3-319-25414-2_12

resources. Despite the benefits promised by Cloud computing, we see that essential improvement on technologies and operations governance are needed to enable widely adoption of Cloud services [2].

The best way to protect data outside organization premises is to define a policy to organize the relation between the owner and service provider. Policy definition requires well-developed information security governance framework [3].

It is mandatory for any organization to follow a framework for establishing information security governance environment. The framework will be utilized by the business across the organization [4]. We create a new Cloud governance framework for helping organization to govern the Cloud services. It is a measurable, sustainable, continually improving and cost effective framework on an ongoing basis [5, 6].

The rest of this paper is organized into six sections. Section 2 discusses related works in governance and Cloud computing. We will go through existing Guo's Model and show the gap between its theoretical model and practical world, and will go through the pros and cons of the model. We propose our new Cloud Computing definition in Sect. 3. Section 4 illustrates our proposed new model of Cloud Governance. Our new governance framework is introduced in Sect. 5. Finally, conclusion and future work are presented in Sect. 6.

2 Related Work

Cloud Computing is a relatively new term in the computing world. The definition of Cloud Computing from NIST (2009) is very common and almost all other definitions are part of this definition [7].

Cloud Computing becomes a huge market. Relations between services inside the Cloud are complicated. Virtualization vendors use different APIs. This creates many obstacles and challenges when moving between Clouds. Infrastructure inside the Cloud contains many layers of shared resources. Software licensing and end users license and agreement have many parameters and stages [8]. Federations and access control between service provider premises and end user premises become vague [9].

The Cloud services become a self-service through websites. Customers can customize orders by themselves, which mean that they need to access the Cloud via all connectivity facilities. The user can increase or decrease the usage of the resources that is distributed across all provider premises.

Cloud Computing service models (SaaS, PaaS, IaaS) can be deployed in public, private or mixed model. User Control is varying from model to other and increasing or decreasing depending on the features and capabilities provided by the service provider or needed by the customer, (Fig. 1) [10].

In SaaS model as an example, the Cloud user accesses the web service through any type of connectivity via web browsers, and he does not have control to the infrastructure or applications running in the Cloud.

All of these features and facilities maximize security risks on the Cloud, open many doors for hijacking, and increase possible system vulnerabilities. Risks will be eliminated or mitigated by a robust governance framework [11, 12].

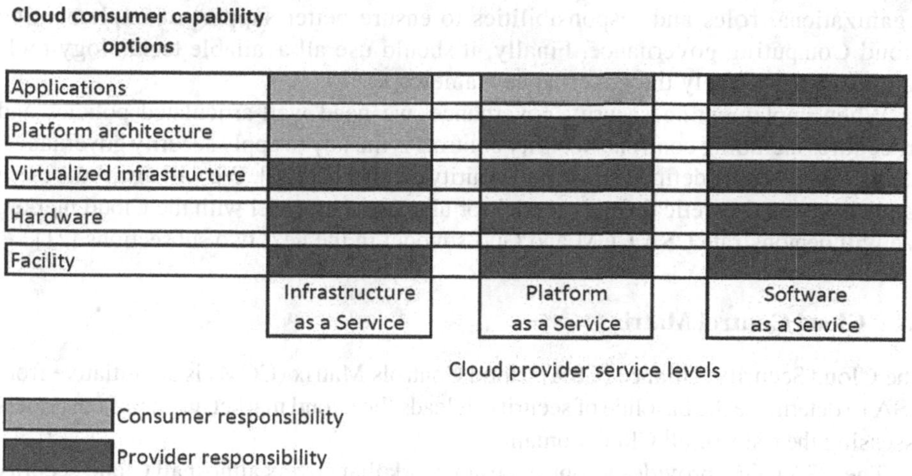

Cloud consumer capability
options

	Infrastructure as a Service	Platform as a Service	Software as a Service
Applications			
Platform architecture			
Virtualized infrastructure			
Hardware			
Facility			
	Infrastructure as a Service	Platform as a Service	Software as a Service

Cloud provider service levels

Consumer responsibility

Provider responsibility

Fig. 1. Control level of Cloud Computing.

Governance consists of policies, guidance, processes and decision-rights for a given area of responsibility. Corporate governance is to align processes and policies with business to ensure arrival to the business objectives. IT governance is part of the corporate governance and focuses on IT decisions and policies to ensure that IT assets are used according to the approved policies and procedures [13].

IT assets are huge and distributed between customer and service provider premises. They are classified into many types like people, policies, and equipment. It may be inside the organization or outsourced. Here, governance is required to control and maintain assets.

In many organization success stories, there is a harmony between managing the IT assets and decisions made by management. DELL Supply chain success story is an example of this harmony [14].

IT governance is responsible for aligning the IT assets with the business goals and strategy to deliver values to the entity. Cloud Computing Governance is part of the IT governance in the organization's governance hierarchy.

Governance is to control and secure our data outside our organization premises. It will align business speed to the Cloud and will cope with market demands. It helps also to initiate a new IT operating model [15].

Organizations must ensure that the level of access they request is guaranteed into the Service-Level Agreement (SLA); uptime must be audited regularly to ensure that it conforms to the SLA [16]. There are many ways to mitigate risks in the Cloud using technologies and policies [17]. Cloud governance makes the decision easier and balances the investments and risks while gaining the Cloud benefits [18, 19].

Processes, policies, tools and even organization personnel will be unified under one framework that makes the workflow easier and give the business some elasticity on applying the framework.

A Cloud governance should contain processes to apply Cloud Computing inside the organizations and applied controls to facilitate it. Moreover, it must adopt the organizational roles and responsibilities to ensure better support of implementing Cloud Computing governance. Finally, it should use all available technology tools that will help to apply the governance framework.

When implementing security governance, we need well-articulated policies and procedures including controls. Security controls is the key to apply security governance. CSA CCM is a well-defined industrial security control list [20]. We will distribute these controls on the theoretical Guo's model for aligning the model with the Cloud market. We will demonstrate CSA CCM and Guo's model in the next two subsections [21].

2.1 Cloud Control Matrix

The Cloud Security Alliance (CSA) Cloud Controls Matrix (CCM) is an initiative from CSA to determine the baseline of security. It leads the Cloud market and helps customers assessing the risks of all Cloud domains.

The CSA CCM provides a controls framework that covers almost all Cloud security domains. CSA relates it to the standards already in the market for IT Governance like COBIT. They mapped controls to the industry and practical life that help during the process of transferring the Guo's Model from theoretical model to practical model.

As a framework, the CSA CCM offers to the organization the required structure and details related to information security tailored to the Cloud industry. It covers all Cloud aspects and controls. Some controls are covered in IT governance models and other controls, related to the Cloud system, are brand new.

By mapping these controls to security standards that are already implemented in the market like COBIT and HIPPA, it helps in pointing to information security control required by business and management strategy [22].

The main target of CSA CCM is to provide a standard management to security and operational risk that will face any organization implementing Cloud Computing in its infrastructure. This matrix is mitigating and minimizing security threats and vulnerabilities in the Cloud by providing controls to each domain that covers almost all Cloud security related topics.

CSA CCM contains eleven domains that cover all security issues related to Cloud computing. They divide it by function. It means that controls related to legal issues will be a domain and controls related to data governance will be a domain and so on.

Compliance is the first domain. It has six controls that cover audits, regulations, and intellectual property. It also reviews legislative, regulatory and contractual requirement. Data governance has eight controls that manage data objects containing information. It classifies and assigns responsibilities, communication, labelling, policies, and data destruction. Facility security has eight controls that secure working environment like physical access, site authorization and asset management. Human resource security has three controls that cover aspects related to humans like background screening and employment termination.

Information security is the largest domain in CSA CCM; it has thirty-four controls that take care of security management, policy, user access, training, benchmarking, encryption, security incidents, infrastructure and auditing. Legal is the domain that controls agreements and reviews contracts with the national and international laws. It has only two controls. Operation management is taking care of resources planning and managing procedures and equipment. Risk management is a very important part of the matrix. It predicts all risks happening in the Cloud or the project. It delivers a plan to control and mitigate risks. Release management controls planned changes in production environment and set policies and procedures to apply the new changes. It has five controls.

Resiliency is responsible for business continuity planning and environmental risks mitigation. It has eight controls. Security architecture is the last domain containing fifteen controls that address all regulatory requirements for customer access, data security, network security including infrastructure and applications.

2.2 Guo's Governance Model

The Guo's Governance Model can be identified as the first proposed academic governance model to our knowledge (Fig. 2). It outlines the necessary components for Cloud governance. It was created based on four objectives of Cloud governance, which are service, policy, risk, and compliance management. It classifies the components of Cloud governance into three categories; policy, operational and management activities.

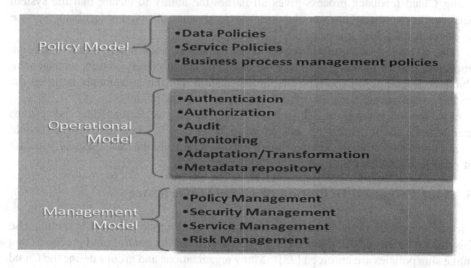

Fig. 2. Guo's governance model

There is a gap between the model and the real world, which we cover in this paper. We contribute in this paper to close this gap. The gap in the model can be identified after we apply controls in the CCM to the Guo's model. The CCM is a list of controls extracted from real Cloud business. We can apply it to any Cloud Computing system and be sure that most security aspects are covered. It helps transferring the theoretical model to an applicable one.

First missing corner in the model is the aligning with business strategy. The gap between IT and organizational alignment obstructs the adoption of Cloud computing. In Cloud Computing system, an organization's IT team has to be upgraded from being only technologists towards being also information and business experts. Therefore, the organization should determine how Cloud Computing could best serve its business needs while addressing how it may affect its current IT organization and governance.

In the Cloud, the traditional roles of CIO, IT support, service provider and even user are changing dramatically. Organization applying security roles should align it with the whole organization's roles. It has to assure the harmony between controls and roles governing the organization. This integration makes implementation easier and changes the way employees can accept and apply these roles and responsibilities. This is the second missing corner.

Roles and responsibilities may change during or after implementation of the Cloud system. Therefore, change management should have a well-defined strategy because of the nature of Cloud. It changes periodically and rapidly more than any other fixed systems. Replacing defective items, applying patches, or upgrading firmware are a few examples of the change procedures needed in Cloud environments. Taking resources down for change, applying efficient change management techniques is a key to survive in the Cloud. Change management is the third missing corner in the model.

Feedback process in a successful system improves the efficiency and reliability. Using Cloud feedback process gives all parties the ability to ensure that the system performs as expected. Guo's model does not clearly state this type of feedback. Service feedback is the fourth missing point in the model.

Due to asset distribution in the Cloud environment, asset management will be an important part of Cloud governance. It should be stated clearly. Assets management changes depending on the type of implementation and the agreements between the parties. Asset management is another missing point in the model.

Last missing point is the exit strategy. It contains contract ending, data and systems maintenance and it manages assets before and after exit. A Cloud exit strategy should be as simple as putting data in the Cloud, but this is far from the case, especially in case of proprietary public Clouds.

3   Our Proposed Definition of Cloud Governance

Cloud governance definition is still in the developing mode. Cloud Computing Use Discussion Group (2010) defines Cloud governance as "the controls and processes that make sure policies are enforced [23]". Many organizations and groups define the Cloud Computing governance in a different way.

According to our definitions, defining policies is important, but defining processes to apply these policies is more important. Cloud governance model should be aligned with corporate governance and IT governance. Moreover, it has to comply with organization strategy to accomplish business goals.

In our experience, Cloud governance has to support business strategy and to ensure service value, service quality and security irrespective of the control and locations of the services. Therefore, we define Cloud governance as:

> "Cloud governance is a framework applied to all related parties and business processes in a secure way, to guarantee that the organization's Cloud supports the goals of organization strategies and objectives."

4 New Model Prespective

Cloud governance is challenging. Technology is faster than the standards. We have to take into consideration the future expansion and update.

Building Cloud governance increases the ability to its technology to grow not to hinder it [24]. The governance process guarantees the rights of all stakeholders.

The challenge is the trade-off to achieve a governance model's implementation plan agreed by all parties. The plan should be elastic and customizable to all models and business cases. The plan has to tolerate moving between the Service Providers (SP) and their customers.

The vague nature of information interchange, the ubiquitous connectivity and the old static controls, all require new thinking with regard to Cloud computing. How can we implement the governance model without knowing the practical controls from real world and its implementation?

Therefore, what we already did is transforming the Guo's model to an applicable framework. We distribute controls under each model and its components to illustrate the practical implementation of the governance. We categorize the controls into two main categories, normal controls and key controls. We reserve developing the criteria to measure each control for future publications.

As we have seen, the Guo's model is not a process oriented. To overcome the problem, we redefine its three models (policy, operational, and management) to be processes. Then, we correlate the different CCM controls to each relevant process. Thereafter, we create new processes for the controls that are not relevant to any existing process.

We have to go deeply inside each model to determine the related controls to achieve the goal of this model. The model should be understandable and the structure of the model should be logical and reasonable.

To solve these issues we add, modify and update few categories of the Guo's model (Table 1). In the Management Model, we define clearly the Roles and Responsibilities under the Security Management. We use it in aligning Cloud system roles with the organization's roles and responsibilities. In addition, we have added Service improvement to the Service Management to be used as a key of the feedback to increase system reliability and efficiency.

Change Management will be part of the Management Model due to the rapid changes in the Cloud service either from the customer side or from the provider side.

Under the Operational Model, we define the asset management, configuration management and capacity planning. It supports the organization to operate its own Cloud or the Cloud services they use. Moreover, we have added Capacity planning to enforce changing the way of thinking inside the organization regarding the Cloud service. It helps in the planning phase and it guides the organizations to meet future changing demands of its services. Moreover, it supports the organization to take the right decision about Cloud service.

Finally, we have added the exit policy to be stated clearly and be defined in any contract separately to well define the procedures to be done to maintain user systems and data after ending the Cloud service or moving to a new provider. It supports both sides to be secure before or after service contracting.

Now we have processes in the new model and each process has its own controls.

Each control has inputs and outputs. Control's measures and tools depend on the deployment model. We create a framework and put each process in its suitable stage. The new framework is a conceptual structure to serve and guide organizations in Cloud Computing adoption process.

Table 1. New cloud governance model.

New Governance Model		
Policy Model	Operational Model	Management Model
Data Policy	Authentication	**Policy Management**
Service Policy	Authorization	• Generic Policy Ontology
Business Process Management Policy	Audit	• Application Specification Ontology
Exit Policy	Monitoring	• Policy Repository
	Adaptation/ Transformation	• Policy Specification Service
	Metadata repository	**Security Management**
	Asset Management	• Integration
	• Human resources	• Privacy
	• IT Assets	• Access
	Configuration management and documentation	• Jurisdiction
	Capacity planning	• Roles and responsibilities
		Service Management
		• Service Discovery
		• Service Delivery
		• SLAs management
		• Errors and exceptions management
• Note Grey cell is the identified gap. Bullet is a sub items		• Auditing and Logging
		• Service improvement
		Risk Management
		Change Management

5   New Cloud Governance Framework

The changes being driven by Cloud Computing and the growing sophistication of attackers do represent new challenges. We solve these challenges by creating the Cloud Governance Framework to control people, data, applications and infrastructure. Our security framework provides a more integrated, intelligent approach to Cloud Governance.

An intelligent framework must improve itself continuously; it has to have a feedback and service improvement process. We develop a new framework with five stages to achieve this goal (Fig. 3).

It also solves the weakness of organization strategy alignment. The stages are:

- Strategic trigger
- Define and align
- Build and implement
- Deliver and measure
- Operate and feedback

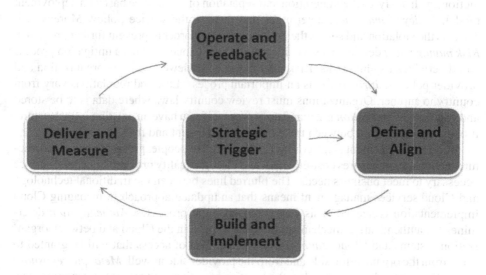

Fig. 3. New Cloud governance framework.

Strategic Trigger is the first stage. It is the event that initiates the need to use the Cloud computing. Business need is the main trigger for using the Cloud services. Other trigger may be gaining market share due to strong competition in market. The company needs a competitive edge. We use Cloud services to comply with a standard or a government rule. The major trigger is the technical need. An SP delivering services needs technically a Cloud service [24]; for example, E-mail services.

This stage contains four processes. *Business process management policy* defines interrelations between Cloud-based services. It analyses the business and considers the service process reuse. *Service discovery* finds and discovers the existing services and available technologies for new services. *Capacity planning* reviews the existing environment and future business extensions to plan the best way technically and financially to achieve business goals. *Exit policy* is mandatory. Business needs changes to cope with the market. It may require ending the Cloud service. Exit the Cloud service is more complicated than joining and entering it. A well-defined plan is mandatory before starting to use Cloud service.

Define and Align stage is the planning phase of adopting the Cloud service or transforming the existing environment to the Cloud. It ensures that the Cloud services are aligned to the business needs and actively supports them. Organizations using a Cloud require their service to be successful. If processes and services are implemented, managed and supported in the right way, the business will be more successful. This means cost reduction, revenue increase, and achieving its business objectives. It is the most important phase helping the decision makers with the economic and technical preparations for Cloud services.

This stage contains six Processes. *Data Policy* defines data's physical and logical model, in addition to data performance and stability. *Service policy* builds a service dictionary. It analyses the integration and separation of the service based on deployment model. *Policy management* determines and reviews the service policy. Moreover, it reviews the violation and solves the policy conflicts in order to prevent further problems. *Risk management* defines risks when moving to the Cloud. It plans a mitigation process and determines residual risks. Risk plan has to be reviewed with the organization and provider policies. *Jurisdiction* is an important process. Law and regulations vary from country to another. Organizations must review country laws where data is to be stored and processed. *Integration* is a mandatory process if you have an existing infrastructure. It plans the integration between the existing environment and the Cloud service.

Build and Implement stage covers issues related to people, processes and infrastructure technology. It ensures cost-effective and the high quality provision of Cloud service necessary to meet business needs. The blurred lines between the traditional technology and Cloud services management means that an updated approach to managing Cloud implementation is needed. This stage contains eight processes. *Authentication* determines the authentication mechanism that will be used in the Cloud and between organization systems and Cloud. *Authorization* is the level of access that will be granted to users from the organization side and from the provider side as well. *Metadata repository* is the storage of policy. It considers the location of polices and roles. *Asset management* monitors and maintains things of value to an organization. It manages the logical and physical assets and even human assets. *Configuration management and documentation* establishes and maintains performance, functional and physical attributes. It also establishes and maintains configurations within Cloud service throughout its life. *Roles and responsibility* is a dictionary, which determines the roles and the responsibility of each contributor in the Cloud service. *Privacy* considers the data encryption and the location privacy. *Access* takes care of the access policy in the Cloud because of using shared resources.

Deliver and Measure stage ensures that the implemented service is aligned with the planned services. It measures and compares the outputs with the references that were determined before. This stage contains four processes. *Service delivery* is moving the service to the execution environment. *SLA Management* ensures that all service levels are met. It reviews contract for penalties. *Errors and expectation management* reviews the current environment with the planned one. It analyses the running systems and reports the existing errors. *Auditing and logging track* all the activities and defines whom, when and where this activity was done. It helps during external and internal auditing.

Operate and Feedback stage is the final stage in the framework. Feedback for many organizations becomes a temporary project recalled only in case of malfunction or failure that affects the business. After resolving the issue, the concept is forgotten until the next failure occurs. The most important task starts after implementation. How do we gain benefits of using the new service? How do we measure, report and operate the new service to improve the service delivery? This requires wise decisions to operate and control feedback. It clearly defines goals, documented procedures, and identified roles and responsibilities.

This stage contains four processes. *Monitoring* collects transaction and access data to present a service statistics. It helps the management to review the existing environment and to plan for the future expansion. *Adaptation/transformation* manages the unavoidable consequences and changes in the running service. *Service improvement* assesses measures and improves all the system components. It uses the data collected in the execution phase. *Change management* transforms the service to a desired future state. Due to rapid changes in technology, the organization must cope with these changes. All changes have to be approved from all parties.

We can apply this framework to any Cloud system. We need controls and tools that can activate each process inside the framework. We have to state controls under each model and its components. We classify the controls into two types, key control and normal control. **Key control** is the control that will be mandatory and necessary to apply this process into the framework. **Normal control** is the control that has some inputs but is not mandatory to achieve the main goals of the process. We have distributed ninety-eight controls from CSA-CCM on each process in the framework. Then, we determine the key and normal control. We can use this framework in the future to serve the "the Security as a Service" model (SecaaS). So the SecaaS providers will have much wider view and capabilities than any customer to provide such a service to customers and will have the ability technically and financially to facilitate all of these controls. Due to limited space, we reserve publishing the process controls details to future publications with a detailed explanation to each control and its relation and impact to the processes.

6   Conclusion and Future Work

A Cloud system has different deployment models and architecture. Although it offers an economy of scale solution to the market, it creates new risks and challenges in the IT environment. In this paper, we introduce our new Cloud Computing governance model that represents a perspective combination of theoretical and practical implementation. We turn the Guo's theoretical model to a practical model to enable applying it to the industry. We identify the gap using CCM, and then identify controls related to each process and its effect using CCM. We add, modify and update the missing corners in the model. We create a new governance framework. It is a five stages framework with a service feedback. Each stage has few processes. Each process contains controls. Each control has inputs, outputs, and tools to activate and measure it. The framework is suitable for all Cloud deployment models. In the future, we will apply the new governance model and framework to all Cloud models (SaaS, PaaS, and IaaS). We will specify inputs and outputs to each control. We will define the RACI (Responsible, Accountable, Consulted, and Informed) Model and identify persons that must be informed and accountable based on the deployment model. In addition, we will extract and develop SLA from the new Cloud governance model. We will relate controls effect directly to the SLA.

References

1. Foster, I., Zhao,Y., Raicu, I., Lu, S.: Cloud computing and grid computing 360-degree compared. In: Grid Computing Environments Workshop, GCE 2008, pp. 1–10, 12–16 Nov 2008
2. Popović, K., Hocenski, Z.: Cloud computing security issues and challenges. In: MIPRO, Proceedings of the 33rd International Convention, pp. 344, 349, 24–28 May 2010
3. Borgman, H.P., Bahli, B., Heier, H., Schewski, F.: Cloudrise: exploring cloud computing adoption and governance with the TOE framework. In: 46th Hawaii International Conference Fiona System Sciences (HICSS) (2013)
4. Mukherjee, K., Sahoo, G.: Cloud computing: future framework for e-Governance. Int. J. Comput. Appl. 7(7), 0975–8887 (2010)
5. Li, X.-Y., Zhou, L.-T., Shi, Y., Guo, Y.: A trusted computing environment model in cloud architecture. In: International Conference on Machine Learning and Cybernetics (ICMLC), pp. 2843–2848, 11–14 July 2010
6. Ahmad, R., Janczewski, L.: Governance life cycle framework for managing security in public cloud: from user perspective. In: 2011 IEEE International Conference on Cloud Computing (CLOUD), pp. 372–379, 4–9 July 2011
7. NIST, The NIST Definition of Cloud Computing (NIST Special Publication 800-145), Sep 2012
8. Li, J.Z., Chinneck, J., Woodside, M., Litoiu, M.: Deployment of services in a cloud subject to memory and license constraints. In: IEEE International Conference on Cloud Computing, CLOUD 2009, pp. 33–40, 21–25 Sept 2009
9. Copie, A., Fortis, T., Munteanu, V.I., Negru, V.: From cloud governance to IoT governance. In: 27th International Conference on Advanced Information Networking and Applications Workshops (WAINA), pp. 1229–1234, 25–28 March 2013
10. NIST, NIST Cloud Computing Security Reference Architecture (NIST Special Publication 500-299) (2012)
11. Furht, B., Escalante, A.: Handbook of Cloud Computing. Springer, Heidelberg (2010)
12. Sixth Annual Meeting of the Internet Governance Forum, SOP Workshop 116: Cloud governance (2011)
13. McWiliams, G., White, J.: Dell to derail: Get into gear online. Wall Street J. Bl, 1 December 1999
14. Mather, T., Kumaraswamy, S., Latif, S.H.: Cloud Security and Privacy. Oreilly, Sebastopol (2009)
15. ISACA (Information Systems Audit and Control Association): IT control objectives for cloud computing: controls and assurance in the cloud. IN: ISACA (2011)
16. Guidelines on Security and Privacy in Public Cloud Computing (NIST Special Publication 800-144), NIST (2012)
17. ENISA, Cloud Computing Risk Assessment (2009). http://www.enisa.europa.eu/act/rm/files/deliverables/cloudcomputing-risk-assessment

18. Morin, J., Aubert, J., Gateau, B.: Towards cloud computing SLA risk management: issues and challenges. In: 2012 45th Hawaii International Conference on System Science (HICSS), pp. 5509–5514, 4–7 Jan 2012
19. Cloud Security Alliance (2012). https://cloudsecurityalliance.org/research/ccm/
20. Guo, Z., Song, M., Song, J.: A governance model for cloud computing. In: 2010 International Conference on Management and Service Science (MASS), pp. 1–6, 24–26 Aug 2010
21. Sahibudin, S., et al.: Combining ITIL, COBIT and ISO/IEC 27002 in Order to Design a Comprehensive IT Framework in Organizations. In: Second Asia International Conference on Modeling & Simulation, AICMS 2008, pp. 749–753 (2008)
22. Cloud Computing Use Cases group (2011). http://cloudusecases.org/
23. Internet Governance Forum (IGF), workshop 116, Security, Openness and Privacy – Cloud Governance (2011). http://www.intgovforum.org/cms/component/chronocontact/?chronoformname=WSProposals2011View&wspid=116
24. Borgman, H.P., Heier, H., Bahli, B.: Cloudrise: opportunities and challenges for IT governance at the dawn of cloud computing. In: 45th Hawaii International Conference on System Sciences, Big Island (2012)

Towards Modelling Support for Multi-cloud and Multi-data Store Applications

Marcos Aurélio Almeida da Silva[✉] and Andrey Sadovykh

Research and Development, SOFTEAM, 8 Parc Ariane Immeuble Le Jupiter, SOFTEAM, 78284 CEDEX, Guyancourt, France
{marcos.almeida,andrey.sadovykh}@softeam.fr

Abstract. The support to cloud enabled databases varies from one cloud provider to another. Developers face the task of supporting applications living in different clouds, and therefore of supporting different database management systems. To these developers, the challenge lies in understanding the differences in expressivity between data stores and the impact of such differences on the rest of the application. The advent of the NoSQL movement increased the complexity of this task by leveraging the creation of a large number of cloud enabled database management systems employing slightly different data models. In this paper, we will present a modelling approach that will allow developers to consider the impact of these features to different concrete deployment scenarios in multiple clouds. This approach is currently being developed on the JUNIPER and MODA-Clouds FP7 projects.

Keywords: Data stores · NoSQL · Data migration · Modelling

1 Introduction

A decade after the advent of the first cloud based solutions, it is clear to companies that migrating to cloud platforms is cost effective [1]. The success of the cloud lead to the advent of multiple cloud provider offerings. As in any nascent market, there are no established standards. Economically speaking, on the one hand, the multiplication of offerings reduces the prices and makes cloud and multi-cloud applications more and more interesting to companies. On the other hand, the consequent fragmentation of the market, makes the life of cloud developers harder, since it increases the complexity of the development and maintenance of applications.

In this paper we focus on the challenges related to data stored on the cloud. The problem stems from the fact that different cloud providers support different database management systems (DMS). Developers have then a high degree of flexibility, ranging from the one they have on Infrastructure As a Service providers, in which virtually any DMS can be installed; to the one they have in the Platform as A Service providers, which usually support only a very specific subset of DMSs. Finally, in Software as a Service providers, developers are usually only able to store data opaquely behind provider specific APIs.

© Springer International Publishing Switzerland 2015
M. Helfert et al. (Eds.): CLOSER 2014, CCIS 512, pp. 200–212, 2015.
DOI: 10.1007/978-3-319-25414-2_13

The consequences of the fragmentation of the support of DMSs by cloud providers are amplified by the so-called NoSQL "movement". It consists of a series of DMSs that strip the well-known SQL based relational DMSs from some for their characteristics in order to increase their performance. The problem is that different applications usually have different performance bottlenecks, which leads to different sets of optimizations that need to be applied to SQL DMSs to make them adapted to each application. This lead to the existence of a myriad of NoSQL DMSs, based on slightly different sets of optimizations upon traditional DMSs or even based on completely different data models, fine-tuned to specific applications.

For a developer, building and maintaining a cloud application means dealing with all this fragmentation. **The main hypothesis of this paper is that in order to deal with these concerns, one, first of all, needs to understand the differences in expressivity between the data models provided by different DMSs.** In this paper we are going to present the main concepts behind most used cloud DMSs. We'll use this classification in a case study in which we identify the best DMSs to support parts of the data manipulated by an application. These concepts will then be applied on a concrete modelling approach to describe static and dynamic aspects of DMSs.

The present work presents part of the ongoing work in the EU FP7 projects MODA-Clouds and JUNIPER. These projects intend to tackle multi DMS challenges by means of model driven approaches to allow developers to model applications on a very high level. Developers can then have their models analysed by automated tools and to have code automatically generated from it. The MODAClouds project focuses on public clouds and in providing automated tools to help data design. The JUNIPER project focuses on private clouds and in providing analysis tools to make sure that a particular set of DMSs respects a given set of real time constraints.

This paper is structured as follows. Section 2 details the context of data management in multi cloud applications and introduces the fragmentation of databases in this domain. This section also presents a motivating example on these kinds of applications. Section 3 presents the most important concepts used in multi-cloud DMSs, and a modelling approach to support them. Finally, Sect. 3 applies the modelling approach to the motivating example. To conclude, Sects. 4 and 5 present related works and conclusions of this paper.

2 Multi-cloud Applications and the NoSQL "Movement"

2.1 Overview

Clouds started as ways to offer all this as a service, in a "pay as you" go way. That means that a cloud provider would create a big data centre, and would use it to offer virtual machines to clients. On top of purely infrastructure driven cloud solutions, platform driven ones came into being. In this case, cloud providers do not offer virtual machines and storage device, but instead, they offer software platforms. The customer then is only responsible for installing their application on the provided platform while the cloud provider will dimension the needed machines, storage and load balance strategies for the user's application [2].

The main disadvantage of clouds is that users have much less flexibility than in a "on premises" solution. Each cloud provider provides only a limited set of configurations of machines, storage and platforms, while on premise solutions allow for unlimited sets of configurations. Each cloud is also optimized for a limited range of applications, i.e. some clouds are optimized to running applications involving fast running queries and long running background processes; while others may also accept long running queries over data. One way to mitigate this heterogeneity problem is to use multiple cloud providers, putting parts of the application on each provider, trying to find the best match between the cloud and the application [3, 4].

As one could expect, the data storages supported by each cloud provider vary from one offering to another. This is so, because data storage is nowadays a much complicated matter than it was years ago. It doesn't consist anymore of choosing between traditional relational databases or home grown file based data formats. Now, developers have a myriad of Data Management Systems (DMS), each of them optimized to a particular set of data structures. This is the result of the NoSQL "movement", which in fact intends to improve the efficiency of relational DMSs by constraining the data structures they support and the queries that they can answer.

The downside for the programmer is that designing a cloud application is not only a matter of choosing the "cheapest cloud provider", but choosing the provider that supports the DMSs backed by the best data structures to represent the application data. One still needs to think about the cost and performance costs involved in transferring data from one cloud to another, and consequently from one DMS and backed data structure to another.

The main objective of this paper is helping developers in choosing the best DMSs for their data and in understanding, by the use of models, the **performance and expressiveness trade-offs** involved in moving data from one DMS to another. In order to do so, we intend to provide a model of the data structures and queries supported by existing NoSQL and SQL based DMS. Developers will then be able to develop high performance applications, losing as least as possible when moving data from one DMS to another.

2.2   Motivating Example: The MiC Application

The MiC (Meeting in the Cloud) application [5] is a social network which allows users to maintain user profiles in which they register they topics of interests. The MiC application then groups users by similarity, allowing users to interact with their "best contacts", based on the answers given by each user in their profiles.

Figure 1 presents a simplified view of the data model behind the MiC application. It stores, Messages posted by `UserProfiles` in `Topics` associated to `Questions`. `UserRatings` store ratings given by `UserProfiles` to `Topics`. `UserRatings` also include `Pictures` of users. Finally, and `UserSimilarity` stores pairs of similar users.

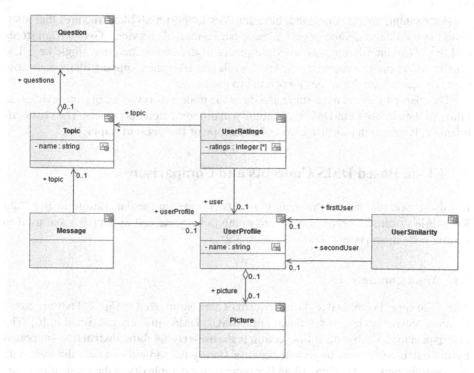

Fig. 1. The data model of the MiC Application.

When developing the MiC application, developers need to decide on using an infra-structure or platform as a service solution; and then on which specific provider the application is going to be deployed. When it comes to designing the data layer of the application, the developer has to decide on which DMSs will be reused and which part of the data is going to be stored on each DMS.

In order to illustrate the complexity of these choices, let us suppose the developers want to use platform as a service cloud providers, in order to reduce the cost of managing the infrastructure and to focus on the application design. Suppose they want to choose between Microsoft Azure, Heroku and Google App Engine.

Without going into the details on each DMS, Table 1 shows that each provider includes a variety of different data stores. Each DMS supports slightly different kinds of data, with different levels of details.

Table 1. Comparing possible platform as a service providers for the MiC application.

Provider	DMS
Microsoft azure	Table Service, Blob Service
Heroku	Postgres, Cloudant add-on
Google app engine	Datastore, Blobstore

For example, on the one hand, blob services support hash like structures that associate binary data to unique keys. On the other hand, table services, Google Datastores and the Cloudant add-on store multiple pieces of data associated to a single key. The former are optimal for queries on leys, while the later may support filters and more complex queries on the values associated to each key.

This paper focuses on the static and dynamic trade-offs involved in storing different kinds of data in different DMSs, eventually in different cloud providers. The cost optimization involved in this task **is out of the scope of the present paper.**

3   Cloud Based DMS Concepts and Comparison

In this section we present the main concepts concerning the data design in Big Data Real-time systems. These concepts are going to be presented in Sect. 3.1 and used to compare the most popular DMSs in Sect. 3.2.

3.1   Main Concepts

The main concepts related to **data structures** are summarized in Fig. 2. They are based on an extensive review of relational and NoSQL DMSs initially published in [6]. The first aspect to be dealt with at this section is the **underlying data abstraction** supported by the database. That is important because storing the same data under different data abstractions may lead to data loss and/or increase the complexity of the application code.

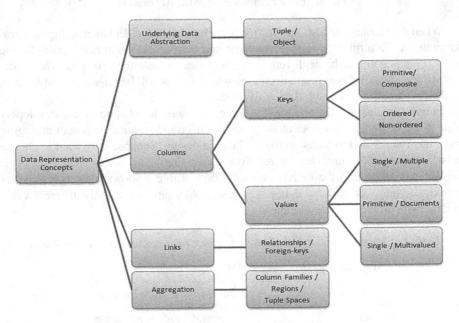

Fig. 2. Kinds of Data Structure related concepts.

The next aspect is the one of how each system **uniquely identifies** data stored in it. This is usually done by means of a piece of data called **Key**. Notice that keys are dispensable in object oriented databases; because objects are unique by themselves, no matter the data they contain. Keys may be atomic or composed of many pieces of data (they are then called **Composite keys**). Additionally, **File paths** are special kinds of keys that uniquely identify documents in file systems. Finally, keys may be **Ordered** or not.

The **Values** stored in the database are represented differently from one system to another. They can represent **Single** or **Multiple** columns containing primitive types only or **Documents,** which stand for non-structured blobs of information. Finally, columns may be **Single** or **Multi-valued.**

Links between different pieces of information are established differently in different kinds of database. In tuple based ones, **Foreign-keys** are generally used, while in object oriented ones **Relationships** are used. A relationship is a direct link from an object to another, allowing navigation usually in constant time. Foreign-keys link two tuples by adding the key from one tuple as part of the columns represented in another. Lookups from tuples using foreign-keys may vary from logarithm time complexity in single primitive ordered keys, to linear time in non-ordered keys.

Different tools also provide different strategies for **Aggregating** data. **Tuple spaces** and **Regions** group objects or tuples in different containers, so that items that are most accessed together (from a single region) can be retrieved more quickly. Tuple spaces differ from regions by the fact that they are also a concurrent programming mechanism: processes can **put** and **take** tuples from the tuple space, i.e. no two processes can take the same tuple at the same time. The third aggregation technique is called **Column families.** In this case, the columns that form each tuple are grouped into families of columns that should be stored together, accelerating analysis over the whole column (e.g. summing all values).

3.2   Comparing Cloud Based DMSs

Table 2 presents and compares the main kinds of Big Data databases based on the concepts presented in the previous section and presents the main implementations for each category of database.

Distributed file systems represent data as an association between file paths (used as keys) and documents (that represent file content). The underlying data abstraction paradigm is the object oriented one, i.e. files are not uniquely identified by their content, but only by their paths (usually, several paths may point to a single file).

The **Key-value stores** represent data as simple tuples containing simple primitive keys and a single column of data. **Ordered key-value** stores support ordered keys, and therefore allow retrieval of ranges in linear time on the length of the range, whereas in Key-value systems this operation may be quadratic. **Document stores** are also a special case of key-value stores in which the single column in each row (apart from the key) can store an arbitrarily complex document. Notice that these four kinds of data stores may be referred to generally as **Key-value stores.**

Table 2. Comparing cloud enabled databases.

Category	Data Abstr.	Keys	Values	Links	Aggregation	Examples
Distributed file systems	Object	Primitive (File Path)	Document	–	–	HDFS, Lustre
Key-value store	Tuple	Primitive	Single Column	–	–	Amazon DynamoDB
Ordered key-value store	Tuple	Ordered	Single Column	–	–	Memcache DB, Redis
Document store	Tuple	Primitive	Document	–	–	MongoDB, CouchDB, Riak SimpleDB
Big table	Tuple	Primitive	Multiple Columns	–	Column Families, Regions	Google BigTable, Cassandra, HBase
Object database/RDF store	Object	–	Multiple Columns	Relationships	–	Neo4j, RavenDB, FlockDB, InfiniteGraph
Multivalued databases	Tuple		Multiple Multivalued Columns		–	jBASE, Caché
Tuple store	Tuple	–	Multiple Columns	–	Tuple Spaces	Gigaspace, Javaspaces, Tarantool
Relational database	Tuple	Composite Primitive	Multiple Columns	Foreign Keys	–	MySQL

Big tables are tuples with a primitive key and multiple columns aggregated in families and rows that can be grouped into regions. **Object databases** represent objects which contain multiple columns (or fields) and are connected by means of relationships. **Multivalued databases** are systems that allow more than one value to be stored at a time for a column. Expressiveness and Performance Trade-offs

Tuple stores are databases that support tuple spaces. Finally, **Relational databases** are tuple based databases supporting composite keys and foreign keys.

3.3 Modelling Approach

Figure 3 shows the basis of the modelling approach developed in the JUNIPER project applied to the MiC application. The JUNIPER project deals with the problem of multiple clouds and multiple data stores by means of a modelling approach describing applications in terms of big computation and storage units called programs. Programs communicate by means of well-defined interfaces, and communication overhead is dealt with by means of code generation.

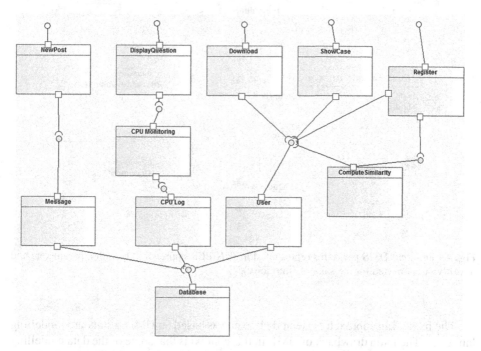

Fig. 3. JUNIPER modelling approach applied to the MiC example.

11 programs compose the MiC application. The NewPost, DisplayQuestion, Download, ShowCase, and Register programs provide, each of them, part of the interface to the user. The Message, CPU Log and User programs, implement business logic and interface with the DMS program (called Database). The CPU monitoring and Compute Similarity programs are responsible respectively of computing monitoring information (for bug fixing purposes, and similarity information between user profiles). UML ports and lollipop notations are used to represent the communication channel between programs.

As shown in Fig. 4, DMSs are represented by means of programs specialized in data storage. The interface of these DMS programs is tailored to support the data modelling concepts under each DMS. For example, ordered and unordered key value stores differ on the supported methods, since the former are able to perform sequential searches on data while the later are not. Under the JUNIPER modelling approach, specific implentations of the different concrete DMSs under the interfaces provided in Fig. 4, will be provided. This will allow application developers to interoperate similar databases located in different clouds and to promptly notice the semantic difference between the DMSs supported by each cloud and to adapt the application code appropriately.

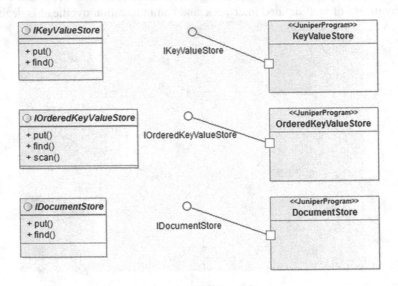

Fig. 4. Different DMS programs represented in JUNIPER approach (Operation parameters and return values omitted for the sake of simplicity).

The modelling approach presented up to now is based on UML, a standard modelling language. The main drawback of UML in this context is that some of the data modelling related concepts presented at this section are not supported by UML. That is why, in the JUNIPER project, we extend UML with the missing concepts.

Three big data related concepts are not supported by UML: (i) the concept of **Key** is not supported. Since UML is an object-oriented language, instances are objects by default. The concepts of (ii) **vertical** and (iii) **horizontal partitions** are also not supported by UML since for UML they are regarded as concepts too specific to be dealt by UML.

In JUNIPER, we use the standard mechanism of profiles provided by UML to extend the language. Table 3 presents the four new stereotypes will be added to the language, and the existing concepts they extend. The **key** stereotype will be added to .entity attributes, indicating that the tagged attributes identify uniquely the object. The **VerticalPartition** stereotype will be added to classes representing such partitions. UML Dependencies will be used to link vertical partitions to the columns on the same family. The **HorizontalPartition** stereotype will be added to an entity class stating that the instance of this classes will be partitioned according to the values of their keys.

Table 3. UML profile with missing concepts.

Stereotype	UML meta-class
Key	Attribute
VerticalPartition	Class
HorizontalPartition	Class

Figure 5 illustrates the use of the mapping presented on the current and previous subsections. The UserProfile entity got an id attribute that uniquely identifies the UserProfiles (i.e. it is a key for this entity), the topics of a UserProfile can be stored on an external vertical partition (i.e. not on the same partition as the rest of the user profile information) and the UserProfile is tagged as having horizontal partitions enabled, i.e. instances may be partitioned on different machines to make access to their information faster.

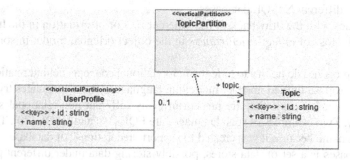

Fig. 5. Extension of the MiC application data model with (big) data modelling concepts.

With a combination of an extended UML profile for data modelling, and a library of DMS high level instantiable DMSs models, our approach will allow developers to represent either static (data types, structure and partitioning concerns) and dynamic (DMS available interfaces and parameters). Designers and developers can therefore support multiple clouds and (big) data stores. They can support different stores implementing the same/similar interfaces and without drastic changes on the applications code, or support different DMSs and know, because of the models, the semantic differences between DMSs.

4   Related Work

The main problem addressed by this paper is the one of understanding and documenting the trade-offs between different cloud DMSs, in order to optimize the deployment of application data in multiple clouds. Past work has tried to address this problem but in different ways. We classify these works into two categories: (i) the ones that try to hide this complexity from the developer, (ii) the ones that allow the developer to work on surpassing such complexity.

We consider that approaches in the first category are not best suited to developers that need to extract the most from cloud data stores, since any black box that hides the real complexity of the DMSs is going to be efficient only in a restricted set of situations. The present work falls in the second category, but differently from other works, that try to provide tools under which the developer can himself try to bridge the semantic gap between different tools, we show explicitly the gap and the involved gaps to the developer.

In the first category we would put the systems that try to automatically bridge the gap between different database categories. This group starts out by the tools that facilitate the use of relational data stores by object oriented applications [7–9].

In the non-relational world some tools try to do the same. A first set of tools [10–15] reuses the concepts defined by JPA, which is a very popular system of annotations over Java code (i.e. an object oriented model of data), to translate an object oriented model represented by a set of Java classes into a non-relational databases. Other tools do the same thing for relational models [16, 17]. They provide a relational SQL-based interface to non-relational NoSQL databases, allowing existing relational modelling approaches to be reused to model non-relational databases. Finally, Spring Data [18], provides different interfaces for different NoSQL databases.

This comes with the drawback of the inherent loss of information in the translation process or the loss of *object-orientedness* in the object oriented model in some corner cases.

Other approaches do not try to hide the non-relational concepts behind relational ones, but instead, propose unified abstract modelling languages. These languages try to represent the common concepts that are present in many different non-relational stores in a uniform way. Two examples of such languages are FQL [19] and UnQL [20]. The former received this name because it was created to support "federations" of databases. A federation of databases is a set of data stores, possibly storing data under different paradigms (relational or non-relational). The FQL language is then based on SQL but is able to query non-relational data bases. Its main drawback is that it supports only data retrieval, i.e. it provides no Data Definition Language. A similar approach for dealing with federated databases can be found in [21]. The UnQL language stands for Unstructured Query Language. It follows a similar approach, but is limited to unstructured (and therefore non-relational) databases). It is targeted only to data stores containing JSON documents.

On the second category we will find tools such as such as Pentaho [22] and Yahoo! Pipes [23], which are Data Integration tools. They offer visual editors that allow one to describe how data coming from different sources, following different schemas and data types can be mapped into different data types and then fed to other systems. The semantic gap between different DMSs needs to be understood and filled by the developer.

In scientific literature, some papers also discuss the differences between the offerings of cloud providers and their supported DMSs. A good example of this kind of work is [24]. In this work, the different cloud providers are described along with their features and storage solutions. However the referred paper focuses on runtime characteristics (security, load balancing, fault tolerance etc.) and not on the impact of the design time storage choices to the cloud application.

More recent works such as [25–27] go into the concepts behind different DMSs, their runtime properties, preferred use cases and supported queries. However these works are usually restricted to some specific kinds of cloud storage (usually variations of key-valued stores), and compare tools mostly based on runtime characteristics instead of design time ones.

5 Conclusion

The multiplication of cloud providers has both positive and negative impacts on industrial applications. On the positive side, we have the increasing availability and multiplicity of cloud providers that allows for the existence of clever applications profiting from the best of different providers. On the negative side, we have the fragmentation of the market that makes developing such applications much harder. In particular, maintaining them (fixing bugs and eventually moving to other clouds) becomes much harder than for regular non-cloud applications.

In this paper we investigated this problem in the point of view of the developer that needs to design data structures and applications that will be potentially deployed on different clouds and on different data management systems (DMS). More specifically, we investigated the main concepts behind the different DMS, the semantic gap between different databases, and proposed a modelling approach to take them into account.

The present work is actually being implemented as part of the FP7 projects MODA-Clouds and JUNIPER. Code generation is actually supported as a module to the Modelio open source modelling environment. In MODAClouds, the code and model generators are coupled with architecture and data definition tools that allow the analysis of the application behaviour and the generation of application and data deployment scripts. In JUNIPER, the code and model generation tools described here are coupled with real-time analysis tools, to help developers optimize their design w.r.t the real-time constraints of the applications.

As future works, we are currently working providing a library of DMSs types/interfaces and code generation support from models to actual implantation. Our objective is to allow developers to reuse them on their real-time big data pipelines. An extension of the model presented in this paper with concerns unrelated to data structures (i.e. support to transactions, programming language integration etc.) is also under consideration for future works.

Acknowledgements. The research reported in this article is partially supported by the European Commission grants no. FP7-ICT-2011-8- 318484 (MODAClouds) and FP7-ICT-2011-8- 318763 (JUNIPER).

References

1. Rackspace, 88 per cent of cloud users point to cost savings, according to Rackspace Survey, 13 February 2013. http://blog.rackspace.co.uk/in-the-industry/88-per-cent-of-cloud-users-point-to-cost-savings-according-to-rackspace-survey/. Accessed June 2013

2. Khajeh-Hosseini, A., Greenwood, D., Sommerville, I.: Cloud migration: a case study of migrating an enterprise IT system to IaaS. In: 2010 IEEE 3rd International Conference on Cloud Computing (CLOUD), Miami, FL (2010)
3. Liu, T., Katsuno, Y., Sun, K., Li, Y.: Multi cloud management for unified cloud services across cloud sites. In: IEEE International Conference on Cloud Computing and Intelligence Systems (CCIS), Beijing (2011)
4. Singh, Y., Kandah, F., Zhang, W.: A secured cost-effective multi-cloud storage in cloud computing. In: IEEE Conference on Computer Communications Workshops (INFOCOM WKSHPS), Shanghai (2011)
5. Giove, F., Longoni, D., Shokrolahi Yancheshmeh, M., Ardagna, D., Di Nitto, E.: An approach for the development of portable applications on PaaS clouds. In: Proceedings of the 3rd International Conference on Cloud Computing and Service Science (CLOSER 2013) (2013)
6. SOFTEAM; University of York, D5.1 – Foundations for MDE of Big Data Oriented Real-Time Systems (2013)
7. DB-UML Database Modeling Tool. http://argouml-db.tigris.org/. Accessed 8 November 2013
8. Hibernate: Relational Persistence for Java and .NET. http://hibernate.org. Accessed 8 November 2013
9. DeMichiel, L.: JSR 131:Java Persistence API, Version 2.0, Sun Microsystems (2009)
10. Acid House. https://github.com/eiichiro/acidhouse. Accessed 8 November 2013
11. Kundera. https://github.com/impetus-opensource/Kundera. Accessed 8 November 2013
12. PlayORM. https://github.com/deanhiller/playorm. Accessed 8 November 2013
13. DataNucleus Access Platform. http://www.datanucleus.org/. Accessed 8 November 2013
14. Hibernate Object/Grid Mapper. http://www.hibernate.org/subprojects/ogm.html. Accessed 8 November 2013
15. Morphia. http://code.google.com/p/morphia/. Accessed 8 November 2013
16. Toad for Cloud. http://toadforcloud.com/index.jspa. Accessed 8 November 2013
17. eobjects.org MetaModel. http://metamodel.eobjects.org/index.html. Accessed 8 November 2013
18. Spring Data. http://www.springsource.org/spring-data. Accessed 8 November 2013
19. Federated Unfied Query Language, FunQL. http://funql.org/. Accessed 8 November 2013
20. UnQL Specification. http://www.unqlspec.org. Accessed 8 November 2013
21. JBoss Teiid. http://www.jboss.org/teiid/. Accessed 8 November 2013
22. Pentaho. http://www.pentaho.com/. Accessed 8 November 2013
23. Yahoo Pipes. http://pipes.yahoo.com/pipes/. Accessed 8 November 2013
24. Rimal, B., Choi, E., Lumb, I.: A taxonomy and survey of cloud computing systems. In: Fifth International Joint Conference on INC, IMS and IDC, 2009. NCM 2009, Seoul (2009)
25. Cattell, R.: Scalable SQL and NoSQL data stores. ACM SIGMOD Record **39**, 12–27 (2010)
26. Hecht, R., Jablonski, S.: NoSQL evaluation: a use case oriented survey. In: 2011 International Conference on Cloud and Service Computing (CSC), Hong Kong (2011)
27. Moniruzzaman, A.B.M., Hossain, S.A.: NoSQL database: new era of databases for big data analytics - classification, characteristics and comparison. Int. J. Database Theor. Appl. **6**, 1–14 (2013)

Experimenting with Application-Based Benchmarks on Different Cloud Providers via a Multi-cloud Execution and Modeling Framework

Athanasia Evangelinou[1]([✉]), Nunzio Andrea Galante[2], George Kousiouris[1],
Gabriele Giammatteo[2], Elton Kevani[1], Christoforos Stampoltas[1], Andreas Menychtas[1],
Aliki Kopaneli[1], Kanchanna Ramasamy Balraj[2], Dimosthenis Kyriazis[1],
Theodora Varvarigou[1], Peter Stuer[3], Leire Orue-Echevarria Arrieta[4],
Gorka Mikel Echevarria Velez[4], and Alexander Bergmayr[5]

[1] Department of Electrical and Computer Engineering, NTUA, 9 Heroon Polytechnioy Street,
15773 Athens, Greece
{aevang,gkousiou,ameny,alikikop,dimos}@mail.ntua.gr,
eltonkevani@hotmail.com, stampoltaschris@gmail.com,
dora@telecom.ntua.gr
[2] Research and Development Laboratory, Engineering Ingegneria Informatica S.p.A.,
V. R. Morandi, 32, 00148 Rome, Italy
{NunzioAndrea.Galante,gabriele.giammatteo,
Kanchanna.RamasamyBalraj}@eng.it
[3] Spikes Research Department, Spikes, Mechelsesteenweg 64,
2018 Antwerp, Belgium
peter.stuer@spikes.be
[4] ICT-European Software Institute Division, TECNALIA, Parque Tecnológico Ed #202,
48170 Zamudio, Spain
{Leire.Orue-Echevarria,Gorka.Echevarria}@tecnalia.com
[5] Business Informatics Group, TU Vienna, Favoritenstraße 9-11/188-3,
1040 Vienna, Austria
bergmayr@big.tuwien.ac.at

Abstract. Cloud services are emerging today as an innovative IT provisioning model, offering benefits over the traditional approach of provisioning infrastructure. However, the occurrence of multi-tenancy, virtualization and resource sharing issues raise certain difficulties in providing performance estimation during application design or deployment time. In order to assess the performance of cloud services and compare cloud offerings, cloud benchmarks are required. The aim of this paper is to present a mechanism and a benchmarking process for measuring the performance of various cloud service delivery models, while describing this information in a machine understandable format. The suggested framework is responsible for organizing the execution and may support multiple cloud providers. In our work context, benchmarking measurement results are demonstrated from three large commercial cloud providers, Amazon EC2, Microsoft Azure and Flexiant in order to assist with provisioning decisions for cloud users. Furthermore, we present approaches for measuring service performance with the usage of specialized metrics for ranking the services according to a weighted combination of cost, performance and workload.

© Springer International Publishing Switzerland 2015
M. Helfert et al. (Eds.): CLOSER 2014, CCIS 512, pp. 213–227, 2015.
DOI: 10.1007/978-3-319-25414-2_14

Keywords: Benchmarking · Cloud services · Multi-cloud · Performance benchmarking

1 Introduction

Performance of cloud environments has started to gain significant attention in the recent years and is now related to more extensive concepts such as availability, competency and reliability [4]. After promises for infinite resources and on-demand scalability, the issues of cloud environments instability with regard to performance issues of the allocated resources have begun to arise [3]. Thus, for a successful cloud migration process, the issue of provider performance is a key factor that should be taken into account, in order to save money but also guarantee a (as much as possible) stability in the migrated application with respect to service-level agreements. In [17], both the wide range of applications deployed in cloud environments and the variability of cloud services are detected; thus, measurement practices are required. Cloud benchmarks play a significant role in the wide-spread adoption of cloud services, providing end-to-end performance evaluation across different application areas and pricing of cloud offerings [16]. As identified in our previous work [1], a significant gap in existing research is the lack of such descriptions in current metamodels regarding Cloud infrastructures. However, different providers may have their own metrics and strategies for guaranteeing cloud QoS. Thus, there is the need of a modeling framework in order to incorporate the related information and provide a more abstracted and common way for identifying performance aspects of cloud environments.

In our approach, the benchmarking process is based on the identification of a set of representative application types that correspond to various common applications that can be met in real life. For these types suitable benchmarks are identified that provide representative application scenarios and capture services abilities in the respective field. The main aspect of interest for the selection of the benchmarks was the ability to have application level workloads characterization. The major aim of this process is to abstract performance of cloud services to a suitable degree that can be understood and used by the majority of cloud non performance-aware individuals.

Given the extent of cloud computing environments, many factors can affect the performance of cloud services and their resources. The main performance aspects of cloud computing as analysed by the ARTIST approach can be summarized as:

(a) Heterogeneous and unknown hardware resources: the computing resources offered by the cloud providers are unknown to the external users. Available information may be limited to number of cores for example, memory sizes or disk quotes. According to a study on Amazon platform conducted by Aalto University [5], the variation between the fast instances and slow instances can reach 40 %. In some applications, the variation can even approach up to 60 %.

(b) Different configurations: even in the existence of the same hardware however, the way this resource is configured plays a significant role in its performance. The same applies for software configurations (e.g. a DB instance over a virtual cluster) or variations in the software development.

(c) Multi-tenancy and obscure, black box management by providers: cloud infrastructures deal with multiple different users that may start their virtual resources on the same physical host at any given time. However, the effect of concurrently running VMs for example significantly degrades the actual application performance.

(d) VM interference effects. Studies [6, 7] show that combined performance varies substantially with different combinations of applications. Applications that rarely interfere with each other achieve performance to the standalone performance. However, some combinations interfere with each other in an adverse way.

(e) Virtualization is a technology used in all cloud data centers to ensure high utilization of hardware resources and better manageability of VMs. According to the aforementioned studies despite the advantages provided by virtualization, they do not provide effective performance isolation. While the hypervisor (a.k.a. the virtual machine monitor) slices resources and allocates shares to different VMs, the behaviour of one VM can still affect the performance of another adversely due to the shared use of resources in the system. Furthermore, the isolation provided by virtualization limits the visibility of an application in a VM into the cause of performance anomalies that occur in a virtualized environment.

All these aspects along with the fact that cloud providers are separate entities and no information is available on their internal structure and operation, make it necessary to macroscopically examine a provider's behavior with regard to the offered resources and on a series of metrics. This process should be performed through benchmarking, by using the suitable tools and tests. One of the key aspects is that due to this dynamicity in resources management, the benchmarking process must be iterated over time, so that we can ensure as much as possible that different hardware, different management decisions (e.g., update/reconfiguration/improvement of the infrastructure) are demonstrated in the refreshed metric values, but also observe key characteristics such as performance variation, standard deviation etc. Finally, the acquired information should be represented in a machine understandable way, in order to be used in decision making systems.

In software engineering, metamodeling concepts are increasingly being used for representing a certain kind of information in a more abstracted level. During the last years, several proposals for cloud modeling concepts emerged supporting different scenarios, such as MODAClouds [18], which proposes a model-based migration approach similar to ARTIST. Nevertheless, the first one focusses on the migration of cloud-based software between cloud providers and their interoperability, while ARTIST on the migration of software artefact to cloud-based software as a means of software modernization. With regard to our work, following the metamodel definition, concrete instances for specific cloud providers and services can be created in order to describe the target environments of the migrated applications. Thus, during the deployment phase, the provider that fits best to the application type being migrated will be selected.

The aim of this paper is to provide such mechanisms to address the aforementioned issues. A benchmarking framework designed in the context of the FP7 ARTIST project is presented in order to measure the ability of various cloud offerings to a wide range of applications, from graphics and databases to web serving and streaming. The framework consists of a software suite for benchmarking cloud platforms in order to extract performance-related data and to include it in the cloud models. What is more, we define a metric, namely Service Efficiency (SE), in order to rank different services based on a combination of performance, cost and workload factors. YCSB and DaCapo are the two benchmarks used in the performance testing. The first one is a framework that facilitates comparisons of different NoSQL databases, while DaCapo benchmarking suite measures JVM related aspects. Measurement results are demonstrated after the implementation of Service Efficiency on various known cloud environments.

The paper is structured as follows: In Sect. 2, an analysis of existing work is performed; in Sect. 3, the description of the ARTIST tools for mitigating these issues is presented; in Sect. 4, a case study on three cloud commercial providers Amazon EC2, Microsoft Azure and Flexiant is presented; conclusions and future work is contained in Sect. 5.

2 Related Work

Related work around this paper ranges in the fields of performance frameworks, available benchmark services and description frameworks and is based in the according analysis performed in the context of the ARTIST [1]. With regard to the former, the most relevant to our work is [12]. In this paper, a very interesting and multi-level cloud service comparison framework is presented, including aspects such as agility, availability, accountability, performance, security and cost. Also an analytical hierarchical process is described in order to achieve the optimal tradeoff between the parameters. While more advanced in the area of the combined metric investigation, this work does not seem to include also the mechanism to launch and perform the measurements. Skymark [13] is a framework designed to analyze the performance of IaaS environments. The framework consists of 2 components – Grenchmark and C-Meter. Grenchmark is responsible for workload generation and submission while C-Meter consists of a job scheduler and submits the job to a cloud manager that manages various IaaS Clouds in a pluggable architecture. Skymark focuses on the low level performance parameters of cloud services like CPU, Memory etc. and not on elementary application types.

CloudCmp [14] provides a methodology and has a goal very similar to our approach to estimate the performance and costs of a Cloud deployed legacy application. A potential cloud customer can use the results to compare different providers and decide whether it should migrate to the cloud and which cloud provider is best suited for their applications. CloudCmp identifies a set of performance metrics relevant to application performance and cost, develop a benchmarking task for each metric, run the tasks on different providers and compare. However CloudCmp does not seem to define a common framework for all the benchmark tasks.

With regard to benchmarking services, the most prominent are CloudHarmony.com and CloudSleuth.com. The former utilizes a vast number of benchmarks against various cloud services, offering their results through an API.

However, there are two aspects that can be improved with relation to this approach. Initially it is the fact that too many benchmarks are included in the list. We believe that a more limited scope should be pursued in order to increase the focus of the measurements. Furthermore, the measurement process is not repeated on a regular basis, in order to investigate aspects such as deviation. For CloudSleuth, the focus is solely on web-based applications and their response time/availability. Their approach is very worthwhile, by deploying an elementary web application across different providers and monitoring it constantly, however it is limited to that application type.

With regard to description frameworks, a number of interesting approaches exist. According to the REMICS project [2] PIM4Cloud, which is focused in both private and public Clouds, has been defined to provide support to model the applications and also to describe the system deployment on the cloud environment. PIM4Cloud is implemented as a profile for UML and a metamodel which is capable to describe most of the features of a system that will be deployed in a Cloud environment. It is organized in four packages (Cloud Provider domain, Cloud Application domain, Physical Infrastructure domain and Resource domain).

FleRD [8] is a flexible resource description language for inter-provider communication in virtual networks architectures. It appears enhanced with regard to realism and generality (ability to describe real world topologies), extensibility, grouping and aggregation. FleRD is mainly focused around networking elements, however its concepts of modeling more information for QoS of networks has influenced our approach.

EDML [9] defines a XML syntax for declaring internal and external general parsed entities. VXDL [10] is an XML-based language that describes Virtual Private eXecution Infrastructure (ViPXi) which is a time-limited organized aggregation of heterogeneous computing and communication resources. VXDL can describe resources, networks' topology that are virtual but are also, to some extent, adapted to physical ones and finally to represent timeline.

The implementation of DADL [11] is based on the prediction that future businesses will use allocated resources from different Clouds such as public or private to run a single application. DADL was developed as an extension of SmartFrog (framework for deploying and managing distributed software systems based on java) and it is used to specify application architecture and cloud resources that are necessary for an application to run. There are elements to describe QoS features such as CPU speed, number of cores etc.

The main issue with the aforementioned approaches, which most of them support description of QoS terms, is the fact that in many cases the standard ways (CPU cores, frequency etc.) of describing capabilities are not sufficient to demonstrate the actual performance of virtualized resources. Thus a new approach based on benchmark scores should be pursued that would indicate the direct capability of a resource service to solve a particular computational problem. The descriptions defined in this paper are revolved around this test-based approach.

3 Benchmarking Approach in Artist

The benchmarking approach followed in the context of ARTIST has the following targets:

- Identify a set of common application types and the respective benchmarks to measure the performance of cloud services
- Create a framework that is able to automatically install, execute and retrieve the benchmark results, with the ability to support multiple providers

- Investigate aspects of cloud service performance with regard to variation and ability across a wide range of potential applications
- Define a machine understandable way of representing this information and improved metrics that will characterize more efficiently the services.

The use case diagram for the benchmarking suite appears in Fig. 1. We envisage that the capabilities of the toolkit will be exploited by an entity ("Benchmarks Provider") that will be responsible for performing and obtaining the tests, similar to the role of CloudHarmony.com. This entity will utilize the various aspects of the toolkit in order to create provider models that have concrete results and metrics per service offering, that are stored on the ARTIST repository, so that an external entity ("Model User") may be able to retrieve and consult them. More details on each part of the process are presented in the following paragraphs.

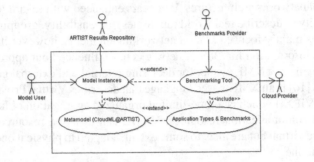

Fig. 1. Use case diagram for the ARTIST Benchmarking process and tools.

3.1 Application Benchmark Types

The main target of the application benchmark types is to highlight a set of common and popular application tests that can be used in order to benchmark provider's offerings. Thus each offering may have a performance vector indicating its ability to solve specific problems or cater for a specific type of computation. The set of application benchmarks used in ARTIST appears in Table 1.

Table 1. Benchmark tests used in the ARTIST platform.

Benchmark test	Application type
YCSB	Databases
Dwarfs	Generic applications
Cloudsuite	Common web aps like streaming, web serving etc.
Filebench	File system and storage
DaCapo	JVM applications

3.2 Models of Necessary Information

In order to exploit the information from the benchmark execution, a suitable machine understandable format should be in place in order to store results and utilize them in other processes like service selection. For achieving this, suitable model templates have been designed. These templates include all the relevant information needed, such as measurement aspects (number of measurements, statistical information like standard deviation etc.), test configurations and workload profiles.

Initially these templates had been defined as an XML schema and in later stages they were incorporated into a suitable sub-metamodel developed in the context of the ARTIST project (CloudML@ARTIST metamodel). In this sub-metamodel, which is portrayed in (Fig. 2), the workloads are static (and the default ones defined by each benchmark) in order to be able to compare the performance of different services on the same examined workload. For simplicity purposes we have defined one universal enumeration that includes the default workloads from all the aforementioned categories. Also for the Cloudsuite case, each category reports a large number of statistics, that are case specific. In order to simplify the descriptions, we have kept only the generic average score to be included in the model instances. However the remaining information will be kept during benchmark execution in a raw data DB, in order to be used in case an interested party needs the entire range of information.

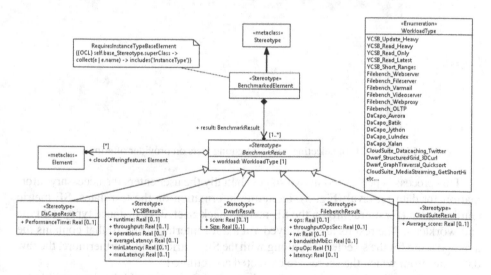

Fig. 2. Performance metamodel for incorporation of application stereotypes information in CloudML@ARTIST.

3.3 Benchmarking Suite Architecture

The Benchmarking Suite Architecture appears in Fig. 3. The user through the GUI (Fig. 4) may set the conditions of the test, selecting the relevant benchmark, workload

conditions, target provider and service offering. Furthermore, through extended interfaces, the results of the benchmarking process may be viewed and categorized based on
different types of workload, VM and test types.

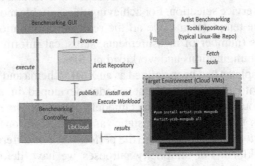

Fig. 3. Overall System Architecture.

Fig. 4. GUI for selecting and configuring tests on provider offerings.

This process is performed in two stages. Initially the user enters the necessary information for data retrieval (Fig. 5), including information on the test dates, SE metric
configuration (for more info on the SE metric check Sect. 3.4), instance type, test type
and workload. The results are displayed via a third interface (Fig. 6) that contains the
average score for the selected test, along with the SE metric result. Furthermore, the raw
data lines from which the scores are extracted are returned.

This information is passed to the Benchmarking Controller which is responsible for
raising the virtual resources on the target provider and executing the tests. The former
is based on the incorporation of Apache LibCloud project, in order to support multiple
provider frameworks. The latter needs to install first the tests, through the utilization of
an external Linux-like repository that contains the scripts related to the different phases
of installation and execution of each test. Once the tests are installed (through a standard
repo-based installation), the workload setup scripts are transferred to the target machines
and the execution begins.

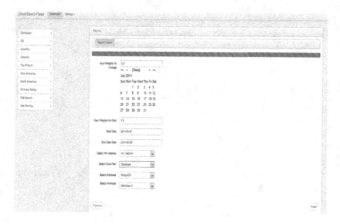

Fig. 5. Filtering information for historical data.

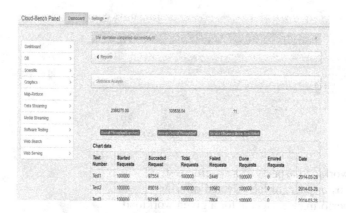

Fig. 6. Result display and statistical information.

The configuration of initial tests was modified in order to achieve some extra desirable figures like the number of iterations and extended run time. After the execution results are transferred back and processed in order to be included in the model descriptions, following the template definition highlighted in Sect. 3.2. In addition, a mysql raw database schema created and provided in case the results from the benchmark tests needed to be stored locally. The database structure is portrayed in Fig. 7.

At the moment the two parts (GUI and Controller) are not integrated, however the benchmarking controller which is the main backend component can also be used standalone to perform measurements on the various application types. Installation instructions can be found in [15].

3.4   Service Efficiency Metric Description

In order to better express the performance ability of a service offering, we considered the usage of a metric that would fulfill the following requirements:

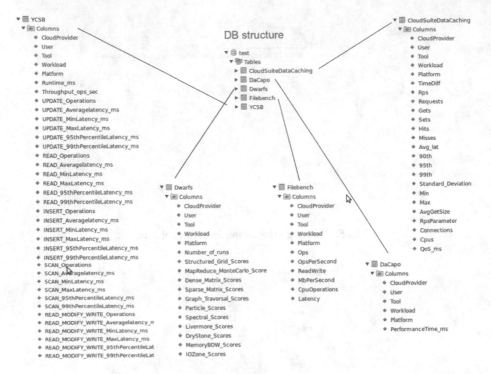

Fig. 7. Raw database structure.

- Include workload aspects of a specific test
- Include cost aspects of the selected offering
- Include performance aspects for a given workload
- Give the ability to have varying rankings based on user interests
- Intuitively higher values would be better

Following these points, we considered that positive factors (e.g. workload aspects) should be used in the numerator and negative on the denominator (cost and Key Performance Indicators that follow a "higher is worse" approach). Furthermore, normalization should be used in order to have a more generic rating. Usage of sum would be preferable over product, since the former enables us to include weight factors. Thus such a metric can answer a potential question of the sort: "what is the best service to run my web streaming application, when I am interested more on a cheap service?".

The resulting formula of Service Efficiency is the following (Eq. 1):

$$SE = \frac{\sum_i s_i l_i}{\sum_j s_j w_j f_j} \qquad (1)$$

Where s scaling factor

   l: workload metric
   f: KPI or cost metric
   w: weight factor

The resulting metric can be compared between different offerings, potentially of different providers but on the same workload basis. However the incorporation of workload is necessary since it affects the performance and thus ranking of the services. Usage of different workloads may display a different optimal selection, based on the anticipated workload conditions for the application that needs to be deployed.

4   Metric Case Study on Three Selected Cloud Providers: Amazon EC2, Microsoft Azure and Flexiant

In order to experiment initially with the defined metrics and investigate differences in VM performance, we utilized workloads from both DaCapo benchmarking suite and YCSB benchmark framework. However the Benchmarking Controller apart from DaCapo and YCSB supports the managing execution of three more benchmarks included in Table 1, such as Dwarfs, CloudSuite and Filebench. Nevertheless, in this work, only the aforementioned ones have been tested.

DaCapo is designed to facilitate performance analysis of Java Virtual Machines, while YCSB measures databases performance. The selected workloads from each test were running on instances in three different cloud environments: Amazon EC2, Microsoft Azure and Flexiant. Regarding Amazon EC2, different types of VM instances were selected while for Microsoft Azure and Flexiant the tests were running on the same VM instances during the entire benchmarking process. Information regarding the selected benchmarking workloads and the VM instance characteristics are presented in Tables 2 and 3 respectively.

The execution of the tests took place at specific hours (daily and at different time intervals) during a period of two weeks and the average values were extracted for each case. Moreover, the different time zones of the three respective regions were taken into consideration so that the peak hours were the same in each zone. Then the metric SE described in Sect. 3.4 was applied with the following form:

$$SE = \frac{1}{w1 * delay + w2 * Cost}$$

Different weights were given to the performance and cost aspects (50–50, 90–10) and a normalization interval was considered (1–10). We avoided using a normalization interval including 0 since it may lead to infinite values for some cases. One should compare between same color bars, indicating similar workloads. From the graphs it is evident how the ranking of a potential VM rating can change based on the aspect that we are most interested in.

For example, both the weighted decision (50–50) and the performance-based selection (90–10) in the DaCapo case for 'workload fop' suggest Azure as the best choice (Fig. 8). However the overall results may not be favorable for Flexiant due to the fact that we only measured large VM instances. Another interesting result derives from the fact that since the Service Efficiency metric includes the cost factor, we conclude that the smaller VMs give better results and the selection of small instances are more efficient. Moreover, it is worthy to mention that for the DaCapo case the Service Efficiency values for the large VM instances which were tested, are lower than the values for small or medium VM instances. Despite the fact that the performance of a large VM instance is approximately double than the performance of a small or medium instance, the cost is significantly higher, approximately 3.5 times (Fig. 9). Thus, taking into consideration that the Service Efficiency is inversely proportional to cost, this is expected.

Table 2. DaCapo and YCSB application benchmark type.

DaCapo	YCSB
xalan: transforms XML documents into HTML ones	**A:** Update heavy workload
tomcat: runs a set of queries against a tomcat server retrieving and verifying the resulting webpages	**B: Read mostly workload**
pmd: analyzes a set of Java classes for a range of source code problems	**C:** Read only
jython: interprets pybench Python benchmark	**D:** Read latest workload
h2: executes a JDBC benchmark using a number of transactions against a banking model application	**E:** Short ranges
fop: parses/formats XSL-FO file and generates a PDF file	**F:** Read-modify-write
eclipse: executes jdt performance tests for the Eclipse IDE	
avrora: simulates a number of programs running on a grid of AVR micro-controllers	

Table 3. VM instance characteristics.

Cloud Provider	VM instance	Region
Amazon EC2	t1.micro	N.Virginia
	m1.medium	N.Virginia
	m1.large	N.Virginia
Microsoft Azure	small Standard	Ireland
Flexiant	4 GB RAM- 3CPU	Ireland

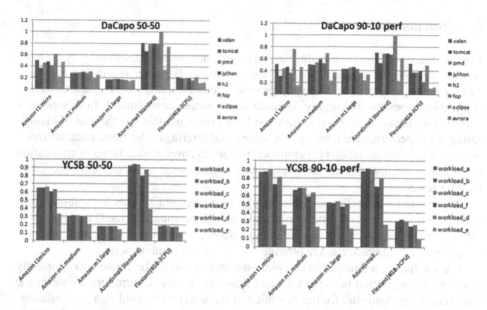

Fig. 8. Implementation of the metric on application-based benchmarks across different cloud providers and different type of VM instances and variable workload (higher score is better). Comparison should be made between columns with similar color (identical workload conditions) (Color figure online).

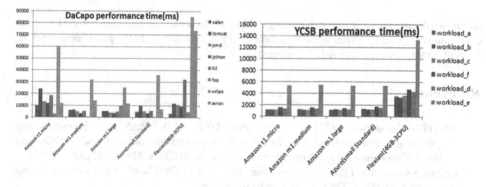

Fig. 9. Performance time in ms for DaCapo and YCSB workloads.

Moreover, the performance for the given workloads is similar across the Amazon and Azure instances. This is probably due to the fact that the maximum computational threshold of the VM was not reached. For Flexiant the performance is significantly lower and this behaviour seems to be related to a configuration of the VM in the Flexiant environment which was outside of our control.

In addition, for all the tested VM instances the performance for the "Short Ranges" workload, 'workload_e', is approximately three times lower than the other workloads. Thus, independently from the VM size (small, medium or large) the 'workload_e' seems to be three times slower than other workloads which were tested.

5   Conclusions

The emergence of cloud computing has led to a plethora of various offerings by multiple providers, covering different needs of the consumer. However significant questions emerge for the efficiency of these pay-per-use resources, mainly with regard to various application types, in this highly dynamic management environment. In this paper a multi-Cloud measurement framework has been presented, that has the aim of investigating these performance issues of the virtualized offerings. The framework utilizes a variety of application related benchmarks in order to cover a wide range of application types and it mainly focuses on investigating aspects such as service efficiency with relation to cost.

A combined metric (Service Efficiency) is also proposed in order to combine workload, performance and cost aspects in a single rating for comparing cloud offerings across different providers. A case study on 3 cloud providers has indicated the application of such a metric to characterize the offerings based on this combination.

For the future, we intend to complete the integration of the framework (currently missing the integration between GUI and Benchmark Suite Controller). However the Benchmarking Controller for the execution of the tests can be used also as standalone, following the instructions in [15]. Another interesting aspect would also be the incorporation of other non-functional aspects such as availability in the main SE metric.

Finally, the implementation of the measurements in more instance types and for all the benchmarks defined in Sect. 3.1 is one of our major goals for the future.

Acknowledgements. The research leading to these results is partially supported by the European Community's Seventh Framework Programme (FP7/2007-2013) under grant agreement n° 317859, in the context of the ARTIST Project.

References

1. ARTIST Consortium (2013), Deliverable D7.2 v1.0- PaaS/IaaS Metamodelling Requirements and SOTA. http://www.artist-project.eu/sites/default/files/D7.2%20PaaS %20IaaS%20metamodeling%20requirements%20and%20SOTA_M4_31012013.pdf
2. REMICS Consortium (2012), Deliverable D4.1 v2.0 - PIM4Cloud. http://www.remics.eu/ system/files/REMICS_D4.1_V2.0_LowResolution.pdf
3. Kousiouris, G., Kyriazis, D., Menychtas, A., Varvarigou, T.: Legacy applications on the cloud: challenges and enablers focusing on application performance analysis and providers characteristics. In: Proceedings of the 2012 2nd IEEE International Conference on Cloud Computing and Intelligence Systems (IEEE CCIS 2012), Hangzhou, China, 30 October–1 November 2012
4. Hauck, M., Huber, M., Klems, M., Kounev, S., Muller-Quade, J., Pretschner, A., Reussner, R., Tai, S.: Challenges and opportunities of Cloud computing. Karlsruhe Reports in Informatics 19, Karlsruhe Institute of Technology - Faculty of Informatics (2010)
5. Ou, Z., Zhuang, H., Nurminen, J.K., Ylä-Jääski, A., Hui, P.: Exploiting hardware heterogeneity within the same instance type of Amazon EC2. In: Proceedings of the 4th USENIX Conference on Hot Topics in Cloud Computing (HotCloud 2012), p. 4. USENIX Association, Berkeley (2012)

6. Kousiouris, G., Cucinotta, T., Varvarigou, T.: The effects of scheduling, workload type and consolidation scenarios on virtual machine performance and their prediction through optimized artificial neural networks. J. Syst. Softw. **84**(8), 1270–1291 (2011). doi:10.1016/j.jss.2011.04.013. Elsevier

7. Koh, Y., Knauerhase, R., Brett, P., Bowman, M., Wen, Z., Pu, C.: An analysis of performance interference effects in virtual environments. In: IEEE International Symposium on Performance Analysis of Systems and Software (ISPASS), pp. 200–209, April 2007

8. Schaffrath, G., Schmid, S., Vaishnavi, I., Khan, A., Feldmann, A.: A resource description language with vagueness support for multi-provider cloud networks. In: International Conference on Computer Communication Networks (ICCCN 2012), Munich, Germany (2012)

9. Charlton, S.: Model driven design and operations for the Cloud. In: OOPSLA 2009, 14th Conference Companion on Object Oriented Programming Systems Languages and Applications, pp. 17–26 (2009)

10. Charão, A.S., Primet, P.V.-B., Koslovski, G.P.: VXDL: virtual resources and interconnection networks description language. In: Kudoh, T., Mambretti, J., Vicat-Blanc Primet, P. (eds.) GridNets 2008. LNICST, vol. 2, pp. 138–154. Springer, Heidelberg (2009)

11. Mirkovic, J., Faber, T., Hsieh, P., Malayandisamu, G., Malavia, R.: DADL: Distributed Application Description Language. USC/ISI Technical report ISI-TR-664 (2010)

12. Garg, S.K., Versteeg, S., Buyya, R.: A framework for ranking of Cloud computing services. Future Gener. Comput. Syst. **29**(4), 1012–1023 (2013). ISSN 0167-739X http://dx.doi.org/10.1016/j.future.2012.06.006

13. Iosup, A., Prodan, R., Epema, D.: Iaas cloud benchmarking: approaches, challenges, and experience. In: Proceedings of the International Conference on High Performance Networking and Computing (SC), MTAGS 2012, pp. 1–8. IEEE/ACM (2012)

14. Li, A., Yang, X., Kandula, S., Zhang, M.: CloudCmp: comparing public Cloud providers. In: Proceedings of the 10th ACM SIGCOMM Conference on Internet measurement (IMC 2010), pp. 1–14. ACM, New York (2010). doi:10.1145/1879141.1879143, http://doi.acm.org/10.1145/1879141.1879143

15. ARTIST Consortium, Deliverable D7.2.1 v1.0- Cloud services modelling and performance analysis framework (2013). http://www.artist-project.eu/sites/default/files/D7.2.1%20Cloud%20services%20modeling%20and%20performance%20analysis%20framework_M12_30092013.pdf

16. Folkerts, E., Alexandrov, A., Sachs, K., Iosup, A., Markl, V., Tosun, C.: Benchmarking in the Cloud: what it should, can, and cannot be. In: Nambiar, R., Poess, M. (eds.) TPCTC 2012. LNCS, vol. 7755, pp. 173–188. Springer, Heidelberg (2013)

17. Milenkoski, A., Iosup, A., Kounev, S., Sachs, K., Rygielski, P., Ding, J., Cirne, W., Rosenberg, F.: Cloud Usage Patterns: A Formalism for Description of Cloud Usage Scenarios. Technical report SPEC-RG-2013-001 v.1.0.1, SPEC Research Group - Cloud Working Group, Standard Performance Evaluation Corporation (SPEC), April 2013

18. Ardagna, D., Di Nitto, E., Casale, G., Petcu, D., Mohagheghi, P., Mosser, S., Matthews, P., Gericke, A., Balligny, C., D'Andria, F., Nechifor, C.-S., Sheridan, C.: MODACLOUDS: a model-driven approach for the design and execution of applications on multiple clouds. In: ICSE MiSE: International Workshop on Modelling in Software Engineering, pp. 50–56. IEEE/ACM (2012)

Author Index